To Gary Steam –
Joanna, Mercedes, Stephen, Keith –

With many thanks
for the repeated encouragements
of your phone – calls
and our conversations

Warmest wishes,

Philip (Seddon)

Thanks for the pleasure
of working with you!

Christmas
1996

THE LORD
of the
JOURNEY

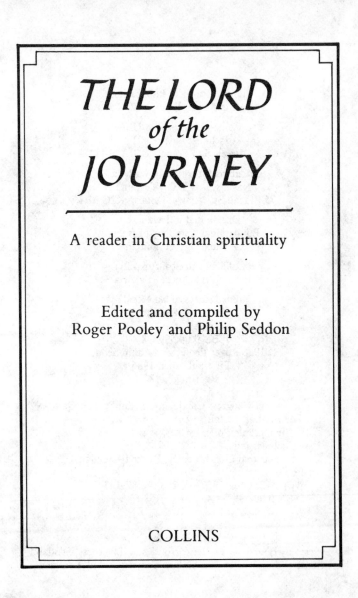

THE LORD
of the
JOURNEY

A reader in Christian spirituality

Edited and compiled by
Roger Pooley and Philip Seddon

COLLINS

Collins Liturgical Publications
8 Grafton Street, London W1X 3LA

Collins Liturgical in USA
Icehouse One — 401
151 Union Street, San Francisco, CA 94111-1299

Collins Liturgical in Canada
Novalis, Box 9700, Terminal,
375 Rideau St, Ottawa, Ontario K1G 4B4

Distributed in Ireland by
Educational Company of Ireland
21 Talbot Street, Dublin 1

Collins Liturgical Australia
PO Box 316, Blackburn, Victoria 3130

Collins Liturgical New Zealand
PO Box 1, Auckland

ISBN 0 00 599834 4
© 1986 Roger Pooley and Philip Seddon
First published 1986
Reprinted 1987

Library of Congress Cataloging-in-Publication Data
The Lord of the Journey
  Bibliography: p.
  Includes index
  1. Spiritual Life. I. Pooley, Roger II. Seddon,
Philip.
BV4501.2.L665-1987   248   87-14343
ISBN 0 00 599834 4

Typographical design by Colin Reed
Typeset by Bookmag, 13 Henderson Road, Inverness, Scotland
Made and printed by Wm Collins Sons & Co Ltd, Glasgow

Contents

Acknowledgements

The Publishers are grateful to the following for permission to reproduce copyright material:

Banner of Truth Trust, Edinburgh for John Newton, *Letters*; Robert Murray M'Cheyne, *Sermons*; Arthur Bennett, *The Valley of Vision*; Richard Sibbes, *The Bruised Reed and the Smoking Flax*; William Bridge, *A Lifting Up for the Downcast*.

Blackwells (Publishers) for Marie-Louise Martin, *Kimbangu: An African Prophet and his Church*.

Patrick Carpmael for *Conversion*.

Geoffrey Chapman and Orbis Books for Aylward Shorter, *African Christian Spirituality*.

T & T Clark Ltd for H.U. von Balthasar, *The Glory of the Lord: a Theological Aesthetics*.

Wm Collins & Co Ltd for Simone Weil *Waiting on God*; Hans Küng, *Does God Exist?*; Henri Nouwen, *Reaching Out*; Thomas à Kempis, *The Imitation of Christ*.

Wm Collins, The Harvill Press for *Poems of St John of the Cross* tr. Roy Campbell.

Concordia Publishing House for volume 21 (© 1956) and volume 26 (© 1963) of *Luther's Works*, ed. J. Pelikan & Helmut T. Lehmann.

Darton, Longman & Todd for Frank Lake, *Clinical Theology*; Metropolitan Anthony Bloom, *God and Man*.

Gaba Publications for Christopher Mwoleka in *African Ecclesial Review* No. 17.

Hassan B. Dehqani-Tafti for his work *The Hard Awakening*.

Dimension Books for *Intoxicated with God: The Fifty Spiritual Homilies of Macarius*, tr. George A. Maloney SJ; *Hymns of Divine Love* tr. George A. Maloney.

Epworth Press for John Wesley, *Letters*.

Faber & Faber and Farrar Straus & Giroux for John Berryman, 'Eleven addresses to the Lord' in *Love and Fame*.

Faber and Faber and Alfred A. Knopf Inc for Dag Hammarskjöld, *Markings*, tr. Leif Sjöberg and W.H. Auden.

Fortress Press for volumes 31-54 of *Luther's Works*, ed. J. Pelikan & Helmut T. Lehmann.

Franciscan Herald Press for *St Francis of Assisi, Omnibus of Sources*, ed. M.A. Habig.

Harper & Row Inc for Edith Cherry, quoted in Elisabeth Elliott, *Through Gates of Splendour*.

Hodder & Stoughton for Geoffrey T. Bull, *When Iron Gates Yield*; Steve Turner, *Up to Date: Poems 1968-1972*.

Hodder and Stoughton and OMF for Ayako Miura, *The Wind is Howling*, tr. Valerie Griffiths.

I.V.P. for D.M. Lloyd Jones, *Christ Our Sanctification*.

Jubilate Hymns © Mrs Mavis Seddon for James E. Seddon in *Hymns for Today's Church*.

Kingsway Publications and Fleming H. Revell Company for Bilquis Sheikh, *I Dared to Call Him Father*.

Lion Publishing for Jim Wallis, *The Call to Conversion*.

Lutterworth Press and Christian Literature Crusade Inc for N.P. Grubb, *C.T. Studd, Cricketer and Pioneer*.

Lutterworth Press for Dorothee Sölle, *Revolutionary Patience*.

Macmillan Publishers for R.S. Thomas, *Suddenly*.

Mowbray A.R. & Co. for *The Life and Letters of Fr Andrew* ed. Kathleen E. Burne.

OMF Books for Dr & Mrs Hudson Taylor, *Biography of James Hudson Taylor*.

Oxford University Press and Clarendon Press for Thomas Traherne, *Poems, Centuries and Three Thanksgivings* ed. A. Ridler; *Iacopone da Todi: Laudi* ed. F. Ageno in John Saward, *Perfect Fools*; Melito of Sardis *On Pascha*, tr. S.G. Hall; George Herbert, *Works* ed. F.E. Hutchinson; John Bunyan *The Pilgrim's Progress*, ed. J.B. Wharey and Roger Sharrock; Robert Southwell, *The Poems of Robert Southwell SJ*, ed. James H. McDonald and Nancy Pollard Brown.

Penguin Books for Augustine, *Confessions*, tr. R.S. Pine-Coffin; Pascal, *Pensées*, tr. A.J. Krailsheimer; John Donne, *Complete English Poems*, ed. A.J. Smith; Richard Rolle, *Fire of Love*, tr. Clifton Wolters; St Anselm, *Prayers and Meditations of St Anselm*, tr. Sister B. Ward; *Early Christian Writings: the Apostolic Fathers* tr. Maxwell Staniforth; F.D. Maurice in *Sermons and Society*, ed. Paul Welsby; Julian of Norwich, *Revelations of Divine Love*, tr. Clifton Walters.

Paulist Press for *The Martyrdom of St Polycarp* from Vol. 6 *Ancient Christian Writers*, ed. J. Quasten & J.C. Plumpe.

Princeton University Press for Søren Kierkegaard, *Parables of Kierkegaard*, ed. Thomas C. Oden.

Society of Biblical Literature and Scholars Press for *The Odes of Solomon: The Syriac Texts*, ed. and tr. J.H. Charlesworth.

SCM Press for J.V. Taylor, *The Primal Vision*.

SCM Press and Westminster Press for Klaus Klostermaier, *Hindu and Christian in Vrindaban*. Published in USA under the title *In the Paradise of Krishna: Hindu and Christian Seekers*.

SCM Press and Macmillan Inc for D. Bonhoeffer, *Letter and Papers from Prison*.

SCM Press and OUP Inc for J.V. Taylor, *The Go-Between God*.

SCM Press and Orbis Books for V. Donovan, *Christianity Rediscovered: An Epistle from the Masai*.

SCM Press and Wm. B. Eerdmans Inc for T.F. Torrance, *Theology in*

Acknowledgements

Reconstruction.

SCM Press and Harper & Row for Dietrich Bonhoeffer, *Life Together.*

Search Press Ltd for Martin Luther King in Stephen B. Oates, *Let the Trumpet Sound: The Life of Martin Luther King Jr*; Ernesto Cardenal, *Marilyn Monroe and Other Poems.*

Sheed & Ward for Helder Camara, *The Desert is Fertile*, tr. Dinah Livingstone.

S.P.C.K. for Lesslie Newbigin, *The Open Secret*; Amy Carmichael, *Towards Jerusalem*; Michael Hare Duke, *The Break of Glory*; *The Way of a Pilgrim*, anon. Russian, tr. R.M. French.

S.P.C.K. and Paulist Newman Press for *Francis and Clare: the Complete Works*, ed. Regis J. Armstrong O.M.F. and Ignatius C. Brady O.F.M. from the Classics of Western Spirituality Series, © 1982 by the Missionary Society of St Paul the Apostle in the State of New York; *Bonaventure: the Soul's Journey to God*, trans. E. Cousins from the Classics of Western Spirituality, © 1978 by The Missionary Society of St Paul the Apostle in the State of New York; John Wesley, *John & Charles Wesley*, ed. Frank Whaling.

Donald E. Stanford for Edward Taylor, *Poems*. ed. Donald E. Stanford (1960).

University of California Press for *The Sermons of John Donne*, ed. G.R. Potter & E.M. Simpson.

Verlag Evangelische Marienschwesternschaft for Basilea Schlink, *A Foretaste of Heaven.*

Veritas Publications Ltd for Simon Tugwell, *Prayer Vol. 2: Prayer in Practice.*

Preface

The idea of making this selection arose out of our association with the Grove Books Spirituality Group; we'd like to thank its Chairman, Ian Bunting, and its publisher, Colin Buchanan, for their encouragement, and the members of the group who've helped us with their suggestions and expertise – Richard Bauckham, Michael Botting, Richard Burton, Jane Hatfield, Anne Long, Mark Mills-Powell, Graham Pigott, Michael Vasey and Ian Williams. We are also indebted to David Bebbington, Martin Dent, Eamon Duffy, Denis Feeney, John Goldingay, Michael Insley, Christopher Lamb, John Lloyd and John Walsh for suggesting or lending material and other expert advice. Needless to say, responsibility for gaps and inadequacies remains with us. We thank our respective parent institutions, the University of Keele and Magdalene College, Cambridge, who gave us useful support with facilities and secretarial assistance; we are particularly grateful for Caryl Lowe's help with typing. Finally, we both thank Debbie Seddon very warmly for her patient encouragement and support during the crucial part of the book's gestation.

September 1985

Roger Pooley
Philip Seddon

How to use this book

Our arrangement begins with God and ends with praise, but our central informing metaphor, of the life of the Christian as a pilgrimage, gives us a more narrative sequence in the book as a whole. Within each section (or sub-section) we have ordered our material historically. Though we hope there is comprehensiveness within the constraints of space and our ambition to redress balances, it is intended more as a user's guide to spirituality, a set of 'tasters', rather than an academic 'essential documents'.

As we explain more fully in the introductory essay, part of our purpose in assembling the reader was to insert the reformed, evangelical tradition of spirituality into a wider sense of how Christian discipleship has developed. As a result, we hope Evangelicals will feel more confident about exploring other patterns of devotion; and their own traditions will invigorate and enrich the lives of other Christians.

This is a book to dip into, to raid for stimulation and illustrations on a variety of topics. But we also hope that it will be a resource for more serious, applied spiritual reading; a textbook for housegroups and retreats; and (with the help of the footnoted references) a starting-point for an exploration of the great riches that our precursors in the faith have left us. We borrow John Bunyan's confidence, at the end of his introduction to *The Pilgrim's Progress*, that 'this book will make a traveller of thee'.

The extracts are arranged within sections according to the date of publication, or, where possible, date of composition or delivery. Prose extracts have been modernised in spelling and (conservatively) punctuation; most of the poems haven't. Bibliographical details can be found in the footnotes. We apologise to any holders of copyright who have eluded our best efforts at tracing them.

Introduction

CHRISTIAN SPIRITUALITY AND THE EVANGELICAL TRADITION

1. The heart of faith

At the heart of *Christian faith* lies the deep conviction that we can know and love God because God first loved and knew us. The one truly existent God, we believe, has been so poured out, so made known to us in Christ and the Spirit, that we can respond with mutual personal knowledge, and in the intimacy and awe of love.

In terms of the universe, we see Jesus Christ as the personal and eternal Word of God, as creator and redeemer. In terms of his earthly life, we see the cross and the resurrection as the sacrificial climax and achievement, and as the axis of every Christian's understanding of history, from death to life. In terms of application, we see justification by faith and forgiveness as the pattern of God's grace coming as a gift to the undeserving.

It is true that at one time or another in history, and in experience, this work of Father, Son and Spirit has been underemphasised or underestimated. We have therefore tried as best we can to represent a fully Trinitarian spirituality in the pages which follow, believing that only in that way do we experience the richness and diversity both of our experience of God and also of Christian tradition.

So how are these gifts and truths of God to be grasped? The meeting-point has often been the event, or the consciousness of conversion, the idea of joyful repentance and change of direction embedded in the New Testament word *metanoia*. But of course it doesn't stop there, and perhaps part of the hunger for a true spirituality stems from the fear that it might, as well as from the experience and dangers of superficiality. At the heart of a true *Christian spirituality*, however, lies the conviction that the beginning of the Christian life is only a beginning, even if it has touched the End; that not merely outward appearances but hidden bases of false living are to be challenged; that not just ideas but experiences are to be shaped by the Spirit. In short, there is a future: there is a journey, a pilgrimage to be undertaken in Christ who is the Beginning and the End, the Way, the Truth and the Life. Knowledge of and joy in God increasingly take over as the central desire, fed by prayer, Scripture and sacrament; and it does so in the context of the church, that community of believers with whom we experience both mutual solidarity in joy and suffering as well as frustration with the personal and institutional imperfections that remain endemic. And we begin to see that love of God is exercised in loving our neighbours, in witness and service. Christian spirituality is our longing to enter, experience and express the love and the knowledge of God more and more, in ourselves, in the community of faith, and beyond.

Now this may all become ossified and atrophied as doctrine, or habit, or sinfulness overbear Christian practice. But the history of Christianity, and of individual Christians, is full of outbursts of reality, where the experience of forgiveness has ousted grim legalism and the truth underlying the prescriptions has become fresh again.

2. Patterns and practices of evangelical spirituality

Part of our motive in assembling this collection is to place the various strands of evangelical spirituality since the sixteenth century into those of the Christian centuries as a whole. It's often been argued that evangelical spirituality hardly existed; or that it is a culture of feelings; excessively individualistic; anti-sacramental; philistine; and excessively tied up with Scripture. Too often, these accusations have been fully justified; though perhaps they are less valid today. But, on the positive side, what patterns of life and faith can be discerned within this tradition?

A CONVERSION

Anglican and Baptist Evangelicals may have disagreed strongly on the place of baptism, but both have looked alike to the 'awakening' of conversion as a crucial initiatory experience of forgiveness and liberation. At times conversion has become an individual event as isolated as the Platonic 'flight of the soul to God': unrelated to baptism and the church, to the society around, or even the individual's own past. Thankfully, conversion is again being seen as a process as well as an experience, and the Puritan discernment of stages in conversion seems apposite: calling (sometimes 'effectual calling'), conviction of sin, then justification, sanctification (the process of increasing conformity to Christ), and glorification (the final bliss of heaven) completed the soul's return to God which had begun with God's own act of election. This is, first of all, a Calvinist framework, but one with its roots in the experience and teaching of Paul and Augustine, and with considerable influence beyond the seventeenth century.

B PROGRESS

It was in this context of progress within a stance that the inwardness of Puritan thinking about conversion emphasised the need to 'make election sure' by highlighting assurance and perseverance. *Assurance* – a heaven on earth according to Thomas Brooks' account – was usually approached through the exposition of Romans 8 and its teaching of the spiritual life. The tension between the 'perfection' commanded in the New Testament and the stubborn tendency of the 'old man' to sin out of desire or habit has given evangelical spirituality its most intractable problem, and some of its most fruitful ideas.

Apart from assurance, the other concept particularly useful to the Puritan 'experimental' divines was *perseverance*, explained by John Owen as follows: 'such is the love and goodwill towards them in the Covenant of mercy in the blood of Christ, that having appointed good works for them to walk in, for which of themselves they are insufficient, he will graciously continue to them such supplies of his Spirit and grace as they shall never depart from following after him in ways of gospel obedience'.

The Methodist revival and the Wesleys in particular offer a change of perspective. John Wesley was particularly indebted to the mystical traditions of the church, and he was attracted by the ideas of purity and simplicity of intention in Macarius' *Homilies*, Thomas à Kempis' *Imitation of Christ* and Arndt's *True Christianity*. (Indeed Wesley's own devout eclecticism might serve as a model for ours; though his *Christian Library* ran to fifty volumes in 1750!) Just as Luther's conversion had become a pattern for many, so Charles' and John's profound experiences of change after conversion but similar to it was echoed by many of their followers' accounts; a period of darkness, or prolonged seeking, followed by a sense of gift rather than attainment, commonly but not inevitably emotional, and with clear ethical consequences. There are parallels with early Quaker narratives, too.

There are further parallels with the 'second blessing' theology of the Holiness movement of the later nineteenth century and the early Pentecostal movement of the twentieth. But the burgeoning of the Charismatic Renewal movement in all traditional churches and theologies has helped to break down rigid schematisations, to reveal again the sovereignty and particularity of the work of the Spirit, and to demonstrate that all Christian experience is a continuation of the original work of regeneration – 'more of the same' and always 'in Christ'. Paul speaks of growing up into Christ; or taking the Puritan John Preston's image of the baby plant, we might say that it is perfect, but it still needs to grow.

We now turn to the practices which have characterised evangelical discipleship.

C SCRIPTURAL LIVING

Partly in reaction to the decayed sacramentalism of the late medieval period, partly as a result of the invention of printing, but largely as a result of the Reformation rediscovery of the sheer vitality of the Scriptures as the Word of God, the Bible became the basis of Protestant life – memorisation, study, meditation, prayer, conversation. Such an openness to God's ability to speak through the written word could, and still can, give rise to interpretative anarchy; but more important, it could and can shape receptivity.

For a Puritan like Bunyan being a Christian was both a consequence of reading and hearing the Bible, and an incentive to carry on with it. So reading and meditating on the Scriptures became a part of evangelical devotion. The 'quiet time', as it became known later, is characteristically a mixture of Bible reading, using some commentary or scheme which means the whole Bible is read over a period, and prayer. Here is developed a rhythm of listening and talking to God, a growth in knowledgeable obedience, the building of a Christian mind. For the Protestant and Evangelical, all spirituality will be shaped by Scripture, just as Scripture itself is shaped by Christ.

Such is the importance of Scripture and the supportive power of text in experience, that it would be possible to construct a parallel anthology to this consisting almost entirely of key Biblical passages. Certainly the whole structure of the book, its anatomising of the Christian life, is underpinned by Biblical patterns and concepts.

D PRAYING TOGETHER

John Cotton, one of the first New England pastors, wrote 'Would any man or woman know whether they have received a spirit of grace and prayer, or no? Why, ask thine own heart, does thou pray with thy family?' Within the Reformed perspective, the family was seen as a miniature church, with the father as head (and, sometimes, priest). The Methodist class system, the prayer meeting, and the camps and youth groups not invariably associated with one local church all point to a strongly corporate element in evangelical spirituality, one which goes hand in hand with a stress on ministry being the duty and privilege of all, not just an ordained clergy, expressing and reinforcing the Reformation doctrine of 'the priesthood of all believers'. Evangelical churches have always been characterised by a strong element of preaching and worship, with a stress on participation, especially in music, evangelism and mission. Hymns and choruses are a crucial source for evengelical theology and devotion. For Anglican Evangelicals, notably Charles Simeon, the Book of Common Prayer has been a major source of spirituality; for the Free Churches the lack of a fixed liturgy has been a delight.

The role of the communion is less clear. For some, going back to Sibbes and Owen, the Holy Communion is central; for others, quite marginal. An early desire to 'fence the table' in the spirit of 1 Corinthians 10, has sometimes slipped into the practice of thinking of Communion as an optional extra, an appendix to the main body of worship. Today the Lord's Supper is regaining a central place as Eucharist (thanksgiving) and as Communion (sharing); it still falls short of being the constitutive focus of the church's proclamation and anticipation of Christ.

3. Interweaving the strands

The great change that has come about in the last twenty years or so is that Evangelicalism, along with other Christian groupings, has left its island fortress isolation on the field of religious warfare, and begun to parley with its allies. Some have seen this as a failure of nerve, an abandonment of all that was best in order to achieve a false peace. But we would contend that the movement is, largely, recognisable as God's work. There is nothing but gain in a truthful, humble, caring responsiveness between separated children in a family owing common gratitude and commitment to God's parental love.

In some ways this is traceable to the recognition of God's creativity in the Charismatic movement, which transcended many denominational and party lines and built trust and solidarity in place of suspicion. From another point of view it is consistent with history; such figures as Calvin, Baxter and the Wesleys felt themselves to be in touch with some of the great figures of Catholic tradition, like Augustine and Bernard. There has always been widespread discourse between writers on the spiritual life, but the scale and breadth of it seem to be increasing.

Recent research also shows that there were surprisingly close connections between Puritan and Catholic spiritual writing, even though, at the time, the Pope was routinely identified with the Antichrist. Patterns of Puritan meditation are sometimes derived from existing Anglican adaptations of Catholic methods, particularly those derived from Ignatius and Francis de Sales. There is a more unfortunate link – both have fathered unhappy children, plagued by the morbid scrupulosity of some of the devotion of the last century. At other times, there can be common Catholic and Evangelical concern for guarding and enlivening 'the apostles' teaching', or for guarding the sanctity of human life.

But, despite an increasing willingness to learn from each other, there are still understandable hesitations. One stems from the danger of vagueness – that 'spirituality' is already an abstraction from 'The Spirit', and that what is promoted is a vague, over-inclusive other-worldliness, perhaps even self-indulgent religiosity, rather than the distinctive claims of Christ. Indeed, it seems that the word 'spirituality' began as a term of abuse describing a form of devotion in seventeenth century France that seemed to its critics to have no connection with real life. Another is that techniques and practices of the 'science' of spirituality might be practised in a vacuum, and thus the discipline (= ascesis) needed by the Christian in Paul's athletic image (1 Cor 9:25-7) will be perverted into a new legalism. And the third, particularly acute in Reformed circles, is that spirituality might become a religious luxury item, suitable for advanced or sophisticated Christians only, even to the extent of reintroducing unofficially the religious/laity division the Reformation did much to break down.

None of these should be dismissed as backwoodsmanship; they point to real dangers. But we feel they should not engender simply partisan or rejecting attitudes. Certainly in our selection we have felt unable to operate exclusively evangelical parameters. On the contrary, we want to acknowledge and represent the kind of help we have had from retreats in monasteries and convents, Eastern Orthodox discussions of the Jesus Prayer, the poets of High Anglicanism and so on, as well as the faithful Biblical exposition, spontaneous prayer, emphasis on the 'quiet time', impetus to mission and warmth of fellowship that characterise the best of Evangelicalism. So our principles of selection are eclectic; we want to make available a wide range of approaches to Christian spirituality from a number of traditions, and at the same time to counter the implication, present, albeit unconsciously, in books like Bouyer's *History of Christian Spirituality*, that evangelical spirituality has little to offer to the rest of the church. Rather, we feel, all Christians need to be both evangelical and catholic, in the radical sense of those words, living and bringing the whole gospel to the whole world, aware of all that has not only brought them to life, but also nourished the lives of others.

4. *Contexts for contemporary spirituality*

Christian spirituality no more takes place in a vacuum than (say) modern Islamic spirituality. It is a salutary experience for Western Christians to be taken to task by 'Two Thirds World' Christians for having exported a Gospel already, and probably unconsciously loaded with cultural presuppositions. Perhaps this is inevitable; wheat and tares only become distinguishable towards harvest time. But the criticism hasn't been all fraternal. Just as the Roman Empire was the context for furious persecution of Christians so is, for example, modern Russia. Just as the Athenian intellectual elite were variously scornful or curious of Paul's teaching of the resurrection, so are many of the modern intelligentsia. Indeed, over the past two centuries there has been a series of critiques of religion, which, together with more ostensibly neutral social movements, have eroded the intellectual and social domination of Christianity in the West. However, properly understood, those experiences of persecution, criticism and indifference which we share with the early Church might be seen as purifying experiences as well as attacks to be resisted. In other words, they might help us to see what true Christianity and true spirituality are today; and what they are not.

The critiques of religion offered by Marx, Nietzsche and Freud may have originated in their mistrust of the institutional Christianity of their own time. But the radical nature of their criticisms stems from new analyses of motive; that the root of man's desires is not religious but economic, sexual, or political. Religion is then either an illusion or a personal and social practice entirely explicable in natural terms. There is a Christian apologetic response to these accusations, and they hardly constitute a watertight case against Christianity. But simple rejection of them isn't enough. These critiques point to weaknesses in Christian practice – the promotion of emotional immaturity, or the tendency to support unjust political regimes – which might otherwise have remained invisible. And there is a necessary dialogue between psychological understanding and spirituality, too – in our understanding of depression, to take one example. Again, there may be times when simple defiance, 'here I stand', is appropriate. But we need to be careful where we stand; the materialism of London's Oxford Street or the shopping malls of the USA can be just as corrosive as the ideological materialism of Moscow. More precisely, we need to be more aware of the unconscious influences on Christian spirituality, its often unacknowledged 'background'. We can see such a discerning alertness in much true spirituality – from Jesus confronting Satan to Paul's exposé of Satan as an angel of light, to the Desert Fathers' ascetic watchfulness, to Ignatius' *Rules for the Discernment of Spirits*, to Samuel Rutherford's astringent warnings against false comforts, right up to Richard Foster's *Celebration of Discipline* in our own day.

To take one key example: Christian practice has been, and continues to be thrown out of balance by the various dualisms of Platonism (4th century BC, but resurgent in the 2nd century AD and the Renaissance), Gnosticism (2nd century) and Manichaeism (3rd century) – all variously preaching false divisions of head and heart, thought and action, mind and feelings, soul and body, self and world. Not only are things which Christianly ought to be united set in opposition; but sinfulness is redefined as externals versus essences, which underestimates the rebellion of 'the world' (inner and 'religious' as well as outer and 'profane') against God, in the characteristic formulation of John's Gospel. Quantities of Christian literature are infected with this spirit. Similarly, in the last century, and surviving into this, Idealism has promoted part of this dualism in its exclusive esteem for the realities of the mind. But it is unwise to assume that what can be thought or reasoned is most acceptable to God. In our own generation the culture of the body has resurfaced, and while it continues to engender idolatry of a narcissistic kind, isn't the rediscovery of creation, of human sexual and other felt energies, not just a liberation for many, but a fresh way of understanding bread and wine, the proper relationship between physical and spiritual?

The Romantic movement, particularly in the nineteenth century, did point more positively towards creation, even if acknowledgement of the creator was often vague and perfunctory. The experience of beauty, or the necessity of elevated feelings, which for some Romantics was the criterion for being alive, can be paralleled with the concentration on 'conversion experiences' and 'feelings of holiness' in the Evangelicalism of the period as well as the emotive models of sanctity in Catholicism. On the negative side, the interest in emotional events in their extraordinariness and intensity can be seen as a diversion from perceiving God's communication in the totality of experience. But more positively, this is a necessary reaction to the alienating consequences of the Industrial Revolution and the growth of the big cities, a sign of the survival of the image of God in man. In the end, however, there are deep ambiguities. The releasing of the emotions has been found in this century to be part of Christ's healing work; and yet an over-eager identification of romantic feelings with Christian faith, or the deliberate orchestration of emotionalism, is bound to bring trouble sooner or later.

Two closely linked movements of recent centuries, both of which have affected Christian spirituality more deeply than is usually realised, are those of individualism and Existentialism. The former is already a feature of Reformation thought, but intensified in Romanticism and the strain of agonised inwardness in literary Modernism. This ideological analysis can be complemented by noting the reduction in the size of the nuclear family, not least by divorce, and the accelerating privatisation of most areas of life, from entertainment to death. One Christian response to this has been simply to go with the tide (and against false nostalgia, at times) and concentrate on individual conversion and holiness. But equally there has been a conscious rediscovery of community, in the revival of monastic orders in the nineteenth century, in the recasting of liturgy, in the house church movement, and in numerous experiments in living communally – the appeal of Taizé to young people from all over the world is an outstanding example.

Coupled with this, Existentialism has acquired its Christian exponents. Its prophetic founder, Kierkegaard, is represented below. But the danger with more recent varieties is for appeals to commitment, decision, response, action or authenticity to be dislodged entirely from any historical context, individual or social. There is the additional convenience of sidestepping the results of the questions raised by Biblical criticism, evolution and so on. But while an appeal to minds and emotions is right and proper, the tendency to 'justification by decision' is fraught with peril, not least because it is unlikely to dislodge that pride which preserves the attitudes and consequences of the Fall even into the Christian life.

This discussion could be extended, not least as a comment on Dean Inge's astringent rule, that he who marries the Spirit of the Age soon finds himself a widower. But perhaps these are sufficient examples to reveal the aptness of Christ's command to 'watch and pray', not least because these areas are not always considered to have much relevance for spirituality.

Another question: why is there still a hunger for spirituality – even a vogue for it? Many contemporary analysts have responded with variations on Augustine's analysis, that God has made us for himself, and we are restless until we find our rest in him. True; although not everyone regards that restlessness as religious. It may simply be the case, as a character in Arthur Miller's *The Price* argues, that when people are restless they don't found a religion or start a revolution any more, they go shopping. But the readiness of many modern people to bare their souls to psychiatrists or psychotherapists, or to pay out vast sums to cults and charlatans indicates a deep unfulfilled longing.

The revival of interest in Christian spirituality may also be in response to the renewed appeal of the East – gurus, Transcendental Meditation, and other paths to spiritual fulfilment. The assumption that Western Christianity had run dry had been encouraged by the practice and pronouncements of many Western Christians; and even for those who wanted to go deeper, theology seemed to be arid and lifeless. At best it offered a Christianity heavily weighted towards Christ's second commandment, to love our neighbour, without the dynamism to be gained from observing the first, to love God. So, the search for the specifically spiritual roots of Christianity became urgent.

These two response models of Christian spirituality – response to modern life, and to 'Eastern religion' – can be seen in the path taken by T.S. Eliot. In *The Waste Land* he depicted the disintegration felt in the modern city and psyche, 'I can connect nothing with nothing', and concluded with a despairing lunge towards Buddhism. But in the last of his *Four Quartets* he describes something close to mystical union with God in the context of the seventeenth century Christian community of Little Gidding and the language of Dame Julian of Norwich. Here the specifically Christian roots of spirituality come to life.

But the Christian historian has another context to delineate. Those movements, or waves of renewal that have come throughout Christian history – the Desert Fathers and the monastic movement of the first five centuries, the 12th century Renaissance, the *devotio moderna* of the 15th century, the Reformation and Counter-Reformation, Puritanism, Pietism, the Methodist movement, the missionary movement of the 19th centuries, the Pentecostal and Ecumenical

movements of our own time – flawed, time-bound as all
human movements are, can also be seen as the irruption of
the Spirit of God working in history. These are all movements we've attempted to represent in this anthology.

5. Conclusion

Ultimately, nothing but the presence of the living God in
human life today – as, once, uniquely, in Jesus of Nazareth –
will satisfy. But everyone's path will be as different as the
details of their own life. This calls us both to flexibility and
sensitivity in ministry and counsel; to wide acquaintance
with the spiritual traditions within Christianity (and
beyond, not least in multiracial areas; we forget the extent to
which even the Christianity of the first four or five centuries
was already in contact with the meditative wisdom of the
East); and to the wisdom, freedom, love and truth which is
most clearly and ultimately expressed in Jesus, for us and for
all. The vital element of the Spirit calls us to a freshness and
adventurousness which accepts labels but is not happy to be
limited by them. The living Spirit is not in conflict with the
Word, but rather the present/historical reality who applies
Christ to us. And God is no respecter of persons. Too often
spirituality has been taken to be for monks, nuns, priests,
and perhaps some rich or leisured lay people. Part of our
motive in collecting this reader has been to extend the range
of spiritual experience and guidance available to all who are
thirsty. And in that catholic and evangelical spirit we conclude with the words of a contemporary Orthodox theologian, Alexander Schmemann:

'Spirituality' is not a separate and self-contained pursuit
whose techniques it suffices to master in order to succeed
in it. Ultimately it is the new life itself, stemming from
the Church and thus having its source and also its criteria
where the Church herself has them: in the death in Christ
of the old man, in the rising again in Christ of the new life,

in the gift of the Holy Spirit which makes us 'kings, priests and prophets', in the participation in the hidden, yet real life of the 'eighth day', the day without evening of the Kingdom (*Of Water and the Spirit* SPCK 1976, pp. 153–4).

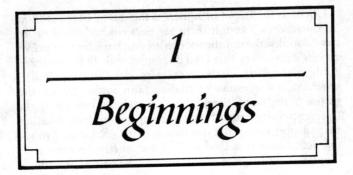

1

Beginnings

'In the beginning, God . . .' The end of Christian spirituality, in the fine, bold words of the Westminster Confession,
is 'to glorify God and enjoy him for ever'; and so we must
begin with the revelation of God's nature. For many it is
God's creation that provides a starting-point of awe and
wonder, and the Thomas Traherne passages in particular
show that this needn't begin only in the face of mighty
mountains and storms, but can equally come in a recognition of the small things, even in the workings of our own
bodies. The poet Jack Clemo reminds us that this mustn't
lead into the idolatry of nature-worship – and indeed his
note of suspicion is perhaps truer to the historic evangelical
teaching of the hostility of 'the world' than to many post-
Romantic rhapsodies. Supremely, though, God is revealed
in Christ, and here, and in the next section, we see the
uniqueness of that revealing. There is a sense in which
Christ's humility is more provocative, more challenging to
our ideas of God than God's power. But wherever we start,
we can start because God comes to us saying 'I am'; God
communicates, divulges his nature (e.g. Exodus 3:14, John
8: 12 and 10:7-11). That is, if we can call God 'him'; as the
passage from Anselm points out, there is a quality of
'motherhood' in God, too.

Christ as the friend of sinners is the theme of the section 'in ourselves'. Though there are patterns we could easily have doubled the number of conversion narratives to prove Baxter's discovery that God does not break all hearts alike. And, particularly in those extracts like Geoffrey Bull's, where it is a question of finding faith again, we see the justice of the word 'break'. God's people are often brought to an extremity before they can be opened to him; whether that opening is no more spectacular than C.S. Lewis' grudging acceptance that God is God, or whether it shows, in Cyprian's words, the exuberance of the Spirit of God.

In God

[Jesus says] I am the hope of the hopeless, the helper of those who have no helper, the treasure of those in need, the physician of the sick, the resurrection of the dead.

Epistle of the Apostles, c. 150 [1]

*
**

When the Lord taught us the doctrine of Father, Son and Holy Spirit, he did not make arithmetic a part of this gift! He did not say, 'In the first, the second, and the third,' or 'In one, two, and three' . . . The Unapproachable One is beyond numbers, wisest sirs . . . There is one God and Father, one Only-Begotten Son, and one Holy Spirit. We declare each Person to be unique, and if we must use numbers, we will not let a stupid arithmetic lead us astray to the idea of many gods.

Basil the Great, 374 [2]

*
**

Eternal Truth, true Love, beloved Eternity – all this, my God, you are, and it is to you that I sigh by night and day. When first I knew you, you raised me up so that I could see that there was something to be seen, but also that I was not yet able to see it. I gazed on you with eyes too weak to resist the dazzle of your splendour. Your light shone upon me in its brilliance, and I thrilled with love and dread alike. I realized that I was far away from you. It was as though I were in a land where all is different from your own and I heard your voice calling from on high, saying 'I am the food of full-grown men. Grow and you shall feed on me. But you shall not change me into your own substance, as you do with the food of your body. Instead you shall be changed into me.'

Augustine, 401 [3]

**
*

But what do I love when I love my God? Not material beauty or beauty of a temporal order; not the brilliance of earthly light, so welcome to our eyes; not the sweet melody of harmony and song; not the fragrance of flowers, perfumes, and spices; not manna or honey; not limbs such as the body delights to embrace. It is not these that I love when I love my God. And yet, when I love him, it is true that I love a light of a certain kind, a voice, a perfume, a food, an embrace; but they are of the kind that I love in my inner self, when my soul is bathed in light that is not bound by space; when it listens to sound that never dies away; when it breathes fragrance that is not borne away on the wind; when it tastes food that is never consumed by the eating; when it clings to an embrace from which it is not severed by fulfilment of desire. This is what I love when I love my God.

Augustine, 401 [4]

**
*

Patrick's Breastplate

I arise today
    through a mighty strength, the invocation of the
      Trinity,
    through belief in the threeness,
    through confession of the oneness
    towards the creator.

I arise today
  through the strength of Christ with his baptism,
  through the strength of his crucifixion with his burial,
  through the strength of his resurrection with his
    ascension,
  through the strength of his descent for the judgment
    of doom.

I arise today
  through the strength of the love of cherubim,
  in obedience of angels,
  in the service of the archangels,
  in hope of resurrection to meet with reward,
  in prayers of patriarchs,
  in predictions of prophets,
  in preachings of apostles,
  in faiths of confessors,
  in innocence of holy virgins,
  in deeds of righteous men.

I arise today
  through the strength of heaven:
  light of sun,
  brilliance of moon,
  splendour of fire,
  speed of lightning,
  swiftness of wind,
  depth of sea,
  stability of earth,
  firmness of rock.

I arise today
  through God's strength to pilot me:
  God's might to uphold me,
  God's wisdom to guide me,
  God's eye to look before me,
  God's ear to hear me,
  God's word to speak for me,

God's hand to guard me,
God's way to lie before me,
God's shield to protect me,
God's host to secure me –
   against snares of devils,
   against temptations of vices,
   against inclinations of nature,
   against everyone who shall wish me ill,
   afar and anear,
   alone and in a crowd.

I summon today all these powers between me and these
   evils –
   against every cruel and merciless power that may
     oppose my body and my soul,
   against incantations of false prophets,
   against black laws of heathenry,
   against false laws of heretics,
   against craft of idolatry,
   agsinst spells of women and smiths and wizards,
   against every knowledge that endangers man's body
     and soul.

Christ to protect me today
   against poison, against burning,
   against drowning, against wounding,
   so that there may come abundance of reward.
Christ with me, Christ before me, Christ behind me,
Christ in me, Christ beneath me, Christ above me,
Christ on my right, Christ on my left,
Christ where I lie, Christ where I sit, Christ where I
   arise,
Christ in the heart of every man who thinks of me,
Christ in the mouth of every man who speaks of me,
Christ in every eye that sees me,
Christ in every ear that hears me.

I arise today
   through a mighty strength, the invocation of the
      Trinity,
   through belief in the threeness,
   through confession of the oneness
   towards the creator.

Salvation is of the Lord.
Salvation is of the Lord.
Salvation is of Christ.
May thy salvation, O Lord, be ever with us.

? from Patrick (5th cent.), but mainly 6th cent. [5]

***

Humility is the garment of the Deity.

Isaac of Nineveh, 7th cent. [6]

***

And you, Jesus, are you not also a mother?
   Are you not the mother who, like a hen,
   gathers her chickens under her wings?
Truly, Lord, you are a mother;
   for both they who are in labour
   and they who are brought forth
      are accepted by you.
You have died more than they, that they may labour to
      bear.
   It is by your death that they have been born,
   for if you had not been in labour,
      you could not have borne death;
and if you had not died, you would not have brought
      forth.
   For, longing to bear sons into life,
      you tasted of death,

34

and by dying you begot them.
You did this in your own self,
   your servants by your commands and help.
You as the author, they as the ministers.
So you, Lord God, are the great mother.
Then both of you are mothers.
Even if you are fathers, you are also mothers.
For you have brought it about that those born to death
   should be reborn to life –
   you by your own act, you by his power.
Therefore you are fathers by your effect
   and mothers by your affection.
Fathers by your authority, mothers by your kindness.
Fathers by your teaching, mothers by your mercy.
Then you, Lord, are a mother,
   and you, Paul, are a mother too.
If in quantity of affection you are unequal,
   yet in quality you are not unalike.
Though in the greatness of your kindness
   you are not co-equal,
   yet in will you are of one heart.
Although you have not equal fullness of mercy,
   yet in intention you are not unequal . . .

And you, my soul, dead in yourself,
   run under the wings of Jesus your mother
and lament your griefs under his feathers.
Ask that your wounds may be healed
and that, comforted, you may live again.

Christ, my mother,
   you gather your chickens under your wings;
this dead chicken of yours puts himself under those
     wings.
For by your gentleness the badly frightened are
     comforted,
   by your sweet smell the despairing are revived,

your warmth gives life to the dead,
your touch justifies sinners.
Mother, know again your dead son,
both by the sign of your cross and the voice of his
    confession.
Warm your chicken, give life to your dead man,
    justify your sinner.
Let your terrified one be consoled by you;
despairing of himself, let him be comforted by you;
and in your whole and unceasing grace
let him be refashioned by you.
For from you flows consolation for sinners;
to you be blessing for ages and ages. Amen.

Anselm, 1070[7]

**

He himself is my contemplation;
he is my delight.
Him for his own sake
I seek above me;
from him himself I feed within me.
He is the field in which I labour;
he is the fruit for which I labour.
He is my cause;
he is my effect.
He is my beginning;
he is my end without end.
He is for me eternity.

Isaac of Stella, 1165-9[8]

**

You are holy, Lord, the only God, You do wonders.
You are strong, you are great, you are the most high,
You are the almighty King.

36

You, Holy Father, the King of heaven and earth.
You are Three and One, Lord God of gods.
You are good, all good, the highest good,
Lord, God, living and true.
You are love, charity.
You are wisdom; you are humility; you are patience;
you are beauty; you are meekness; you are security;
you are inner peace; you are joy; you are our hope and
  joy;
you are justice; you are moderation, you are all our
  riches
you are enough for us.
You are beauty, you are meekness;
you are the protector,
you are our guardian and defender;
you are strength; you are refreshment.
You are our hope, you are our faith, you are our
  charity,
you are all our sweetness,
you are our eternal life:
great and wonderful Lord,
God almighty, Merciful Saviour.

Francis, 1224 [9]

*
**

With a glad countenance our Lord looked at his side,
rejoicing as he gazed. And as he looked, I, with my limited
understanding, was led by way of this same wound into his
side. There he showed me a place, fair and delightful, large
enough for all saved mankind to rest in peace and love. I was
reminded of the most precious blood and water that he shed
for love of us. And, gazing still, he showed me his blessed
heart riven in two. In his sweet enjoyment he helped me to
understand, in part at any rate, how the blessed Godhead
was moving the poor soul to appreciate the eternal love of

God that has neither beginning nor end. At the same time our good Lord said, most blessedly, 'See, how I have loved you.' As if to say, 'My dearest, look at your Lord, your God, your Maker, and your endless joy. See the delight and happiness I have in your salvation; and because you love me, rejoice with me.'

Julian of Norwich, 1373 [10]

*
* *

Welcome to earth, thou noble guest,
Through whom e'en wicked men are blest!
Thou com'st to share our misery,
What can we render, Lord, to Thee!

Ah, Lord, who hast created all,
How hast thou made thee weak and small,
That thou must choose thy infant bed
Where ass and ox but lately fed!

Were earth a thousand times as fair
Beset with gold and jewels rare,
She yet were far too poor to be,
A narrow cradle, Lord, for thee.

For velvets soft and silken stuff
Thou hast but hay and straw so rough,
Whereon thou king, so rich and great,
As 'twere thy heaven, art throned in state.

Thus hath it pleased thee to make plain
The truth to us poor fools and vain,
That this world's honour, wealth and might
Are nought and worthless in thy sight.

Ah dearest Jesus, holy child,
Make thee a bed, soft, undefiled,
Within my heart, that it may be
A quiet chamber kept for thee.

Martin Luther, 1531 tr. Catherine Winkworth, 1855 [11]

True Christian theology, as I often warn you, does not present God to us in his majesty, as Moses and other teachings do, but Christ born of the Virgin as our Mediator and High Priest . . .

Therefore if you want to be safe and out of danger to your conscience and your salvation, put a check on this speculative spirit . . . begin where Christ began – in the Virgin's womb, in the manger, and at his mother's breasts. For this purpose he came down, was born, lived among men, suffered, was crucified, and died, so that in every possible way he might present himself to our sight. He wanted us to fix the gaze of our hearts upon himself and thus to prevent us from clambering into heaven and speculating about the Divine Majesty.

Therefore whenever you consider the doctrine of justification and wonder how or where or in what condition to find a God who justifies or accepts sinners, then you must know that there is no other God than this Man Jesus Christ. Take hold of him; cling to him with all your heart, and spurn all speculation about the Divine Majesty; for whoever investigates the majesty of God will be consumed by his glory. I know from experience what I am talking about . . .

This is why Paul makes such a frequent practice of linking Jesus Christ with God the Father, to teach us what is the true Christian religion. It does not begin at the top, as all other religions do; it begins at the bottom. It bids us climb up by Jacob's ladder; God himself leans on it, and its feet touch the earth, right by Jacob's head (Gen. 28:12). Therefore whenever you are concerned to think and act about your salvation, you must put away all speculations about the Majesty, all thoughts of works, traditions and philosophy – indeed, of the Law of God itself. And you must run directly to the manger and the mother's womb, embrace this Infant and Virgin's Child in your arms, and look at him – born, being nursed, growing up, going about in human society, teaching, dying, rising again, ascending above all the heavens, and having authority over all things. In this way you can shake off all terrors and errors.

Martin Luther, 1531 [12]

*
**

This little Babe, so few days old,
Is come to rifle Satan's fold;
All hell doth at his presence quake,
Though he himself for cold do shake;
For in this weak unarmed wise
The gates of hell he will surprise.

With tears he fights and wins the field,
His naked breast stands for a shield;
His battering shot are babish cries,
His arrows looks of weeping eyes,
His martial ensigns cold and need,
And feeble flesh his warrior's steed.

His camp is pitched in a stall,
His bulwark but a broken wall;
The crib his trench, hay-stalks his stakes,
Of shepherds he his muster makes;
And thus, as sure his foe to wound,
The angels' trumps alarum sound.

My soul, with Christ join thou in fight;
Stick to the tents that he hath pight;
Within his crib is surest ward,
This little Babe will be thy guard;
If thou wilt foil thy foes with joy,
Then flit not from this heavenly boy.

Robert Southwell, early 1590's [13]

Q. What is the chief end of man?

A. Man's chief end is to glorify God, and to enjoy him for ever.

Westminster Assembly, 1644 [14]

*
**

If there were no obscurity man would not feel his corruption: if there were no light man could not hope for a cure. Thus it is not only right but useful for us that God should be partly concealed and partly revealed, since it is equally dangerous for man to know God without knowing his own wretchedness as to know his wretchedness without knowing God.

Blaise Pascal, 1658 [15]

*
**

God is an universal excellency. All the particular excellencies that are scattered up and down among angels, men, and all other creatures, are virtually and transcendently in him, he hath them all in his own being, Ephes. 1:3. All creatures in heaven and earth have but their particular excellencies; but God hath in himself the very quintessence of all excellencies. The creatures have but drops of that sea, that ocean, that is in God, they have but their parts of that power, wisdom, goodness, righteousness, holiness, faithfulness, loveliness, desirableness, sweetness, graciousness, beauty, and glory that is in God. One hath this part, and another hath that; one hath this particular excellency, and another hath that; but the whole of all of these parts and excellencies are to be found only in God.

Thomas Brooks, 1666 [16]

All my hope on God is founded:
  He doth still my trust renew.
Me thro' change and chance he guideth,
  Only good and only true.
    God unknown,
    He alone
    Calls my heart to be his own.

Pride of man and earthly glory,
  Sword and crown betray his trust:
What with care and toil he buildeth,
  Tower and temple, fall to dust.
    But God's pow'r,
    Hour by hour,
    Is my temple and my tow'r.

God's great goodness aye endureth,
  Deep his wisdom passing thought:
Splendour, light and life attend him,
  Beauty springeth out of nought.
    Evermore
    From his store
    Newborn worlds rise and adore.

Daily doth th' Almighty Giver
  Bounteous gifts on us bestow.
His desire our soul delighteth,
  Pleasure leads us where we go.
    Love doth stand
    At his hand:
    Joy doth wait on his command.

Still from man to God eternal
  Sacrifice of praise be done,
High above all praises praising
  For the gift of Christ his Son.
    Christ doth call
    One and all:

Ye who follow shall not fall.
Joachim Neander, 1679 tr. Robert Bridges, 1899 [17]

***

Let earth and heaven combine,
  Angels and men agree.
To praise in songs divine
  The incarnate Deity,
Our God contracted to a span,
Incomprehensibly made man.

He laid his glory by
  He wrapped him in our clay;
Unmarked by human eye,
  The latent Godhead lay;
Infant of days he here became,
And bore the mild Immanuel's name.

Unsearchable the love
  That hath the Saviour brought;
The grace is far above
  Or man or angel's thought;
Suffice for us that God, we know,
Our God, is manifest below.

He deigns in flesh to appear,
  Widest extremes to join;
To bring our vileness near,
  And make us all divine:
And we the life of God shall know,
For God is manifest below.

Made perfect first in love,
  And sanctified by grace,
We shall from earth remove,
  And see his glorious face:
Then shall his love be fully showed,
And man shall then be lost in God.
Charles Wesley, 1746 [18]

43

Nothing is inexorable but love.

George MacDonald, 1867 [19]

*
**

All that is not God is death.

George MacDonald, 1885 [19]

*
**

To bring sin home, and to bring grace home, we need that something else should come home which alone gives meaning to both – the holy. The grace of God cannot return to our preaching or to our faith till we recover what has almost clean gone from our general, familiar, and current religion, what liberalism has quite lost – I mean a due sense of the holiness of God. This sense has much gone from our public worship, with its frequent irreverence; from our sentimental piety, to which an ethical piety with its implicates is simply obscure; from our rational religion, which banishes the idea of God's wrath; from our public morals, to which the invasion of property is more dreadful than the damnation of men. If our Gospel be obscure it is obscure to them in whom the slack God of the period has blinded their minds, or a genial God unbraced them, and hidden the Holy One who inhabits eternity. This holiness of God is the real foundation of religion – it is certainly the ruling interest of the Christian religion. In front of all our prayer or work stands 'Hallowed be thy name'. If we take the Lord's Prayer alone, God's holiness is the interest which all the rest of it serves. Neither love, grace, faith, nor sin have any but a passing meaning except as they rest on the holiness of God, except as they arise from it, and return to it, except as they satisfy it, show it forth, set it up, and secure it everywhere and for ever. Love is but its outgoing; sin is but its defiance; grace is but its action on sin; the cross is but its victory; faith is but its worship. The preacher preaches to the divinest purpose only when his lips are touched with the red coal from the altar of the thrice holy in the innermost place. We must rise beyond social righteousness and universal justice to the holiness of an infinite God. What we on earth call righteousness among men, the saints in heaven call holiness in him.

P.T. Forsyth, 1909 [20]

*
**

Grace is the majesty, the freedom, the undeservedness, the unexpectedness, the newness, the arbitrariness, in which the relationship to God and therefore the possibility of knowing him is opened up to man by God himself . . . Grace is God's good-pleasure.

Karl Barth, 1940 [21]

*
**

The holiness of God consists in the unity of his judgment with his grace. God is holy because his grace judges and his judgment is gracious.

Karl Barth, 1940 [22]

*
**

A true doctrine of the divine attributes must in all circumstances attest and take into account both factors – God's self-disclosure and his self-concealment. The knowledge of God must not be swallowed up in the ignorance. Nor, again, must the ignorance be swallowed up by the knowledge. Both demands are laid upon us by God himself in his revelation: the obedience of knowledge and the humility of ignorance. And in laying down both requirements God is equally the one true God. The one grace of his self-revelation is at the root of both, and, because his self-revelation is his truth, we must add: he himself, his own most proper reality. And in both ways, through his self-disclosure and his concealment, he is at one and the same time knowable and unknowable to us . . . At every point, therefore, we have to be silent, but we have also to speak.

Karl Barth, 1940 [23]

***

The Trinity is, for the Orthodox Church, the unshakeable foundation of all religious thought, of all piety, of all spiritual life, of all experience. It is the Trinity that we seek in seeking after God, when we search for the fullness of being, for the end and meaning of existence . . .

Between the Trinity and hell there lies no other choice. This question is, indeed, crucial – in the literal sense of that word. The dogma of the Trinity is a cross for human ways of thought. The apophatic ascent is a mounting of Calvary. This is the reason why no philosophical speculation has ever succeeded in rising to the mystery of the Holy Trinity. This is the reason why the human spirit was able to receive the full revelation of the Godhead only after Christ on the cross had triumphed over death and over the abyss of hell. This, finally, is the reason why the revelation of the Trinity shines out in the Church as a purely religious gift, as the catholic truth above all other.

Vladimir Lossky, 1944 [24]

***

The heart of the gospel was revealed to me as 'the pain of God' . . . . I am filled with gratitude because I was allowed to experience the depth of God's heart with Jeremiah . . . .

We dare to speak about this 'pain of God,' for, to use Calvin's words, 'God does not express his great love for us in any other way!' We dare to see with Jeremiah God's grace in his 'pain'. Are not the eyes which saw God's pain frozen? '. . . his appearance was so marred, beyond human semblance, and his form beyond that of the sons of men . . .' (Isa. 52:14). We cannot behold his pain without risking our life. We must pronounce the words 'pain of God' as if we are allowed to speak them only once in our lifetime. Those who have beheld the pain of God cease to be loquacious, and open their mouths only by the passion to bear witness to it.

Those who have seen the pain of God can live without dying, because the 'pain' is at once 'love'. By this 'love', man's pain is purified and becomes like God's 'pain'.

'Love rooted in the pain of God' cannot be observed objectively outside of our human experience. There is no way to see it other than experiencing it in our own life.

Kazoh Kitamori, 1946 [25]

*\
**

Children of men, lift up your hearts. Laud and magnify God, the everlasting Wisdom, the holy, undivided and adorable Trinity.

Praise him that he hath made man in his own image, a maker and craftsman like himself, a little mirror of his triune majesty.

For every work of creation is threefold, an earthly trinity to match the heavenly.

First: there is the Creative Idea; passionless, timeless, beholding the whole work complete at once, the end in the beginning; and this is the image of the Father.

Second: there is the Creative Energy, begotten of that Idea, working in time from the beginning to the end, with sweat and passion, being incarnate in the bonds of matter; and this is the image of the Word.

Third: there is the Creative Power, the meaning of the work and its response in the lively soul; and this is the image of the indwelling Spirit.

And these three are one, each equally in itself the whole work, whereof none can exist without other; and this is the image of the Trinity.

Dorothy Sayers, 1952 [26]

*
**

The God who appeared in Jesus Christ is where people suffer and struggle and thirst and hunger. He is a provoking God. He is a God who can cope with vultures and dogs and jackals. He is a God indifferent to nothing; on the contrary, he is light and life and the inexorable enemy of darkness and death. The God manifest in Jesus Christ is not one who watches from afar and develops a new theory about God, but he is a living God, a God who proves to the world that there is sin and justice. He is a God become man not in the circles of pharisees and politicians, but in those circles where hunger and thirst, toil and work, grief and death are well-known. He did not appeal to his divinity but gave his humanity for his brethren. Perhaps the people living in a temperature of 120° F in the shade, where there are vultures and jackals, are also in need of one who, of his free volition, will take upon him what, to them, is cruel destiny; perhaps they are in need of one who will deliver them from the caprice of gods and men; perhaps they are in need of one who knows that life is better than death, that God and Satan are not one and the same. Perhaps they are in need of a God who follows them right into death, when all the beautiful speculations burst like a soap bubble and nothing remains but a dirty little drop of water. He would not give them air-conditioners so that they, too, could live at 70° F, nor guns with which to shoot vultures and jackals. But he would bring them the consolation Christ had brought, a consolation that has little to do with what the world considers consoling. And they would understand. Better than the 70° F theologians.

Klaus Klostermaier, 1969 [27]

*
**

In God we find three things. We find the exulting joy of three Persons who love in giving perfectly and receiving perfectly, but who being a Trinitarian relationship, if I may put it in this form of speech, are not in the way of each other, in which each of them accepts every single moment not to exist for the two others to be face to face – the miracle of total communion and oneness. Speaking of God we must consider things in the simultaneity of events and not in temporal succession. The three simultaneously give, the three simultaneously receive, the three simultaneously place themselves in such a situation that the others are alone with each other. But that means death because self-annihilation, sacrifice, means self-negating death and the Cross is inscribed in the mystery of the Holy Trinity.

Metropolitan Anthony, 1971 [28]

*
**

When you're little you 'understand' Mr God . . . Later on you understand him to be a bit different . . . Even though you understand him, he doesn't seem to understand you! . . . In whatever way or state you understand Mister God, so you diminish his size . . .

So Mister God keeps on shedding bits all the way through your life until the time comes when you admit freely and honestly that you don't understand Mister God at all. At this point you have let Mister God be his proper size and wham, there he is laughing at you.

Fynn, 1974 [29]

God is not a person as man is a person. The all-embracing and all-penetrating is never an object that man can view from a distance in order to make statements about it. The primal ground, primal support and primal goal of all reality, which determines every individual existence, is not an individual person among other persons, is not a superman or superego. The term 'person' also is merely a cipher for God. God is not the supreme person among other persons. God transcends also the concept of person. God is *more than person*.

A God who founds personality cannot himself be nonpersonal. Just because God is not a 'thing', just because – as is stressed in the East – he cannot be seen through, controlled, manipulated, he is not impersonal, not infrapersonal. God transcends also the concept of the impersonal. God is also *not less than a person*.

God is not neuter, not an 'it', but a God of men, who provokes the decision for belief or unbelief. He is spirit in creative freedom, the primordial identity of justice and love, one who faces me as founding and embracing all interhuman personality. If, with the religious philosophers of the East, we want to call the absolutely last and absolutely first reality the 'void' or 'Absolute Nothingness,' then we must also call it 'being itself,' which manifests itself with an infinite claim and with infinite understanding. It will be better to call the most real reality not personal or nonpersonal but – if we attach importance to the terminology – *transpersonal or suprapersonal*.

The Bible shows that there is someone who faces us as benevolent and absolutely reliable: not an object, not an empty, unechoing universe, not a merely silent infinite, not an indefinable, nameless Gnostic chasm, not an indeterminate, dark abyss that might be confused with nothingness, still less an anonymous interpersonal something that could be mistaken for man and his very fragile love. God is *one who faces me, whom I can address.*

Hans Küng, 1980 [30]

***

This truly living God is not bound in the fixed necessity of the logic of either Islam or eastern religion. Rather, he holds together in one, at infinite cost, both justice and mercy, necessity and contingency, order and freedom. Here God is disclosed as a 'new Love' holding together both law and free play, the spiritual and the material. He is both beyond us and yet all pervading, supreme and yet, for the sake of a great good, willing to limit his own sovereignty and omniscience, to be vulnerable and responsive to his creatures.

What [world-wide witnesses] find in Jesus is essentially a new love, in which that justice and mercy, beyondness and closeness, utter consistency to itself and yet freedom and openness to the novel, are marvellously combined and relate heaven and earth in a new way – but only through the infinite pain of God realised on the cross itself . . . [where] this essential nature of God is here directly, accessibly and unmistakably present. He can only be with us and for us unmistakably and completely in this crucified One.

This understanding of God shows him as essentially Love, a realistic love which risks and gives its all in a material creation, and in bearing with and seeking to overcome the tragic nature of that creation from the beginning. He brings into being the possibility of a freely participating community of autonomous beings made to be like himself and to share in his divine life. In realising this union of order and freedom in himself in the person of Christ, he opens up the possibility of order and freedom for his creatures.

The Holy Spirit is the continuing realisation of this possibility through Christ.

Simon Barrington-Ward, 1984 [31]

In Creation

Question the beautiful earth; question the beautiful sea; question the beautiful air, diffused and spread abroad; question the beautiful heavens; question the arrangement of the constellations; question the sun brightening the day by its effulgence; question the moon, tempering by its splendour the darkness of the ensuing night; question the living creatures that move about in the water, those that remain on land, and those that flit through the air, their souls hidden but their bodies in view, visible things which are to be ruled and invisible spirits doing the ruling; – question all these things and all will answer: 'Behold and see! We are beautiful.' Their beauty is their acknowledgment. Who made these beautiful transitory things unless it be the unchanging Beauty?

Augustine, 393-403 [32]

*

Learn in the creature to love the creator; and in the work him who made it.

Augustine, 420 [33]

*

The Canticle of Brother Sun

Most high, all-powerful, all good, Lord!
    All praise is yours, all glory, all honour
    and all blessing.
To you, alone, Most High, do they belong.

No mortal lips are worthy
to pronounce your name.
All praise be yours, my Lord, through all that you have
made,
and first my lord Brother Sun,
who brings the day; and light you give to us
through him.
How beautiful is he, how radiant in all his splendour!
Of you, Most High, he bears the likeness.
All praise be yours, my Lord, through Sister Moon and
Stars;
in the heavens you have made them, bright
and precious and fair.
All praise be yours, my Lord, through Brothers Wind
and Air,
and fair and stormy, all the weather's moods,
by which you cherish all that you have made.
All praise be yours, my Lord, through Sister Water,
so useful, lowly, precious and pure.
All praise be yours, my Lord, through Brother Fire,
through whom you brighten up the night.
How beautiful is he, how gay! Full of power and
strength.
All praise be yours, my Lord, through Sister Earth, our
mother,
who feeds us in her sovereignty and produces
various fruits with coloured flowers and herbs.
All praise be yours, my Lord, through those who grant
pardon
for love of you; through those who endure
sickness and trial.
Happy those who endure in peace,
by you, Most High, they will be crowned.
All praise be yours, my Lord, through Sister Death,
from whose embrace no mortal can escape.
Woe to those who die in mortal sin!

Happy those She finds doing your will!
  The second death can do no harm to them.
Praise and bless my Lord, and give him thanks,
  and serve him with great humility.

Francis, 1225 [34]

***

And he showed me more, a little thing, the size of a
hazelnut, on the palm of my hand, round like a ball. I looked
at it thoughtfully and wondered, 'What is this?' And the
answer came, 'It is all that is made.' I marvelled that it
continued to exist and did not suddenly disintegrate; it was
so small. And again my mind supplied the answer, 'It exists,
both now and for ever, because God loves it.' In short,
everything owes its existence to the love of God.

Julian of Norwich, 1373 [35]

***

That God, all Spirit, served with Spirits, associated to
Spirits, should have such an affection, such a love to this
body, this earthly body, this deserves this wonder. The
Father was pleased to breathe into this body, at first, in the
Creation; The Son was pleased to assume this body himself,
after, in the Redemption; The Holy Ghost is pleased to
consecrate this body, and make it his Temple, by his
sanctification . . .

John Donne, 1625 [36]

***

There is not so poor a creature but may be thy glass to see
God in. The greatest flat glass that can be made cannot
represent any thing greater than it is. If every gnat that flies
were an Archangel, all that could but tell me, that there is a

God; and the poorest worm that creeps tells me that. If I should ask the basilisk, how camest thou by those killing eyes, he would tell me, thy God made me so; and if I should ask the slow-worm how camest thou to be without eyes, he would tell me, thy God made me so. The cedar is no better a glass to see God in, than the hyssop on the wall; all things that are, are equally removed from being nothing; and whatsoever hath any being, is by that very being a glass in which we see God, who is the root, and the fountain of all being. The whole frame of nature is the theatre, the whole volume of creatures is the glass, and the light of nature, reason, is our light.

John Donne, 1628 [37]

**
*

Such was the freedom of God's will, that no necessity could constrain him to the production of anything; such the bounty, that none could restrain him from the voluntary profusion of his goodness. When 'twas indifferent to him, or to constitute a world, or to continue alone; he yet was pleased to follow the propensity of his own infinite benignity, and create.

Walter Charleton, 1652 [38]

**
*

To think well is to serve God in the interior court: to have a mind composed of divine thoughts, and set in frame, to be like him within. To conceive aright and to enjoy the world, is to conceive the Holy Ghost, and to see his love; which is the mind of the Father. And this more pleaseth him than many worlds, could we create as fair and great as this. For when you are once acquainted with the world, you will find the goodness and wisdom of God so manifest therein that it was impossible another, or better should be made. Which being made to be enjoyed, nothing can please or serve him more than the soul that enjoys it. For that soul doth accomplish the end of his desire in creating it.

Thomas Traherne, 1670's [39]

**

You never enjoy the world aright, till you see how a sand exhibiteth the wisdom and power of God . . .

You never enjoy the world aright, till the sea itself floweth in your veins, till you are clothed with the heavens, and crowned with the stars: and perceive yourself to be the sole heir of the whole world: and more than so, because men are in it who are every one sole heirs, as well as you. Till you can sing and rejoice and delight in GOD as misers do in gold, and kings in sceptres, you will never enjoy the world.

Thomas Traherne, 1670's [40]

**

Thanksgiving for the Body

O what Praises are due unto thee,
     Who hast made me
          A living Inhabitant
               Of the great World.
          And the Centre of it!
     A sphere of Sense,
          And a mine of Riches,
Which when Bodies are dissected fly away.
     The spacious Room
          Which thou hast hidden in mine Eye,
     The Chambers for Sounds

Which thou hast prepar'd in mine Ear,
The Receptacles for Smells
Concealed in my Nose;
The feeling of my Hands,
The taste of my Tongue.
But above all, O Lord, the Glory of Speech, whereby thy Servant is enabled with Praise to celebrate thee.
For
All the Beauties in Heaven and Earth,
The melody of Sounds,
The sweet Odours
Of thy Dwelling-place.
The delectable pleasures that gratifie my Sense,
That gratify the feeling of Mankind.
The Light of History,
Admitted by the Ear.
The Light of Heaven,
Brought in by the Eye.
The Versatility and Liberty
Of my Hands and Members.
Fitted by thee for all Operations;
Which the Fancy can imagine
Or Soul desire:
From the framing of a Needle's Eye,
To the building of a Tower:
From the squaring of Trees,
To the polishing of Kings' Crowns.
For all the Mysteries, Engines, Instruments, wherewith the World is filled, which we are able to frame and use to thy Glory.

Thomas Traherne, 1670's [41]

*

What do you think especially gives me comfort at this time? The Creation! – the view of God in his work of Creation!

Did Jehovah create the world, or did I? I think he did; now if he made the *world*, he can sufficiently take care of *me*.

Charles Simeon, 1836 [42]

***

Turning sadly away we mounted the pagoda, and what a contrast was the scene outspread before our eyes! Here nature seemed to be offering that worship to her creator which man refused, and with surprise and delight we involuntarily exclaimed, 'How beautiful!' No words can describe the landscape, and the more one looked the more fresh beauties lay revealed. The day was so clear that with the telescope the most distant objects were well-defined, and the brilliant sunlight threw an air of gladness over everything.

Hudson Taylor, 1855 [43]

***

Imagine yourself midway between heaven and earth, the sharp point of rock on which we stood hardly seeming more of earth than if we had been in a balloon, the whole space around, above, and below filled with wild, weird, spectral clouds, driving and whirling in incessant change and with tremendous rapidity; horizon *none*, but every part of where horizon should be, crowded with unimaginable shapes of unimagined colours, with rifts of every shade of blue, from indigo to pearl, and burning with every tint of fire, from gold to intensest red; shafts of keen light shot down into abysses of purple thousands of feet below, enormous surging masses of grey hurled up from beneath, and changing in an instant to glorified brightness of fire as they seemed on the point of swallowing up the shining masses above them; then, all in an instant, a wild grey shroud flung over us, as swiftly passing and leaving us in a blaze of sunshine; then a bursting open of the very heavens, and a vision of what might be celestial heights, pure and still and shining, high above it all; then, an instantaneous cleft in another wild cloud, and a revelation of a perfect paradise of golden and rosy slopes and summits; then, quick gleams of white peaks through veilings and unveilings of flying semi-transparent clouds; then, as quickly as the eye could follow, a rim of dazzling light running round the edges of a black castle of cloud, and flaming windows suddenly pierced in it; oh, mother dear, I might go on for sheets, for it was never twice the same, nor any single minute the same, in any one direction. . .

Frances Ridley Havergal, 1874 [44]

***

God's Grandeur

The world is charged with the grandeur of God.
 It will flame out, like shining from shook foil;
 It gathers to a greatness, like the ooze of oil
Crushed. Why do men then now not reck his rod?
Generations have trod, have trod, have trod;
 And all is seared with trade; bleared, smeared with toil;
 And wears man's smudge and shares man's smell: the soil
Is bare now, nor can foot feel, being shod.

And for all this, nature is never spent;
 There lives the dearest freshness deep down things;
And though the last lights off the black West went
 Oh, morning, at the brown brink eastward, springs –
Because the Holy Ghost over the bent
 World broods with warm breast and with ah! bright
  wings.

Gerard Manley Hopkins, 1877 [45]

What would the world be, once bereft
Of wet and of wildness? Let them be left,
O let them be left, wildness and wet;
Long live the weeds and the wilderness yet.

Gerard Manley Hopkins, 1881 [46]

**

Man is matter and spirit, both real and both good.

Eric Gill, 1938 [47]

**

The love we feel for the splendour of the heavens, the plains,
the sea and the mountains, for the silence of nature which is
borne in upon us by its thousands of tiny sounds, for the
breath of the winds, or the warmth of the sun, this love of
which every human being has at least an inkling, is an
incomplete, painful love, because it is felt for things which
are incapable of responding, that is to say for matter. Men
want to turn this same love towards a being who is like
themselves and capable of answering to their love, of saying
yes, of surrendering. When the feeling for beauty happens
to be associated with the sight of some human being, the
transference of love is made possible, at any rate in an
illusory manner. But it is all the beauty of the world, it is
universal beauty, for which we yearn . . .

The longing to love the beauty of the world in a human
being is essentially the longing for the Incarnation. It is
mistaken if it thinks it is anything else. The Incarnation
alone can satisfy it . . .

Beauty is eternity here below.

Simone Weil, 1942 [48]

For a man in his wife's arms to be hankering after the other world is, in mild terms, a piece of bad taste, and not God's will.

We ought to find and love God in what he actually gives us; if it pleases him to allow us to enjoy some overwhelming earthly happiness, we mustn't try to be more pious than God himself and allow our happiness to be corrupted by presumption and arrogance, and by unbridled religious fantasy which is never satisfied with what God gives. God will see to it that the man who finds him in his earthly happiness and thanks him for it does not lack reminder that earthly things are transient, that it is good for him to attune his heart to what is eternal, and that sooner or later there will be times when he can say in all sincerity, 'I wish I were home.' But everything has its time, and the main thing is that we keep step with God, and do not keep pressing on a few steps ahead – nor keep dawdling a step behind. It's presumptuous to want to have everything at once – matrimonial bliss, the cross, and the heavenly Jerusalem, where they neither marry nor are given in marriage.

Everything has its time.

Dietrich Bonhoeffer, 1943 [49]

**
*

Christ himself was obviously not at peace with nature, any more than he was at peace with human nature. He often acted in open defiance of the 'majesty' of creation. When the storm arose on Gennesaret he did not bid the disciples to humble themselves devoutly before the 'great Being' who was trying to drown them. He lashed back at the elements from his bridgehead in the divine kingdom: 'Be still!' To him the storm was the work of an evil life force, a demonic convulsion that needed cure. All natural catastrophes are symptoms of nature's sickness – fevers, vomits, shiverings: they are not growing pains through which God is slowly evolving a perfect world, but mere reminders that we live in an enemy-occupied zone and that in so far as we are subject to its laws we share its tragedy. Christ has set an example of revolt against the sick rebel, and spiritually our revolt can be an exhilarating success. We can transcend our bond with nature, not through stoicism or courage, but through intimations of the new creation, the kingdom of God.

Jack Clemo, 1958 [50]

**
*

If you love both a human being and music, are you to say you must reject the human love that is more dangerous but you may keep the love of music because though dangerous it is less so? Or are you to outlaw everything? If so, what of the parable of the man who hid his talent in a napkin? . . .

At the bar of heaven shall we be expected only to say how we have done with our fastings and almsdeeds, our pursuit of virtue? Shall we not also be expected to say, You gave me a love of music, and I have tried a little to deepen and sanctify it: to love the magic you put into the souls of your children – John Sebastian and Wolfgang and Ludwig and Johannes – and to praise you through it; you gave me a love of words, and of the magic you make through men's lips, and I have tried not to belittle your gift; you gave me a love of colour, and I have tried to use your gift creatively in a sad, drab world? And shall we not, still more, be expected to say: You gave me, though unworthy, the love of these your children, to keep me young and gay in heart and to help me in the dark places, and I tried to be prudent and to let no harm come thereby to them or to me, but also I tried not to disparage the gift nor refuse its responsibilities? Be constant, gay, prudent: if . . . you grow more and more free from egoism and greed and rapacity, then you have less and less cause for fear: you can find a better motive in all that you do than the cult of safety . . .

Every love you have – of nature, of art, of men, of wisdom – is an added way of loving and worshipping him,

an additional gift to offer him. But that means in the last
resort a gift to give back to him.

Gerald Vann, 1960 [51]

*
**

When God pauses before he composes man into his creation, we sense that there is a risk connected with it: will the
creation of man mean the coronation of creation or its
crucifixion? Will creation reach its pinnacle when there is
added to its creatures a being who rises above the dull level
of reflex and instinct, who is endowed with mind and will,
and is capable of living as a partner and co-worker of God
his creator? Or is the creation of this being called 'man' the
first stage in a tremendous descent that starts in the Garden
of Eden and leads to a disturbed and desolated earth, that
transforms the child and image of God into a robber and a
rebel, and through him carries war and rumours of war to
the farthest planets?

Coronation or crucifixion of creation – that is the question here. And we understand why God pauses and hesi-
tates, for he is facing a risk. What a breath-taking thought! Is
it not almost blasphemous even to think of such a thing?

And this is the way it was. In setting over against himself
a being to whom he gave freedom and power he risked the
possibilities that the child would become a competitor, that
the child would become a megalomaniacal rival of the
creator.

Helmut Thielicke, 1964 [52]

*
**

Suddenly

Suddenly after long silence
he has become voluble.
He addresses me from a myriad
directions with the fluency

of water, the articulateness
of green leaves; and in the genes,
too, the components
of my existence. The rock,
so long speechless, is the library
of his poetry. He sings to me
in the chain-saw, writes
with the surgeon's hand
on the skin's parchment messages
of healing. The weather
is his mind's turbine
driving the earth's bulk round
and around on its remedial
journey. I have no need
to despair; as at
some second Pentecost
of a Gentile, I listen to the things
round me: weeds, stones, instruments,
the machine itself, all
speaking to me in the vernacular
of the purposes of One who is.

R.S. Thomas, 1983 [53]

In Ourselves: Programme

Great indeed is the baptism which is offered you. It is a ransom to captives; the remission of offences; the death of sin; the regeneration of the soul; the garment of light; the holy seal indissoluble; the chariot to heaven; the luxury of paradise; a procuring of the kingdom; the gift of adoption.

Cyril, 347-8 [54]

**

What is good for us to believe and to keep firm and unshaken in our hearts is that the humility whereby God was born of a woman and brought by mortal men to that shameful way of death, is the supreme medicament for the healing of the cancer of our pride, and the profound mystery that can loose the fetters of sin.

Augustine, 417 [55]

**

Even when [God] is found he must be sought. Enquiry concerning the incomprehensible is justified, and the enquirer has found something, if he has succeeded in finding how far what he sought passes comprehension. Comprehending the incomprehensibility of what he seeks, yet he will go on seeking, because he cannot slacken his pursuit so long as progress is made in the actual enquiry into things incomprehensible: so long as he is continually bettered by the search after so great a good – both sought that it may be found, and found that it may be sought: still sought that the finding may be sweeter, still found that the seeking may be more eager.

Augustine, 417 [56]

Repentance is the renewal of baptism and is a contract with God for a fresh start in life. Repentance goes shopping for humility and is ever distrustful of bodily comfort. Repentance is critical awareness and a sure watch over oneself. Repentance is the daughter of hope and the refusal to despair.

John Climacus, 7th cent. [57]

*

The significance of baptism is a blessed dying unto sin and a resurrection in the grace of God, so that the old man, conceived and born in sin, is there drowned, and a new man, born in grace, comes forth and rises . . .

As we can plainly see, the sacrament or sign of baptism is quickly over. But the spiritual baptism, the drowning of sin, which it signifies, lasts as long as we live and is completed only in death. Then it is that a person is completely sunk in baptism, and that which baptism signifies comes to pass.

Therefore this whole life is nothing else than a spiritual baptism which does not cease till death . . .

Then shall we be truly lifted up out of baptism and be completely born, and we shall put on the true baptismal garment of immortal life in heaven.

Martin Luther, 1519 [58]

*

A Christian life is nothing else but a daily baptism, once begun and to be always continued . . . Repentance is nothing but a return and re-entry into baptism, that we may repeat what was once begun and let drop . . . therefore everyone should regard baptism as a garment for everyday use, which he should always have on, that he may ever be in the midst of faith and its fruits, in order to be able to subdue the old Adam and go forward in the new man.

Martin Luther, 1529 [59]

*
**

God hath made no decree to distinguish the seasons of his mercies; in paradise, the fruits were ripe the first minute, and in heaven it is always autumn, his mercies are ever in their maturity. We ask *panem quotidianum*, our daily bread, and God never says you should have come yesterday, he never says, you must again tomorrow, but *today if you will hear his voice*, today he will hear you. If some king of the earth have so large an extent of dominion, in north and south, as that he hath winter and summer together in his dominions, much more hath God mercy and judgement together: he brought light out of darkness, not out of a lesser light; he can bring thy summer out of winter, though thou have no spring; though in the ways of fortune, or understanding, or conscience, thou have been benighted till now, wintered and frozen, clouded and eclipsed, damped and benumbed, smothered and stupified till now, now God comes to thee, not as in the dawning of the day, not as in the bud of the spring, but as the sun at noon to illustrate all shadows, as the sheaves in harvest, to fill all penuries. All occasions invite his mercies, and all times are his seasons.

John Donne, 1624 [60]

*
**

Urge God upon his promise, wrestle with God, as Jacob did, and let him not go without a blessing; wrestling implies resisting, it is a sign God resisted him for a time: so, it may be, God will deny thee a great while, yet continue to seek him, let him not go, he cannot deny thee in the end, thou shalt have the blessing at the last. We should learn thus to importune God; tell him, 'Lord, I have a sure promise, and thou hast made the pardon general, and I am sure I come within the number of that commission: "Go and preach the gospel to every creature," go and tell every man under heaven that Christ is offered to him, he is freely given to him by God the Father, and there is nothing required of you but that you marry him, nothing but to accept of him; here is a word sure enough, if there were nothing else but this.'

John Preston, 1630 [61]

*
**

Repentance unto life is a saving grace, whereby a sinner out of a true sense of his sin, and apprehension of the mercy of God in Christ, doth with grief and hatred of his sin, turn from it unto God, with full purpose of and endeavour after new obedience.

Westminster Assembly, 1644 [62]

*
**

'Tis to be feared that some have gone too far towards directing the Spirit of the Lord, and marking out his footsteps for him, and limiting him to certain steps and methods. Experience plainly shows, that God's Spirit is unsearchable and untraceable, in some of the best of Christians, in the method of his operations, in their conversion. Nor does the Spirit of God proceed discernibly in the steps of a particular established scheme, one half so often as is imagined. A scheme of what is necessary, and according to a rule already received and established by common opinion, has a vast (though to many a very insensible) influence in forming persons' notions of the steps and method of their own experiences.

Jonathan Edwards, 1746 [63]

There are no neutral zones or areas of life left untouched by biblical conversion. It is never solely confined to the inner self, religious consciousness, personal morality, intellectual belief, or political opinion.

If we believe the Bible, every part of our lives belongs to the God who created us and intends to redeem us. No part of us stands apart from God's boundless love; no aspect of our lives remains untouched by the conversion that is God's call and God's gift to us. Biblically, conversion means to surrender ourselves to God in every sphere of human existence: the personal and social, the spiritual and economic, the psychological and political.

Conversion is our fundamental decision in regard to God. It marks nothing less than the ending of the old and the emergence of the new. 'When anyone is united to Christ, there is a new world; the old has gone, and a new order has already begun' (2 Cor. 5:17, New English Bible). Heart, mind, and soul, being, thinking, and doing – all are remade in the grace of God's redeeming love. This decision to allow ourselves to be remade, this conversion, is neither a static nor a once-and-finished event. It is both a moment and a process of transformation that deepens and extends through the whole of our lives. Many think conversion is only for nonbelievers, but the Bible sees conversion as also necessary for the erring believer, the lukewarm community of faith, the people of God who have fallen into disobedience and idolatry.

Conversion means a radical reorientation in terms of personal needs and ideas of personal fulfillment. When we enter community we bring with us an emptiness that seeks filling, but we also bring clear notions of what we think might fill that emptiness. We know our own needs best of all, and we are fairly sure about how they can be met. All of us, sooner or later, have to put aside the primacy of our own needs; we have to relinquish our narrow expectations of self-fulfillment and our agendas for self-assertion. Conversion is ultimately dying to self and becoming part of something that is larger than any of us. Community is the environment which can enable that conversion, and community is the fruit of that conversion. Our perspective changes from 'what can the community do for me?' to 'what can I do to best serve the community?' The ramifications of this conversion are profound. The change affects us spiritually in terms of our identities, politically in terms of our loyalties, economically in terms of our securities, socially in terms of our commitments, and personally in terms of our vocations. Through it all, the most profound change is finally the most simple: discovering the meaning of love.

Jim Wallis, 1981 [64]

In Ourselves: Narrative

After that life-giving Water succoured me, washing away
the stain of former years, and pouring into my cleansed and
hallowed breast the light which comes from heaven, after
that I drank in the heavenly Spirit, and was created into a
new man by a second birth, – then marvellously what
before was doubtful became plain to me, what was hidden
was revealed, what was before difficult now had a way and
means, what had seemed impossible now could be achieved
. . . For there is no measure or rule, as is the way of earthly
gifts, in dispensing of the gift from heaven; the Spirit is
poured forth liberally, not confined by limits, not hindered
in its course by the restraint of barriers or by definitely
measured goals. It flows on without a stop, it flows over
without stint.

Cyprian, c. 246 [65]

*
**

I probed the hidden depths of my soul and wrung its pitiful
secrets from it, and when I mustered them all before the eyes
of my heart, a great storm broke within me, bringing with it
a great deluge of tears. I stood up and left Alypius so that I
might weep and cry to my heart's content, for it occurred to
me that tears were best shed in solitude. I moved away far
enough to avoid being embarrassed even by his presence.
He must have realized what my feelings were, for I suppose
I had said something and he had known from the sound of
my voice that I was ready to burst into tears. So I stood up
and left him where we had been sitting, utterly bewildered.
Somehow I flung myself down beneath a fig tree and gave
way to the tears which now streamed from my eyes, the

71

sacrifice that is acceptable to you. I had much to say to you, my God, not in these very words but in this strain: *Lord, will you never be content? Must we always taste your vengeance? Forget the long record of our sins.* For I felt that I was still the captive of my sins, and in my misery I kept crying 'How long shall I go on saying "tomorrow, tomorrow"? Why not now? Why not make an end of my ugly sins at this moment?'

I was asking myself these questions, weeping all the while with the most bitter sorrow in my heart, when all at once I heard the sing-song voice of a child in a nearby house. Whether it was the voice of a boy or a girl I cannot say, but again and again it repeated the refrain 'Take it and read, take it and read'. At this I looked up, thinking hard whether there was any kind of game in which children used to chant words like these, but I could not remember ever hearing them before. I stemmed my flood of tears and stood up, telling myself that this could only be a divine command to open my book of scripture and read the first passage on which my eyes should fall. For I had heard the story of Antony, and I remembered how he had happened to go into a church while the Gospel was being read and had taken it as a counsel addressed to himself when he heard the words *Go home and sell all that belongs to you. Give it to the poor, and so the treasure you have shall be in heaven; then come back and follow me.* By this divine pronouncement he had at once been converted to you.

So I hurried back to the place where Alypius was sitting, for when I stood up to move away I had put down the book containing Paul's Epistles. I seized it and opened it, and in silence I read the first passage on which my eyes fell: *Not in revelling and drunkenness, not in lust and wantonness, not in quarrels and rivalries. Rather, arm yourselves with the Lord Jesus Christ; spend no more thought on nature and nature's appetites.* I had no wish to read more and no need to do so. For in an instant, as I came to the end of the sentence, it was as though the light of confidence flooded into my heart and all the darkness of doubt was dispelled.

Augustine, 401 [66]

***

How late I came to love you, O beauty so ancient and so fresh, how late I came to love you! You were within me while I had gone outside to seek you. Unlovely myself, I rushed towards all those lovely things you had made. And always you were with me, and I was not with you. All these beauties kept me far from you – although they would not have existed at all unless they had their being in you. You called, you cried, you shattered my deafness. You sparkled, you blazed, you drove away my blindness. You shed your fragrance, and I drew in my breath, and I pant for you. I tasted and now I hunger and thirst. You touched me, and now I burn with longing for your peace.

Augustine, 401 [67]

***

I hated that word 'righteousness of God', which, according to the use and custom of all the teachers, I had been taught to understand philosophically regarding the formal or active righteousness, as they call it, with which God is righteous and punishes the unrighteous sinner.

Though I lived as a monk without reproach, I felt that I was a sinner before God with an extremely disturbed conscience. I could not believe that he was placated by my satisfaction. I did not love, yes, I hated the righteous God who punishes sinners, and secretly, if not blasphemously, certainly murmuring greatly, I was angry with God, and said, 'As if, indeed, it is not enough, that miserable sinners, eternally lost through original sin, are crushed by every kind of calamity by the law of the decalogue, without having God add pain to pain by the gospel and also by the gospel threatening us with his righteousness and wrath!' Thus I raged with a fierce and troubled conscience. Nevertheless, I beat importunately upon Paul at that place, most ardently desiring to know what St Paul wanted.

At last, by the mercy of God, meditating day and night, I gave heed to the context of the words, namely, 'In it the righteousness of God is revealed, as it is written, "He who through faith is righteous shall live".' There I began to understand that the righteousness of God is that by which the righteous lives by a gift of God, namely by faith. And this is the meaning: the righteousness of God is revealed by the gospel, namely, the passive righteousness with which merciful God justifies us by faith, as it is written, 'He who through faith is righteous shall live.' Here I felt that I was altogether born again and had entered paradise itself through open gates. There a totally other face of the entire scripture showed itself to me. Thereupon I ran through the scriptures from memory. I also found in other terms an analogy, as, the work of God, that is, what God does in us, the power of God, with which he makes us strong, the wisdom of God, with which he makes us wise, the strength of God, the salvation of God, the glory of God.

And I extolled my sweetest word with a love as great as the hatred with which I had before hated the word 'righteousness of God'. Thus that place in Paul was for me truly the gate to paradise. Later I read Augustine's *The Spirit and the Letter*, where contrary to hope I found that he, too, interpreted God's righteousness in a similar way, as the righteousness with which God clothes us when he justifies us. Although this was heretofore said imperfectly and he did not explain all things concerning imputation clearly, it nevertheless was pleasing that God's righteousness with which we are justified was taught.

Martin Luther, 1545 [68]

Drown that body of sin which thou hast built up in thee, drown that world of sin which thou hast created (for we have a creation as well as God) *hominem fecit Deus, peccatorem homo*, man is God's creature and the sinner is man's creature, spare thy world no more than God spared his, who drowned it with the flood, drown thine too with repentant tears. But when that work is religiously done, *miserere animae tuae*, be as merciful to thy soul as he was to mankind, drown it no more, suffer it not to lie under the water of distrustful diffidence, for so thou mayest fall too low to be able to tug up against the tide again, so thou mayest be swallowed in Cain's whirlpool, to think thy sins greater than can be forgiven.

John Donne, 1618 [69]

*
**

So God was pleased on the sudden, and as it were in an instant, to alter the whole course of his former dispensation towards me, and said of and to my soul 'yea live, yea live I say' said God: and as he created the world and the matter of all things by a word, so he created and put a new life and spirit into my soul, and so great an alteration was strange to me.

The word of promise which he let fall into my heart, and which was but as it were softly whispered to my soul; and as when a man speaks afar off, he gives a still, yet a certain sound, or as one hath expressed the preachings of the gospel by the Apostles, that God whispered the gospel out of Sion, but the sound whereof went forth over the whole earth; so this speaking of God to my soul, although it was but a gentle sound, yet it made a noise over my whole heart, and filled and possessed all the faculties of my whole soul. God took me aside, and as it were privately said unto me, 'Do you now turn to me, and I will forgive all your sins though never so many, as I forgave and pardoned my servant Paul, and convert you unto me . . .'

I remember some two years after, preaching at Ely . . . I told the auditory, meaning myself in the person of another, that a man to be converted, who is ordinarily ignorant of what the work of conversion should be, and what particular passages it consists of, was yet guided through all the dark corners and windings of it, as would be a wonder to think of, and would be as if a man were to go to the top of that Lantern, and to bring him into all the passages of the Minster, within doors and without, and knew not a jot of the way, and were in every step in danger to tread awry and fall down. So it was with me . . . and it became one evidence of the truth of the work of grace upon me, when I reviewed it, that I had been so strangely guided in the dark.

Thomas Goodwin, 1620s [70]

**
*

The Memorial

A piece of parchment recording the decisive experience of 1654 was found sewn into Pascal's clothing after his death, and it seems that he carried it with him at all times.

The year of grace 1654.
   Monday, 23 November, feast of Saint Clement, Pope
      and Martyr, and of others in the Martyrology.
   Eve of Saint Chrysogonus, Martyr and others.
   From about half past ten in the evening until half past
      mid-night.

Fire.

'God of Abraham, God of Isaac, God of Jacob,' not of
      philosophers and scholars.
Certainty, certainty, heartfelt, joy, peace.
God of Jesus Christ.
God of Jesus Christ.
My God and your God.
'Thy God shall be my God.'

The world forgotten, and everything except God.
He can only be found by the ways taught in the
  Gospels.
Greatness of the human soul.
'O righteous Father, the world had not known thee,
  but I have known thee.'
Joy, joy, joy, tears of joy.
I have cut myself off from him.
They have forsaken me, the fountain of living waters.
'My God wilt thou forsake me?'
Let me not be cut off from him for ever!
'And this is life eternal, that they might know thee,
  the only true God, and Jesus Christ whom thou hast
  sent.'
Jesus Christ.
Jesus Christ.
I have cut myself off from him, shunned him, denied
  him, crucified him.
Let me never be cut off from him!
He can only be kept by the ways taught in the Gospel.
Sweet and total renunciation.
Total submission to Jesus Christ and my director.
Everlasting joy in return for one day's effort on earth.
I will not forget thy word. Amen.

Blaise Pascal, 1654 [71]

*
**

At another time I remember I was again much under the
Question, Whether the blood of Christ was sufficient to
save my Soul? In which doubt I continued from morning till
about seven or eight at night; and at last, when I was, as it
were, quite worn out with fear lest it should not lay hold on
me, those words did sound suddenly within me, *He is able*:
but me thought this word *able*, was spoke so loud unto me,

it shewed such a *great word*, it seemed to be writ in *great* letters, and gave such a justle to my fear and doubt, (I mean for the time it tarried with me, which was about a day) as I never had from that, all my life either before or after that, *Heb. 7:25.*

But one morning when I was again at prayer and trembling under the fear of this, that no word of God could help me, that piece of a sentence darted in upon me, *My Grace is sufficient.* At this me thought I felt some stay, as if there might be hopes. But O how good a thing is it for God to send his Word! for about a fortnight before, I was looking on this very place, and then I thought it could not come near my Soul with comfort, and threw down my Book in a pet; then I thought it was not large enough for me; no, not large enough; but now it was as if it had arms of grace so wide, that it could not only inclose me, but many more besides.

By these words I was sustained, yet not without exceeding conflicts, for the space of seven or eight weeks: for my peace would be in and out sometimes twenty times a day: Comfort now, and Trouble presently; Peace now, and before I could go a furlong, as full of Fear and Guilt as ever heart could hold; and this was not only now and then, but my whole seven weeks' experience; for this about the sufficiency of grace, and that of *Esau's* parting with his Birth-right, would be like a pair of scales within my mind, sometimes one end would be uppermost, and sometimes again the other, according to which would be my peace or trouble.

Therefore I still did pray to God, that he would come in with this Scripture more fully on my heart, to wit, that he would help me to apply the whole sentence, for as yet I could not: that he gave, I gathered; but farther I could not go, for as yet it only helped me to hope there might be mercy for me, *My grace is sufficient*; and tho it came no farther, it answered my former question; to wit, that there was hope; yet, because *for thee* was left out, I was not contented, but prayed to God for that also: Wherefore, one day as I was in a Meeting of God's People, full of sadness and terror, for my fears again were strong upon me, and I was now thinking, my soul was never the better, but my case most sad and fearful, these words did with great power suddenly break in upon me, *My grace is sufficient for thee, my grace is sufficient for thee, my grace is sufficient for thee*; three times together; and, O me-thought that every word was a mighty word unto me; as *my*, and *grace*, and *sufficient*, and *for thee*; they were then, and sometimes are still, far bigger than others be.

At which time, my Understanding was so enlightned, that I was as though I had seen the Lord Jesus look down from Heaven through the Tiles upon me, and direct these words unto me; this sent me mourning home, it broke my heart, and filled me full of joy, and laid me as low as the dust, only it stayed not long with me, I mean in this glory and refreshing comfort, yet it continued with me for several weeks, and did encourage me to hope.

John Bunyan, 1666 [72]

*
**

And as for those doubts of my own salvation, which exercised me many years, the chiefest causes of them were these:
1. Because I could not distinctly trace the workings of the Spirit upon my heart in that method which Mr Bolton, Mr Hooker, Mr Rogers and other divines describe; nor know the time of my conversion, being wrought on by the forementioned degrees. But since then I understood that the soul is in too dark and passionate plight at first to be able to keep an exact account of the order of its own operations . . .
2. My second doubt was as aforesaid, because of the hardness of my heart or want of such lively apprehensions of things spiritual which I had about things corporal. And

though I still groan under this as my sin and want, yet I now perceive that a soul in flesh doth work so much after the manner of the flesh that it much desireth sensible apprehensions; but things spiritual and distant are not so apt to work upon them, and to stir the passions, as things present and sensible are . . . and this is the ordinary state of the believer.

3. My next doubt was lest education and fear had done all that ever was done upon my soul, and regeneration and love were yet to seek; because I had found convictions from my childhood, and found more fear than love in all my duties and restraints.

But I afterwards perceived that education is God's ordinary way for the conveyance of his grace, and ought no more to be set in opposition to the Spirit than the preaching of the Word; and that it was the great mercy of God to begin with me so soon . . . And I understand that though fear without love be not a state of saving grace, . . . the soul of a believer groweth up by degrees from the more troublesome (but safe) operations of fear to the more high and excellent operations of complacential love . . .

But I understood at last that God breaketh not all men's hearts alike . . .

Richard Baxter, 1696[73]

***

One morning, while I was walking in a solitary place, as usual, I at once saw that all my contrivances and projects to effect or procure deliverance and salvation for myself were utterly *in vain*; I was brought quite to a stand, as finding myself totally *lost* . . . While I remained in this state, my *notions* respecting my *duties* were quite different from what I had ever entertained in times past. Before this, the more I did in duty, the more hard I thought it would be for God to cast me off . . . Now I saw that there was no necessary connection between my prayers and the bestowment of divine mercy . . . I saw that I had been heaping up my devotions before God, fasting, praying, etc., pretending, and indeed really thinking sometimes, that I was aiming at the glory of God; whereas I never once *truly* intended it, but only for my own happiness . . . the whole was nothing but *self-worship*, and an horrid abuse of God . . .

I continued, as I remember, in this state of mind, from Friday morning till the Sabbath evening following (July 12, 1739), when I was walking again in the same solitary place . . . I thought that the spirit of God had *quite* left me; but still was not distressed; yet disconsolate, as if there was nothing on heaven and earth could make me happy. Having been thus endeavouring to pray – though, as I thought, very stupid and senseless – for nearly half an hour; then, as I was walking in a dark, thick grove, *unspeakable glory* seemed to open to the view and apprehension of my soul. I do not mean any *external* brightness, for I saw no such thing; nor do I intend any imagination of a body of light, some where in the third heavens, or any thing of that nature; but it was a new inward apprehension or view that I had of *God*, such as I never had before, nor any thing which had the least resemblance to it. I stood still; wondered; and admired! . . . My soul rejoiced with joy unspeakable, to see such a God, such a glorious divine Being; and I was inwardly pleased and satisfied, that he should be *God over all* for ever and ever. My soul was so captivated and delighted with the excellency, loveliness, greatness, and other perfections of God, that I was even swallowed up in him; at least to that degree, that I had no thought (as I remember) at first, about my own salvation, and scarce reflected that there was such a creature as myself.

Thus God, I trust, brought me to a hearty disposition to *exalt him*, and set him on the throne, and principally and ultimately to aim at his honour and glory, as king of the universe . . . At this time, the *way of salvation* opened to me with such infinite wisdom, suitableness, and excellency, that I wondered I should ever think of any other way of salvation; was amazed that I had not dropped my own contrivances, and complied with this lovely, blessed, and excellent way before. If I could have been saved by my own duties, or any other way that I had formerly contrived, my whole soul would now have refused it. I wondered that all the world did not see and comply with this way of salvation, entirely by the *righteousness of Christ* . . .

David Brainerd, 1739 [74]

*
**

My distress of mind continued for about three months, and well might it have continued for years, since my sins were more in number than the hairs of my head, or than the sands upon the sea shore . . . But in Passion week, as I was reading Bishop Wilson on the Lord's Supper, I met with an expression to this effect: 'That the Jews knew what they did when they transferred their sin to the head of their offering.' The thought rushed into my mind, What! may I transfer all my guilt to another? Has God provided an offering for me, that I may lay my sins on his head? then, God willing, I will not bear them on my own soul one moment longer. Accordingly I sought to lay my sins upon the sacred head of Jesus; and on the Wednesday began to have a hope of mercy; on the Thursday that hope increased; on the Friday and Saturday it became more strong; and on the Sunday morning (Easterday, April 4) I awoke early with those words upon my heart and lips, 'Jesus Christ is risen to-day! Hallelujah! Hallelujah!' From that hour peace flowed in rich abundance into my soul; and at the Lord's table in our chapel I had the sweetest access to God through my blessed Saviour.

Charles Simeon, c. 1779 [75]

Christianity is a *personal* matter, not to be commended merely to others, but to be experienced in your own soul: and though you may confound your opponents by your arguments, you will never do any essential good, and much less will you reap any saving benefit to your own soul, till you can say, 'What mine eyes have seen, mine ears have heard, and mine hands have handled of the word of life, that same declare I unto you'.

Charles Simeon, 1822 [76]

*
**

And now, now that in many ways I have been brought to the last extremity, now (since last Easter, though with intervals) a hope has awakened in my soul that God may desire to resolve the fundamental misery of my being. That is to say, now I am in faith in the profoundest sense. Faith is immediacy after reflection. As poet and thinker I have represented all things in the medium of the imagination, myself living in resignation. Now life comes closer to me, or I am closer to myself, coming to myself. – To God all things are possible, that thought is now, in the deepest sense, my watch-word, has acquired a significance in my eyes which I had never imagined it could have. That I must never, at any moment, presume to say that there is no way out for God because I cannot see any. For it is despair and presumption to confuse one's pittance of imagination with the possibility over which God disposes.

Søren Kierkegaard, 1848 [77]

*
**

And while I was reading the Gospel, I thought, well, I will just say a few words in explanation of this, and then I will dismiss them. So I went up into the pulpit and gave out my text. I took it from the gospel of the day – 'What think ye of Christ?' (Matt. 22:42).

As I went on to explain the passage, I saw that the Pharisees and scribes did not know that Christ was the Son of God, or that he was come to save them. They were looking for a king, the son of David, to reign over them as they were. Something was telling me, all the time, 'You are no better than the Pharisees yourself – you do not believe that he is the Son of God, and that he is come to save you, any more than they did.' I do not remember all I said, but I felt a wonderful light and joy coming into my soul, and I was beginning to see what the Pharisees did not. Whether it was something in my words, or my manner, or my look, I know not; but all of a sudden a local preacher, who happened to be in the congregation, stood up, and putting up his arms, shouted out in Cornish manner, 'The parson is converted! the parson is converted! Hallelujah!' and in another moment his voice was lost in the shouts and praises of three or four hundred of the congregation. Instead of rebuking this extraordinary 'brawling', as I should have done in a former time, I joined in the outburst of praise; and to make it more orderly, I gave out the Doxology – 'Praise God, from whom all blessings flow' – and the people sang it with heart and voice, over and over again. My Churchmen were dismayed, and many of them fled precipitately from the place. Still the voice of praise went on, and was swelled by numbers of passers-by, who came into the church, greatly surprised to hear and see what was going on.

When this subsided, I found at least twenty people crying for mercy, whose voices had not been heard in the excitement and noise of thanksgiving. They all professed to find peace and joy in believing. Amongst this number there were three from my own house; and we returned home praising God.

The news spread in all directions that 'the parson was converted', and that by his own sermon, in his own pulpit!

William Haslam, 1851 [78]

Though, according to my ideas at that time, I thought I had done a good deed in burning the Gospel, yet my unrest of heart increased, and for two days after that I was very miserable. On the third day, when I felt I could bear it no longer, I got up at three in the morning, and after bathing, I prayed that if there was a God at all he would reveal himself to me, and show me the way of salvation, and end this unrest of my soul. I firmly made up my mind that, if this prayer was not answered, I would before daylight go down to the railway, and place my head on the line before the incoming train.

I remained till about half past four praying and waiting and expecting to see Krishna or Buddha, or some other *Avatar* of the Hindu religion; they appeared not, but a light was shining in the room. I opened the door to see where it came from, but all was dark outside. I returned inside, and the light increased in intensity and took the form of a globe of light above the ground, and in this light there appeared, not the form I expected, but the living Christ whom I had counted as dead. To all eternity I shall never forget his glorious and loving face, nor the few words which he spoke: 'Why do you persecute me? See, I have died on the cross for you and for the whole world.' These words were burned into my heart as by lightning, and I fell on the ground before him. My heart was filled with inexpressible joy and peace, and my whole life was entirely changed. Then the old Sundar Singh died and a new Sundar Singh, to serve the Living Christ, was born.

Sadhu Sundar Singh, 1904 [79]

***

Doubtless, by definition, God was Reason itself. But would he also be 'reasonable' in that other, more comfortable, sense? Not the slightest assurance on that score was offered me. Total surrender, the absolute leap in the dark, were demanded. The reality with which no treaty can be made was upon me. The demand was not even 'All or nothing'. I think that stage had been passed, on the bus-top when I unbuckled my armour and the snow-man started to melt. Now, the demand was simply 'All'.

You must picture me alone in that room at Magdalen, night after night, feeling, whenever my mind lifted even for a second from my work, the steady, unrelenting approach of him whom I so earnestly desired not to meet. That which I greatly feared had at last come upon me. In the Trinity Term of 1929 I gave in, and admitted that God was God, and knelt and prayed: perhaps, that night, the most dejected and reluctant convert in all England. I did not then see what is now the most shining and obvious thing; the divine humility which will accept a convert even on such terms. The Prodigal Son at least walked home on his own feet. But who can duly adore that Love which will open the high gates to a prodigal who is brought in kicking, struggling, resentful, and darting his eyes in every direction for a chance of escape? The words *compelle intrare*, compel them to come in, have been so abused by wicked men that we shudder at them; but, properly understood, they plumb the depth of the divine mercy. The hardness of God is kinder than the softness of men, and his compulsion is our liberation.

C. S. Lewis, 1929 [80]

***

Last night, going to bed alone, I suddenly found myself (I was taking off my waistcoat) reciting the Lord's Prayer in a loud, emphatic voice – a thing I had not done for many years – with deep urgency and profound disturbed emotion. While I went on I grew more composed; as if it had been empty and craving and were being replenished, my soul grew still; every word had a strange fullness of meaning which astonished and delighted me. It was late; I had sat up reading; I was sleepy; but as I stood in the middle of the floor half-undressed, saying the prayer over and over, meaning after meaning sprang from it, overcoming me again with joyful surprise; and I realized that this simple petition was always universal and always inexhaustible, and day by day sanctified human life.

Edwin Muir, 1939 [81]

***

More and more painfully we saw that we had utterly failed in the hour of trial. We had not devoted ourselves to God in prayer and fervent entreaty, humbled before the holiness of God when his judgement fell upon our nation. We had not interceded for our brothers and sisters, who entered eternity by the thousand each night. Seldom, if ever, were we at hand to show what help we could when the 'apple of God's eye', the Jews, were so cruelly maltreated.

Yet outwardly we seemed so religious. Every morning we read God's Word; every week we attended the Bible study and participated in intercession for the war. Now the scales fell from our eyes and we could scarcely comprehend our blindness. Struck by the seriousness of our sin, we were driven by the thought to make amends by standing in the breach for our people from then on (Ezekiel 22:30) and devoting ourselves to prayer.

One Sunday in February 1945 we were gathered together for the youth Bible study in the Steinberg House in a small room called the 'blue room' – the badly damaged roof had not yet been repaired, but here the rain did not seep through as quickly as in the rooms upstairs. I spoke to the girls about our priestly commission of prayer and adoration as well as about our failure to recognise this commission, let alone perform it. I related how the heathen people of Nineveh repented in sackcloth and ashes when only threatened by God's judgement (Jonah 3). Yet as Christians we had not repented under the judgement of God. All those years we had remained proud and unmoved, although judgement should begin with the household of God.

Suddenly, in the middle of this Bible study, a shower of repentance rained down upon everyone present. Girls who had never prayed aloud in front of others spontaneously began to pray. Genuine tears were shed because of all our sin, because of all that we had failed to do. Before, it was individuals that had come to repentance – and mainly for their personal sins – but now repentance had taken hold of the young people as a whole. We were filled with grief over our lukewarmness, our spiritual death, our failure to fulfil our priestly ministry of prayer for the sin and distress of our nation. Out of this repentance God granted us a new prayer life of intercession and of adoration for the Triune God.

Basilea Schlink, 1945 [82]

*
**

These first days, left so utterly alone in such dark and filthy confinement; subjected to it so suddenly and without reason; cut off from the outside world by immense distances and hedged in by a foe, who as yet did not deign even to speak sensibly to me; together with the absolute shattering of my highest expectation of years, my work amongst the Tibetans cruelly snatched from me, my position of opportunity in Tibet destroyed and myself brought back to Batang a helpless prisoner, now sinking lower and lower in a mire of fateful circumstance in this dismal dungeon out at the back of beyond; all this created an unbearable pressure weighing down upon me, crushing my spirit and rending my soul. The spiritual poverty of my life and service suddenly came before me. All my Christian life seemed just to crumble away. So much of all that I had said and done, ostensibly for his Kingdom, was now, under his rebuke, revealed to be nothing but wood, hay and stubble. With tears, I broke down and knelt trembling on the dusty floor. My mind in a turmoil and overcome by a sense of sin and unworthiness, I wept my way afresh to Calvary. There God met me again. His love to me was wonderful. I thought of the way behind as the way of a prodigal but now, as I knelt in the dust, the Father came running out to meet me where I was. There was no rebuke. I had come to where I had found him at the first. I tried to blurt out: 'I have sinned . . . I am not worthy . . . I am not worthy,' but was only conscious of his great arms around me and his kiss of pardon on my dirty cheeks. And there I knelt and knelt until I heard those matchless words: 'Bring forth the best robe . . . Bring forth the best and put it on him.' It will live with me for ever. Into my heart came a peace and a joy in God's grace and forgiveness, in a measure I had never known before.

Geoffrey Bull, 1950 [83]

*
**

Whitsunday

I don't know Who – or what – put the question, I don't know when it was put. I don't even remember answering. But at some moment I did answer *Yes* to Someone – or Something – and from that hour I was certain that existence is meaningful and that, therefore, my life, in self-surrender, had a goal.

From that moment I have known what it means 'not to look back', and 'to take no thought for the morrow'.

Led by the Ariadne's thread of my answer through the labyrinth of Life, I came to a time and place where I realised that the Way leads to a triumph which is a catastrophe and to a catastrophe which is a triumph, that the price for committing one's life would be reproach, and that the only elevation possible to man lies in the depths of humiliation. After that, the word 'courage' lost its meaning, since nothing could be taken from me.

The Lord of the Journey

As I continued along the Way, I learned, step by step, word by word, that behind every saying in the Gospels, stands *one* man and *one* man's experience. Also behind the prayer that the cup might pass from him and his promise to drink it. Also behind each of the words from the Cross.

Dag Hammarskjöld, 1961 [84]

**

After a Stoic, a Peripatetic, a Pythagorean,
Justin Martyr studied the words of the Saviour,
finding them short, precise, terrible, and full of
    refreshment.
I am tickled to learn this.

Let one day desolate Sherry, fair, thin, tall,
at 29 today her life the Sahara Desert,
who never has once enjoyed a significant relation,
so find his lightning words.

John Berryman, 1971 [85]

**

Suddenly, a breakthrough of hope flooded me. Suppose, just suppose God were like a father. If my earthly father would put aside everything to listen to me, wouldn't my heavenly Father . . . ?

Shaking with excitement, I got out of bed, sank to my knees on the rug, looked up to heaven and in rich new understanding called God 'My Father'.

I was not prepared for what happened.

'Oh Father, my Father . . . Father God.'

Hesitantly, I spoke his name aloud. I tried different ways of speaking to him. And then, as if something broke through for me I found myself trusting that he was indeed hearing me, just as my earthly father had always done.

'Father, oh my Father God,' I cried, with growing confidence. My voice seemed unusually loud in the large bedroom as I knelt on the rug beside my bed. But suddenly that room wasn't empty any more. *He* was there! I could sense his presence. I could feel his hand laid gently on my head. It was as if I could *see* his eyes, filled with love and compassion. He was so close that I found myself laying my head on his knees like a little girl sitting at her father's feet. For a long time I knelt there, sobbing quietly, floating in his love. I found myself talking with him, apologizing for not having known him before. And again, came his loving compassion, like a warm blanket settling around me.

Now I recognized this as the same loving Presence I had met that fragrance-filled afternoon in my garden. The same Presence I had sensed often as I read the Bible.

'I am confused, Father . . .' I said. 'I have to get one thing straight right away.' I reached over to the bedside table where I kept the Bible and the Koran side by side. I picked up both books and lifted them, one in each hand. 'Which, Father?' I said. 'Which one is your book?'

Then a remarkable thing happened. Nothing like it had ever occurred in my life in quite this way. For I heard a voice inside my being, a voice that spoke to me as clearly as if I were repeating words in my inner mind. They were fresh, full of kindness, yet at the same time full of authority.

'In which book do you meet me as your Father?'

I found myself answering: 'In the Bible.' That's all it took.

Bilquis Sheikh, 1979 [86]

*
**

Conversion

In a cold season of the world's turning,
When the air of the night was sharp-edged and clear,
When the evening stars strained together in yearning,
And the planets sang in the youth of the year;

91

When the wind whirled through in the earth's end's
  hunting,
Cried in the crags, moaning down to the sea,
Where the herring-gull screams, with the call of the
  bunting,
I passed through my death-day to life, and was free.
Into darkness the dense air-lord turned, suffocating,
Wrenched, groped out in pain, once more felt his fall.
By the passage of past years a voice came, relating
The deeds of the Ancient of Days, how his call,
Ringing down through the chambers of time, from the
  first
Had smiled on me, blessed by the cross of the cursed.

Patrick Carpmael, 1980s [87]

2

The Way

Jesus' words 'I am the Way' have always been a stumbling-block to those who prefer to deal in religious generalities. But the singularity of Jesus Christ which constitutes him the turning-point of personal and universal history is not selfish and private. He does not exclusively keep himself to himself. Faith grasps that he is unique in that he alone is authorised, because of who he is, to include us in his own identity; that he identified with us in order for us to identify with him; and that we find our true identity not in ourselves, but in being incorporated ('I in you and you in me') in his own inexhaustible life. As we find his life in us, so we learn that he is our true identity. Faith keeps reaching out to seize this extraordinary news.

Where an idealistic modern Liberalism (in Richard Niebuhr's memorable words) offered 'a God without wrath [bringing] men without sin into a Kingdom without judgment through the ministrations of a Christ without a Cross', the New Testament locates the extreme extent of Christ's identification with us on the Cross, in death and sin, our two ultimate negatives. Here we see the moment of absolute truth – for God and mankind, focussed in absolute human and divine vulnerability. Despite the fact that at times 'the Cross' has been divorced from the revelation explicit in Jesus' life, it remains the climax of love and sacrifice, the crucial intersection of light and darkness, the decisive crisis for all truth and lies, and above all the Way of reconciliation and at-one-ment. 'THE CROSS alone is our theology', proclaimed Luther; 'the Cross tests everything'. Precisely so, for it is not only the point where God is handing God over; it is also the point of meeting where we find ourselves again and again drawn to a responsive act of costly self-sacrifice. The paradox above all, however, is that this is precisely 'the attraction of the Cross'.

The work of the Spirit in redemption has often been subordinated to doctrines of the church or the ministry; the genuinely self-effacing creative Spirit has been bound. And yet not. Our repeated attempts to organise God are mercifully thwarted as God confronts us repeatedly in ways beyond our expectation. The One who deals individually with us is the One who breaks down the dividing walls of hostility, because God is the One who creates the Body of Christ, bringing light out of darkness, life out of death, existence out of non-existence. Again, in recent times, we have been learning a new language of experience, learning that there can be an experience of 'more' even where there has not been an experience of 'less'. More importantly, we have been rediscovering a proper Trinitarian doctrine of the Spirit.

All through its history, Christian faith has been tempted to be individualist. A sense of corporate community is essential but fragile. Essential, because the Christian community is called to be – and can be – a reflection of the divine community; fragile, because of all the failings and inadequacies of any visible and earthly (and earthy) community. The Church may be, as Evelyn Underhill reminds us, a flock of sheep rather than a collection of prize specimens; but it is not intended to be monochrome any more than the God who founded it. Rather, all the created variety, diversity, colour and extravagance of human life is intended to be

drawn and fused into a new creation of the Spirit, branded
with the cross and shaped around Christ. That is Christ's
Way. That is Christ's – and our – glory.

Faith in Christ:
Invitation

'Who takes issue with me? – let him stand against me.

I released the condemned;
I brought the dead to life;
I raise up the buried.
   Who is there that contradicts me?
I am the one', says the Christ,

'I am the one that destroyed death
   and triumphed over the enemy
   and trod down Hades
   and bound the strong one
   and carried off man to the heights of heaven;
I am the one', says the Christ.
'Come then, all you families of men who are
   compounded with sins,
   and get forgiveness of sins.
For I am your forgiveness,
   I am the Pascha of salvation,
   I am the lamb slain for you;
   I am your ransom,
   I am your life,
   I am your light,
   I am your salvation,
   I am your resurrection,
   I am your king.
I will raise you up by my right hand;
I am leading you up to the heights of heaven;
   there I will show you the Father from ages past.'

Melito of Sardis, c. 160[88]

The glory of God is man alive;
and the life of man is the vision of God.

Irenaeus, 182–8 [89]

*
**

So doth God almighty to his lovers in contemplation as a taverner that hath good wine to sell doth to good drinkers that will drink well of his wine and largely spend. Well he knoweth what they be when he seeth them in the street. Privily he goeth and whispereth them in the ear and saith to them that he hath a claret and that all fine for their own mouth. He taketh them to house and giveth them a taste. Soon when they have tasted thereof, and they think the drink good and greatly to their pleasure, then they drink day and night and the more they drink, the more they want. Such liking they have of that drink that of none other wine they think, but only for to drink their fill and to have of this drink all their will. And so they spend what they have, and then they spend or pledge their coat or hood and all that they may, to drink with liking as long as they desire. Thus it fareth sometime by God's lovers, that from the time that they had tasted of the sweetness of God, such liking they found therein that as drunken men they did spend what they had and gave themselves to fasting and to keeping vigil and to doing other penance.

Interpolation in Guigo II, after ?c. 1170 [90]

*
**

Love

Love bade me welcome: yet my soul drew back,
        Guiltie of dust and sinne.
But quick-ey'd Love, observing me grow slack
        From my first entrance in,
Drew nearer to me, sweetly questioning,
        If I lack'd any thing.

A guest, I answer'd, worthy to be here:
    Love said, You shall be he.
I the unkinde, ungratefull? Ah my deare,
    I cannot look on thee.
Love took my hand, and smiling did reply,
    Who made the eyes but I?

Truth Lord, but I have marr'd them: let my shame
    Go where it doth deserve.
And know you not, sayes Love, who bore the blame?
    My deare, then I will serve.
You must sit down, sayes Love, and taste my meat:
    So I did sit and eat.

George Herbert, 1633 [91]

*
**

Wherefore, I beseech you, set your mouths to this fountain, Christ, and so shall your souls be filled with the water of life, with the oil of gladness, and with the new wine of the kingdom of God. From him you shall have weighty joys, sweet embracements and ravishing consolations. And how can it be otherwise when your souls shall really communicate with God and by faith have a true taste, and by the Spirit have a sure earnest of all heavenly preferments, having, as it were, one foot in heaven while you live upon earth? O then what an eucharistical love will arise from your thankful hearts, extending itself first towards God and then towards men for God's sake! . . .

And if you can behold Christ with open face you shall see and feel things unutterable, and be changed from beauty to beauty, from glory to glory by the Spirit of the Lord, and so be happy in this life in your union with happiness, and happy hereafter in the full fruition of happiness: whither the Lord Jesus bring us all in his due time.

The Marrow of Modern Divinity, 1645 [92]

Faith in Christ: Identity

I am putting on the love of the Lord.

And his members are with him,
And I am dependent on them; and he loves me.

For I should not have known how to love the Lord,
If he had not continuously loved me.

Who is able to distinguish love,
Except him who is loved?

I love the Beloved and I myself love him,
And where his rest is, there also am I.

And I shall be no stranger,
Because there is no jealousy with the Lord Most High
   and Merciful.

I have been united to him, because the lover has found
   the Beloved,
Because I love him that is the Son, I shall become a son.

Indeed he who is joined to him who is immortal,
Truly shall be immortal.

And he who delights in the Life
Will become living.

This is the Spirit of the lord, which is not false,
Which teaches the sons of men to know his ways.

Be wise and understanding and vigilant.
   Hallelujah.

Odes of Solomon, early 2nd cent. [93]

For as when a figure which has been painted on wood is spoilt by dirt, it is necessary for him whose portrait it is to come again so that the picture can be renewed in the same material – for because of his portrait the material on which it is painted is not thrown away, but the portrait is redone on it – even so the all-holy Son of the Father, who is the image of the Father, came to our realms to renew man who had been made in his likeness, and, as one lost, to find him through the forgiveness of sins; just as he said in the gospels: '*I have come to save and find that which was lost.*'

Athanasius, 318 or 335-6 [94]

*
* *

The portrait painter is attentive to the face of the king as he paints and, when the face of the king is directly opposite, face to face, then he paints the portrait easily and well. But when he turns his face away, then the painter cannot paint because the face of the subject is not looking at the painter.

In a similar way the good portrait painter, Christ, for those who believe in him and gaze continually toward him, at once paints according to his own image a heavenly man. Out of his Spirit, out of the substance of the light itself, ineffable light, he paints a heavenly image and presents to it its noble and good Spouse.

If anyone, therefore, does not continually gaze at him, overlooking all else, the Lord will not paint his image with his own light. It is, therefore, necessary that we gaze on him, believing and loving him, casting aside all else and attending to him so that he may paint his own heavenly image and send it into our souls. And thus carrying Christ, we may receive eternal life and even here, filled with confidence, we may be at rest.

Macarius, mid 4th cent. [95]

Be thou my vision, O Lord of my heart,
Naught is all else to me, save that thou art.

Thou my best thought by day and by night,
Waking or sleeping, thy presence my light.

Be thou my wisdom, thou my true word;
I ever with thee, thou with me, Lord.

Thou my great Father, I thy dear son;
Thou in me dwelling, I with thee one.

Be thou my battle-shield, sword for the fight,
Be thou my dignity, thou my delight.

Thou my soul's shelter, thou my high tower;
Raise thou me heavenward, power of my power.

Riches I heed not or man's empty praise.
Thou mine inheritance now and always.

Thou, and thou only, first in my heart,
High King of heaven, my treasure thou art.

King of the seven heavens, grant me for dole,
Thy love in my heart, thy light in my soul.

Thy light from my soul, thy love from my heart,
King of the seven heavens, may they never depart.

With the High King of heaven, after victory won,
May I reach heaven's joys, O bright heaven's sun!

Heart of my own heart, whatever befall,
Still be my vision, O ruler of all.

Irish, 8th cent. [96]

*
**

He was suddenly completely there,
united with me in an ineffable manner,
joined to me in an unspeakable way
and immersed in me without mixing

as the fire melds one with the iron,
and the light with the crystal.
And he made me as though I were all fire.
And he showed me myself as light
and I became that which before I saw
and I had contemplated only from afar.
I do not know how to express to you
the paradox of this manner.
For I was unable to know
and I still now do not know
how he entered, how he united himself with me.
I was united with him, how can I tell you?
Who is he who united himself with me
and with whom I was united?
I shudder and I fear lest,
if I tell you, you will doubt,
and you will fall into blasphemy
because of your ignorance of such an experience,
and you may even lose your soul, my brother.
Nevertheless, having become one being,
I and he to whom I was united,
how shall I call myself?
God, having two natures, is one person;
he has made me a double being.

Symeon the New Theologian, late 10th cent. [97]

*
**

Just as a woman knows clearly when she has conceived, because the child leaps in her womb and she could not possibly be unaware that she is carrying it within herself, so he who has Christ formed within himself recognises his movements or illuminations and could not but be fully aware of his leapings or lightnings, and so perceives the shape of Christ within . . . What immense and inexpressible glory! What an excess of love! He who contains all things dwells within a corruptible and mortal humanity, whose whole being is under the ruling power of the One who indwells, so that the person himself becomes like a woman with child. What a wonder of ecstasy! What unthinkable acts and mysteries of an unthinkable God!

Symeon the New Theologian, c. 1010 [98]

*
* *

The mind of a man eager for Christ should part company as sharply as possible both with the actions and the opinions of the general run of people, and not look for an example of virtue from any quarter other than Christ alone . . . I would have you differ radically and weigh all values solely in terms of the fellowship of Christ.

Desiderius Erasmus, 1503 [99]

*
* *

For first through the cross every disciple becomes Christ's twin.

Martin Luther, 1518 [100]

*
* *

A Christian man is righteous and a sinner at the same time, holy and profane, an enemy of God and a child of God. None of the sophists will admit this paradox because they do not understand the meaning of justification.

Martin Luther, 1531 [101]

*
* *

If I am truly a sinner, I am nevertheless not a sinner. I am a sinner in and by myself, apart from Christ. Apart from myself and in Christ I am not a sinner.

Martin Luther, 1533 [102]

But since Christ has been so imparted to you with all his benefits that all his things are made yours, that you are made a member of him, indeed one with him, his righteousness overwhelms your sins; his salvation wipes out your condemnation; with his worthiness he intercedes that your unworthiness may not come before God's sight. Surely this is so: We ought not to separate Christ from ourselves or ourselves from him. Rather we ought to hold fast bravely with both hands to that fellowship by which he has bound himself to us . . .

Christ is not outside us but dwells within us. Not only does he cleave to us by an indivisible bond of fellowship, but with a wonderful communion, day by day, he grows more and more into one body with us, until he becomes completely one with us.

Jean Calvin, 1559 [103]

*
**

I saw in my Dream that the Interpreter took Christian by the hand, and led him into a place where was a Fire burning against a wall, and one standing by it always casting much Water upon it to quench it: yet did the Fire burn higher and hotter.

Then said Christian, 'What means this?'

The Interpreter answered, 'This Fire is the work of Grace that is wrought in the heart; he that casts Water upon it, to extinguish and put it out, is the Devil; but in that thou seest the Fire notwithstanding burn higher and hotter, thou shalt also see the reason of that. So he had him about to the backside of the wall, where he saw a man with a Vessel of Oil in his hand, of the which he did also continually cast, but secretly, into the Fire.'

Then said Christian, 'What means this?'

The Interpreter answered, 'This is Christ, who continually, with the Oil of his Grace, maintains the work already begun in the heart: by the means of which, notwithstanding what the Devil can do, the souls of his people prove gracious still. And in that thou sawest that the man stood behind the wall to maintain the Fire, that is to teach thee that it is hard for the tempted to see how this work of Grace is maintained in the soul.'

John Bunyan, 1678 [104]

*

Now I have found the ground, wherein
   Sure my soul's anchor may remain –
The wounds of Jesus, for my sin
   Before the world's foundation slain:
Whose mercy shall unshaken stay,
When heaven and earth are fled away.

Father, thy everlasting grace
   Our scanty thought surpasses far:
Thy heart still melts with tenderness,
   Thy arms of love still open are
Returning sinners to receive,
That mercy they may taste, and live.

O Love, thou bottomless abyss!
   My sins are swallow'd up in thee:
Cover'd is my unrighteousness,
   Nor spot of guilt remains in me,
While Jesu's blood, through earth and skies.
Mercy, free, boundless mercy, cries!

With faith I plunge me in this sea;
   Here is my hope, my joy, my rest:
Hither, when hell assails, I flee,
   I look into my Saviour's breast!
Away, sad doubt, and anxious fear!
Mercy is all that's written there.

Though waves and storms go o'er my head,
  Though strength, and health, and friends be gone,
Though joys be wither'd all, and dead,
  Though every comfort be withdrawn,
On this my steadfast soul relies,
Father, thy mercy never dies.

Fix'd on this ground will I remain,
  Though my heart fail, and flesh decay:
This anchor shall my soul sustain,
  When earth's foundations melt away;
Mercy's full power I then shall prove,
Loved with an everlasting love.

Johann Andreas Rothe, 1727, tr. John Wesley, 1740 [105]

*
**

Did you ever see my picture? I have it drawn by a masterly
hand. And though another person, and one whom I am far
from resembling, sat for it, it is as like me as one new guinea
is like another. The original was drawn at Corinth, and sent
to some persons of distinction at Rome. Many copies have
been taken, and though perhaps it is not to be seen in any of
the London print-shops, it has a place in most public and
private libraries, and I would hope in most families. I had
seen it a great many times before I could discover one of my
own features in it; but then my eyes were very bad. What is
remarkable, it was drawn long before I was born, but
having been favoured with some excellent eye-salve, I
quickly knew it to be my own. I am drawn in an attitude
which would be strange and singular, if it were not so
common with me, looking two different and opposite ways
at once, so that you would be puzzled to tell whether my
eyes are fixed upon heaven or upon earth: I am aiming at
things inconsistent with each other at the same instant, so
that I can accomplish neither. According to the different

light in which you view the picture, I appear to rejoice and mourn, to choose and refuse, to be a conqueror or a captive. In a word, I am a double person; a riddle. It is no wonder if you know not what to make of me, for I cannot tell what to make of myself. I would and I would not; I do and do not; I can and I cannot. I find the hardest things easy, and the easiest things impossible: but while I am in this perplexity, you will observe in the same piece, a hand stretched forth for my relief, and may see a label proceeding out of my mouth with these words, – 'I thank God, through Jesus Christ my Lord.' The more I study this picture, the more I discover some new and striking resemblance, which convinces me that the painter knew me better than I knew myself.

John Newton, 1773 [106]

*
**

I feel that all earthly connections are unimportant: I am born for God only. Christ is nearer to me than father, or mother, or sister, – a nearer relation, a more affectionate friend; and I rejoice to follow him, and to love him. Blessed Jesus! thou art all I want – a forerunner to me in all I ever shall go through, as a Christian, a minister, or a missionary. Rose in the morning with peacefulness and in prayer; was helped to rest by faith on the promises of God, and to be more serious about the effects of the word on the souls of the poor people, than anxious about their opinions of it. Preached from John 1:29. All very attentive as usual, but no impression seemingly. Read Jeremiah afterwards in my cabin, and was recovering from the ruffled state of mind I am generally in after preaching, when McK. by irrelevant conversation, and bringing full food to my pride, disturbed my peace; but at last it was restored, while praying for grace to live spiritually, above all carnal delights, which alas, I find it very hard to do; most of the prayers I offer up on this subject seeming to pass away like the wind. Read, prayed and sung below in the afternoon to a tolerable number. In prayer afterwards in private, had a most precious view of Christ, as a friend that sticketh closer than a brother. Oh how sweet was it to pray to him. I hardly knew how to contemplate him with praise enough; his adorable excellences more and more seemed to open the longer I spoke to him. Who shall shew forth all his praise? I can conceive it to be a theme long enough for eternity.

Henry Martyn, 1806 [107]

*
*

As kingfishers catch fire, dragonflies draw flame;
   As tumbled over rim in roundy wells
   Stones ring; like each tucked string tells, each hung
     bell's
Bow swung finds tongue to fling out broad its name;
Each mortal thing does one thing and the same:
   Deals out that being indoors each one dwells;
   Selves – goes itself; *myself* it speaks and spells,
Crying *What I do is me: for that I came.*

I say more: the just man justices;
   Keeps gráce: thát keeps all his goings graces;
Acts in God's eye what in God's eye he is –
   Chríst. For Christ plays in ten thousand places,
Lovely in limbs, and lovely in eyes not his
   To the Father through the features of men's faces.

Gerard Manley Hopkins, 1881–2 [108]

*
*

I only met Florence Allshorn . . . a few times – over a supper table, at a bazaar, in church. Each time I had an unforgettable and almost incommunicable impression of something I had never encountered before, a feeling that she was living in two worlds simultaneously, mine and one she brought with her. This seemed to show itself in a strange and delightful contradiction in her personality. She was at once gay and yet profoundly serious around her gaiety. She appreciated and offered the best of material pleasures and comforts and beauties and yet one suspected that they really meant nothing to her. She looked ready to share one's most trivial or sordid experience and one knew she would be untouched by it at the same time as bearing it. She gave me the impression of toughness and delicacy, like silver wire. I believe, of course, that I am trying to describe saintliness.

Athene Seyler, 1951 [109]

*

At rock bottom we are made in the image of God, and this stripping is very much like the cleaning of an ancient, beautiful wall painting, or of a painting by a great master that was painted over in the course of the centuries by tasteless people who had intruded upon the real beauty that had been created by the master. To begin with, the more we clean, the more things disappear, and it seems to us that we have created a mess where there was at least a certain amount of beauty; perhaps not much, but some beauty. And then we begin to discover the real beauty which the great master has put into his painting; we see the misery, then the mess in between, but at the same time we have a preview of the authentic beauty. And we discover that what we are is a poor person who needs God; but not God to fill the gap – God to be met.

Metropolitan Anthony, 1966 [110]

Faith in Christ: Incorporation

I confess, Lord, with thanksgiving,
    that you have made me in your image,
so that I can remember you, think of you, and love you.
But that image is so worn and blotted out by faults,
    so darkened by the smoke of sin,
    that it cannot do that for which it was made,
    unless you renew and refashion it.
Lord, I am not trying to make my way to your height,
for my understanding is in no way equal to that,
but I do desire to understand a little of your truth
    which my heart already believes and loves.
I do not seek to understand so that I may believe,
    but I believe so that I may understand;
        and what is more,
I believe that unless I do believe I shall not understand.

Anselm, 1078 [111]

*
**

Faith is not the human notion and dream that some people
call faith. When they see that no improvement of life and no
good works follow – although they can hear and say much
about faith – they fall into the error of saying, 'Faith is not
enough; one must do works in order to be righteous and be
saved.' This is due to the fact that when they hear the gospel,
they get busy and by their own powers create an idea in their
heart which says, 'I believe'; they take this then to be a true
faith. But, as it is a human figment and idea that never
reaches the depths of the heart, nothing comes of it either,
and no improvement follows.

    Faith, however, is a divine work in us which changes us

and makes us to be born anew of God, John 1:12-13. It kills the old Adam and makes us altogether different men, in heart and spirit and mind and powers; and it brings with it the Holy Spirit. O it is a living, busy, active, mighty thing, this faith. It is impossible for it not to be doing good works incessantly. It does not ask whether good works are to be done, but before the question is asked, it has already done them, and is constantly doing them. Whoever does not do such works, however, is an unbeliever. He gropes and looks around for faith and good works, but knows neither what faith is nor what good works are. Yet he talks and talks, with many words, about faith and good works.

Faith is a living, daring confidence in God's grace, so sure and certain that the believer would stake his life on it a thousand times. This knowledge of and confidence in God's grace makes men glad and bold and happy in dealing with God and with all creatures. And this is the work which the Holy Spirit performs in faith. Because of it, without compulsion, a person is ready and glad to do good to everyone, to serve everyone, to suffer everything, out of love and praise to God who has shown him this grace. Thus it is impossible to separate works from faith, quite as impossible as to separate heat and light from fire.

Martin Luther, 1522 [112]

***

Why, then, are we justified by faith? Because by faith we grasp Christ's righteousness, by which alone we are reconciled to God. Yet you could not grasp this without at the same time grasping sanctification also. For he 'is given unto us for righteousness, wisdom, sanctification, and redemption' (1 Cor. 1:30). Therefore Christ justifies no one whom he does not at the same time sanctify. These benefits are joined together by an everlasting and indissoluble bond, so that those whom he illumines by his wisdom, he redeems;

those whom he redeems, he justifies; those whom he justifies, he sanctifies.

But, since the question concerns only righteousness and sanctification, let us dwell upon these. Although we may distinguish them, Christ contains both of them inseparably in himself. Do you wish, then, to attain righteousness in Christ? You must first possess Christ; but you cannot possess him without being made partaker in his sanctification, because he cannot be divided into pieces (1 Cor. 1:13). Since, therefore, it is solely by expending himself that the Lord gives us these benefits to enjoy, he bestows both of them at the same time, the one never without the other. Thus it is clear how true it is that we are justified not without works yet not through works, since in our sharing in Christ, which justifies us, sanctification is just as much included as righteousness.

Jean Calvin, 1559 [113]

*
**

If Christ Jesus shall have been pleased to come to [a sinner's] door, and to have stood, and knocked, and entered, and supped, and brought his dish, and made himself that dish, and sealed a reconciliation to that sinner, in admitting him to that Table, to that Communion, let us forget the name of publican, the vices of any particular profession; and forget the name of sinner, the history of any man's former life; and be glad to meet that man now in the arms, and to grow up with that man now in the bowels of Christ Jesus; since Christ doth not now begin to make that man his, but now declares to us, that he hath been his from all eternity.

John Donne, 1626 [114]

*
**

It is the heart which perceives God and not the reason. That is what faith is: perceived by the heart, not by the reason.

Blaise Pascal, 1658 [115]

Faith empties the soul, and looks upon itself as dead, and sees its life laid up in Christ; and hence forsakes itself, and embraceth the Lord of glory. Secondly, the Spirit comes and possesseth a forsaken empty house, and there lives and dwells.

Thomas Shepard, 1660 [116]

***

To see the law by Christ fulfill'd,
   And hear his pardoning voice,
Changes a slave into a child,
   And duty into choice.

William Cowper, 1779 [117]

***

I would have the whole of my experience one continued sense – 1st, of my nothingness, and dependence on God; 2d, of my guiltiness, and desert before him; 3d, of my obligations to redeeming love, as utterly overwhelming me with its incomprehensible extent and grandeur . . . In two words, my desire is, 1st, never to forget for a moment what *I* am: and 2dly, never to forget for a moment what *God* is . . .

Charles Simeon, 1834 [118]

***

I trust you will have a pleasant and profitable time in Germany. I know you will apply hard to German; but do not forget the culture of the inner man, – I mean of the heart. How diligently the cavalry officer keeps his sabre clean and sharp; every stain he rubs off with the greatest care. Remember you are God's sword, – his instrument, – I trust a chosen vessel unto him to bear his name. In great measure, according to the purity and perfections of the instrument, will be the success. It is not great talents God blesses so much as great likeness to Jesus. A holy minister is an awful weapon in the hand of God.

Robert Murray M'Cheyne, 1840 [119]

**

The Rigorous Coachman

Of what is the human spirit capable?

Once upon a time there was a rich man who ordered from abroad at a high price a pair of entirely faultless and high-bred horses which he desired to have for his own pleasure and for the pleasure of driving them himself. Then about a year or two elapsed. Anyone who previously had known these horses would not have been able to recognize them again. Their eyes had become dull and drowsy, their gait lacked style and decision, they couldn't endure anything, they couldn't hold out, they hardly could be driven four miles without having to stop on the way, sometimes they came to a standstill as he sat for all he was worth attempting to drive them, besides they had acquired all sorts of vices and bad habits, and in spite of the fact that they of course got fodder in overabundance, they were falling off in flesh day by day. Then he had the King's coachman called. He drove them for a month – in the whole region there was not a pair of horses that held their heads so proudly, whose glance was so fiery, whose gait was so handsome, no other pair of horses that could hold out so long, though it were to trot for more than a score of miles at a stretch without stopping. How came this about? It is easy to see. The owner, who without being a coachman pretended to be such, drove them in accordance with the horses' understanding of what it is to drive; the royal coachman drove them in accordance with the coachman's understanding of what it is to drive.

So it is with us men. . . . Once there was a time when it pleased the Deity (if I may venture to say so) to be himself the coachman; and he drove the horses in accordance with the coachman's understanding of what it is to drive. Oh, what was a man not capable of at that time!

Søren Kierkegaard, 1851 [120]

*
**

You do need a Mediator between yourselves and God, but you do not need a Mediator between yourselves and Christ; you may come to him just as you are.

C.H. Spurgeon, quoting William Jay, early 19th cent. [121]

*
**

I long to see a real and simple imitation of the Life we have shown to us in the Gospels. It seems to me that if people go on allowing themselves to shape their lives so much more by the circumstances of the world than by the Gospel, they will be in danger of disbelieving the truths of the Bible itself.

I am anxious to prove, if it please God, in my own life that the Gospels are true.

Edward King, 1865 [122]

*
**

Again and again kind Christian friends, in sending donations, expressed their fear that I might be suffering from want of funds, on account of the large sums sent out of the country, to relieve the distress occasioned by the war; to which I replied, that we lacked nothing. The blessedness of faith is most seen under such circumstances. Faith is above circumstances. No war, no fire, no water, no mercantile panic, no loss of friends, no death can touch it. It goes on its own steady course. It triumphs over all difficulties. It works most easily in the greatest difficulties. Those who really confide in God, because they know the power of his arm, and the love of his heart, as shown most in the death and resurrection of his only begotten Son, are helped, whatever their trials and difficulties might be.

George Mueller, 1870 [123]

***

'We rest on thee,' our shield and our defender;
  We go not forth alone against the foe;
Strong in thy strength, safe in thy keeping tender
  'We rest on thee, and in thy name we go.'

Yea, 'in thy name', O Captain of salvation!
  In thy dear name, all other names above;
Jesus our righteousness, our sure foundation,
  Our Prince of glory and our King of love.

'We go' in faith, our own great weakness feeling,
  And needing more each day thy grace to know:
Yet from our hearts a song of triumph pealing;
  'We rest on thee, and in thy name we go.'

'We rest on thee,' our shield and our defender;
  Thine is the battle; thine shall be the praise
When passing through the gates of pearly splendour,
  Victors, we rest, *with* thee, through endless days.

Edith Gilling Cherry, 1903 [124]

***

I used to think there was something in me that was too precious to run the risk of mixing with ugly, ordinary things – a kind of mystical dream of something that might grow into something very beautiful, if I kept my mind up in the clouds enough and did not allow it to be soiled. I can't explain it, but it was purely selfish. And now I know that life is clean, dirty, ugly, beautiful, wonderful, sordid – and above all love. Just fancy, I even used to think I was rather good at that. I used to think that being nice to people and feeling nice was loving people. But it isn't, it isn't. Love is the most immense unselfishness and it's so big I've never touched it.

Florence Allshorn, c. 1920 [125]

*
**

Even a child knows that his father is not playing tricks on him when he refuses to grant one of his wishes and thus treats him in a way that is seemingly incompatible with love. The highest love is almost always incognito and therefore we must trust it.

Helmut Thielicke, 1962 [126]

*
**

Go down
into the plans of God.
Go down
deep as you may.
Fear not
for your fragility
under that weight of water.
Fear not
for life or limb
sharks attack savagely.
Fear not the power
of treacherous currents under the sea.
Simply, do not be afraid.
Let go. You will be led
like a child whose mother
holds him to her bosom
and against all comers is his shelter.

Helder Camara, 1971 [127]

I used to think that faith was a head trip, a kind of intellectual assent to the truths and doctrines of our religion. I know better now. When my faith began to be shattered, I did not hurt in my head. I hurt all over.

Months later when all this had passed, I was sitting talking with a Masai elder about the agony of belief and unbelief. He used two languages to respond to me – his own and Kiswahili. He pointed out that the word my Masai catechist, Paul, and I had used to convey *faith* was not a very satisfactory word in their language. It meant literally '*to agree to*'. I, myself, knew the word had that shortcoming. He said 'to believe' like that was similar to a white hunter shooting an animal with his gun from a great distance. Only his eyes and his fingers took part in the act. We should find another word. He said for a man really to believe is like a lion going after its prey. His nose and eyes and ears pick up the prey. His legs give him the speed to catch it. All the power of his body is involved in the terrible death leap and single blow to the neck with the front paw, the blow that actually kills. And as the animal goes down the lion envelops it in his arms (Africans refer to the front legs of an animal as its arms) pulls it to himself, and makes it part of himself. This is the way a lion kills. This is the way a man believes. This is what faith is.

I looked at the elder in silence and amazement. Faith understood like that would explain why, when my own was gone, I ached in every fibre of my being. But my wise old teacher was not finished yet.

'We did not search you out, Padri,' he said to me. 'We did not even want you to come to us. You searched us out. You followed us away from your house into the bush, into the plains, into the steppes where our cattle are, into the hills where we take our cattle for water, into our villages, into our homes. You told us of the High God, how we must search for him, even leave our land and our people to find him. But we have not done this. We have not left our land.

We have not searched for him. He has searched for us. He has searched *us* out and found us. All the time we think we are the lion. In the end, the lion is God.'

Vincent Donovan, 1978 [128]

Salvation through the Cross

The Son of God was crucified; I am not ashamed because
men must needs be ashamed of it. And the Son of God died;
it is by all means to be believed, because it is absurd. And he
was buried, and rose again; the fact is certain, because it is
impossible.

Tertullian, 210–2 [129]

**

He bore with us, and in pity he took our sins upon himself
and gave his own Son as a ransom for us – the Holy for the
wicked, the Sinless for sinners, the Just for the unjust, the
Incorrupt for the corrupt, the Immortal for the mortal. For
was there, indeed, anything except his righteousness that
could have availed to cover our sins? In whom could we, in
our lawlessness and ungodliness, have been made holy, but
in the Son of God alone? O sweet exchange! O unsearchable
working! O benefits unhoped for! – that the wickedness of
multitudes should thus be hidden in the One holy, and the
holiness of One should sanctify the countless wicked!

Epistle to Diognetus, early 3rd cent. [130]

**

Prayer to the Suffering Christ

I worship you, Lord; I bless you, God the good; I beseech
you, Most Holy; I fall down before you, Lover of men.
    I give you glory, O Christ, because you, the Only

Begotten, the Lord of all things, who alone are without sin, gave yourself to die for me, a sinner, unworthy of such a blessing: you died the death of the cross to free my sinful soul from the bonds of sin.

What shall I give you, Lord, in return for all this kindness?

Glory to you for your love.

Glory to you for your mercy.

Glory to you for your patience.

Glory to you for forgiving us all our sins.

Glory to you for coming to save our souls.

Glory to you for your incarnation in the virgin's womb.

Glory to you for your bonds.

Glory to you for receiving the cut of the lash.

Glory to you for accepting mockery.

Glory to you for your crucifixion.

Glory to you for your burial.

Glory to you for your resurrection.

Glory to you that were preached to men.

Glory to you in whom they believed.

Glory to you that were taken up into heaven.

Ephraem, 4th cent. [131]

**
**

The deformity of Christ forms thee. If he had not willed to be deformed, thou wouldst not have recovered the form which thou hadst lost. Therefore deformed he hung upon the Cross. But his deformity is our comeliness. In this life, therefore, let us hold fast to the deformed Christ. . . . We carry the sign of this deformity on our forehead. Let us not be ashamed of this deformity of Christ. Let us hold to this way, and we shall arrive where we shall see him; we shall see the perfect justice of God.

Augustine, ?393-403 [132]

What strength is there in such weakness, what height in such lowliness? What is there to be venerated in such abjection? Surely something is hidden by this weakness, something is concealed by this humility. There is something mysterious in this abjection. O hidden strength: a man hangs on a cross and lifts the load of eternal death from the human race; a man nailed to wood looses the bonds of everlasting death that hold fast the world. O hidden power: a man condemned with thieves saves men condemned with devils, a man stretched out on the gibbet draws all men to himself. O mysterious strength: one soul coming forth from torment draws countless souls with him out of hell, a man submits to the death of the body and destroys the death of souls.

Anselm, 1099 [133]

*
**

Jesus Nailed to the Cross

When the wicked men were sated with insulting the meekest King, our King was again clothed in his own garments, which would be stripped off a second time; and bearing his cross for himself, he was led forth to the place of Calvary (John 19:17). There he was stripped completely and covered only with a cheap loincloth. Thrown roughly upon the wood of the cross, spread out, pulled forward and stretched back and forth like a hide, he was pierced by pointed nails, fixed to the cross by his sacred hands and feet and most roughly torn with wounds. His garments were given away as spoils and were divided into parts, except his seamless tunic which was not divided but went by lot to one man.

See, now, my soul,
how he who is God blessed above all things,
is totally submerged
in the waters of suffering

from the sole of the foot to the top of the head.
In order that he might draw you out totally
from these sufferings,
the waters have come up to his soul.
For crowned with thorns
he was ordered to bend his back
under the burden of the cross
and to bear his own ignominy.
Led to the place of execution,
he was stripped of his garments
so that he seemed to be a leper
from the bruises and cuts in his flesh
that were visible over his back and sides
from the blows of the scourges.
And then transfixed
with nails,
he appeared to you as your beloved
cut through with wound upon wound
in order to heal you.
Who will grant me
that my request should come about
and that God will give me
what I long for,
that having been totally transpierced
in both mind and flesh,
I may be fixed
with my beloved
to the yoke of the cross?

Bonaventure, 1259-60 [134]

**

On the fewness of those who love the cross of Jesus

Jesus has in these days many people who love his heavenly
kingdom, but few who bear his cross. He has many who
desire comfort, but few who are ready for trials. He has

found many to share his table, but few to share his fast. Everyone longs to rejoice with him, but few are ready to suffer for him. Many follow Jesus as far as the breaking of the bread, but few go so far as to drink the cup of his passion. Many glory in his miracles, few follow him in the shame of the cross. Many people love Jesus as long as misfortune does not fall on them; they praise him and bless him as long as they are receiving any comfort from him, but if Jesus hides himself or leaves them for a while, they complain bitterly or fall into great despair.

Yet those who love Jesus for his own sake and not for any comfort they can get from him, bless him in every trial and distress of heart, just as they do amidst the highest spiritual comfort. Even if he were never prepared to grant them comfort, they would still be always praising him and always wanting to offer him thanks. What power there is in pure love for Jesus, unmixed with any self-seeking or thought of personal gain!

Surely 'mercenary' is the right name for the people who are always looking for spiritual comforts; and those who are always thinking about their own profit and advantage quite clearly love themselves, not Christ.

Thomas à Kempis, 1418 [135]

**
**

This is that mystery which is rich in divine grace unto sinners: wherein by a wonderful exchange, our sins are no longer ours but Christ's; and the righteousness of Christ is not Christ's but ours. He has emptied himself of his righteousness that he might clothe us with it, and fill us with it: and he has taken our evils upon himself that he might deliver us from them.

Martin Luther, 1519–21 [136]

Christ had within himself the highest pitch of joy and of sadness, of weakness and courage, of glory and confusion, of peace and upheaval, of life and death; and this is amply shown by this verse, where he cries out – as if speaking in opposition to himself – that he has been abandoned by God, and nonetheless calls him 'My God'. . . . What then, shall we say? – that Christ was at once wholly just and wholly a sinner, at once wholly false and wholly truthful, at once wholly glorious and wholly in despair, at once wholly blessed and wholly damned? Yes – for if we do not say that, I do not see in what sense he was abandoned by God, since this was the sense in which many of the saints (Job, David, Hezekiah, Jacob) were abandoned – all the more, then, in the case of Christ, the head of the saints, who bore all our infirmities within himself.

Martin Luther, 1519–21 [137]

**
**

He ran thus till he came at a place somewhat ascending; and upon that place stood a Cross, and a little below in the bottom, a sepulchre. So I saw in my dream, that just as Christian came up with the Cross, his burden loosed from off his shoulders, and fell from off his back; and began to tumble, and so continued to do till it came to the mouth of the sepulchre, where it fell in, and I saw it no more.

Then was Christian glad and lightsome, and said with a merry heart, 'He hath given me rest, by his sorrow, and life, by his death.' Then he stood still a while, to look and wonder; for it was very surprising to him that the sight of the Cross should thus ease him of his burden. He looked therefore, and looked again, even till the springs that were in his head sent the waters down his cheeks. Now as he stood looking and weeping, behold three Shining Ones came to him, and saluted him, with 'Peace be to thee.' So the first said to him, 'Thy sins be forgiven.' The second stripped

him of his rags, and clothed him with change of raiment.
The third also set a mark on his forehead, and gave him a roll
with a seal upon it, which he bid him look on as he ran, and
that he should give it in at the Celestial Gate: so they went
their way. Then Christian gave three leaps for joy, and went
on singing.

> *Thus far did I come loaden with my sin,*
> *Nor could aught ease the grief that I was in,*
> *Till I came hither. What a place is this!*
> *Must here be the beginning of my bliss?*
> *Must here the burden fall from off my back?*
> *Must here the strings that bound it to me, crack?*
> *Blessed Cross! Blessed Sepulchre! Blessed rather be*
> *The man that there was put to shame for me.*

John Bunyan, 1678 [138]

*
**

Christ crucified, the wisdom and power of God

Nature with open volume stands
   to spread her maker's praise abroad,
and every labour of his hands
   shows something worthy of our God.

But in the grace that rescued man
   his brightest form of glory shines;
here on the Cross 'tis fairest drawn
   in precious blood and crimson lines.

Here his whole name appears complete;
   nor wit can guess, nor reason prove
which of the letters best is writ,
   the power, the wisdom, or the love.

Here I behold his inmost heart,
 where grace and vengeance strangely join,
piercing his Son with sharpest smart,
 to make the purchased pleasures mine.

O the sweet wonders of that Cross
 where God the Saviour loved and died;
her noblest life my spirit draws
 from his dear wounds and bleeding side.

I would for ever speak his name
 in sounds to mortal ears unknown,
with angels join to praise the Lamb,
 and worship at his Father's throne.

Isaac Watts, 1707 [139]

**

Crucifixion to the world, by the cross of Christ (Gal. 6:14)

When I survey the wondrous cross
On which the Prince of glory died,
My richest gain I count but loss,
And pour contempt on all my pride.

Forbid it, Lord, that I should boast,
Save in the death of Christ my God;
All the vain things that charm me most,
I sacrifice them to his blood.

See from his head, his hands, his feet,
Sorrow and love flow mingled down!
Did e'er such love and sorrow meet,
Or thorns compose so rich a crown?

His dying crimson, like a robe,
Spreads o'er his body on the tree;
Then I am dead to all the globe,
And all the globe is dead to me.

Were the whole realm of nature mine,
That were a present far too small;
Love so amazing, so divine,
Demands my soul, my life, my all.

Isaac Watts, 1720 [140]

**

Free Grace

And can it be that I should gain
    An interest in the Saviour's blood?
Died he for me, who caused his pain?
    For me? Who him to death pursued?
Amazing love! How can it be
That thou, my God, shouldst die for me?

'Tis myst'ry all: th'Immortal dies!
    Who can explore his strange design?
In vain the firstborn seraph tries
    To sound the depths of love divine.
'Tis mercy all! Let earth adore!
Let angel minds inquire no more.

He left his Father's throne above
    (So free, so infinite his grace!),
Emptied himself of all but love,
    And bled for Adam's helpless race.
'Tis mercy all, immense and free,
For, O my God, it found out me!

Long my imprisoned spirit lay,
    Fast bound in sin and nature's night.
Thine eye diffused a quick'ning ray;
    I woke; the dungeon flamed with light.
My chains fell off, my heart was free,
I rose, went forth, and followed thee.

No condemnation now I dread,
    Jesus, and all in him, is mine.
Alive in him, my living head,
    And clothed in righteousness divine,
Bold I approach th'eternal throne,
And claim the crown, through Christ my own.

Charles Wesley, 1739 [141]

*
**

To the apostles . . . the commission was 'Go ye into all the world, and preach the gospel to every creature', whereas to us is assigned, as it were, a more limited sphere. But the subject of our ministry is the same as theirs. We have the same dispensation committed unto us; and woe will be unto us, if we preach not the gospel . . . The fact is indisputable that the apostle's commission was to preach Christ crucified – to preach, I say, *that* chiefly, *that* constantly, *that* exclusively. And therefore he was justified in his determination to 'know nothing else'. Consequently, to adopt the same resolution is our wisdom also, whether it be in reference to our own salvation, or to the subject of our ministrations in the Church of God.

Charles Simeon, 1811 [142]

*
**

But, it may be said, we rely not on our works alone, nor on our repentance alone, but on *these things and Christ's merits united*. Go, then, and search the records of your life, and see what works you will bring forth in order to eke out the insufficient merits of your Saviour. Bring forth one single work, one only, out of your whole life, one that has no defect and that does not in any respect need the mercy of God to pardon its imperfection. Then carry it to God and say, 'Here, Lord, is a work in which thou thyself canst not find a flaw; it is as perfect as any that my Lord and Saviour himself ever performed, and is therefore worthy to be united to his infinitely meritorious obedience as a joint ground of all my hopes. I am content to stand or fall by this one work. I am aware that, if it is imperfect, it stands in need of mercy for its own imperfection, and consequently can never purchase pardon for all my other offences. But I ask no mercy for that, yea, rather, I claim on account of it all the glory of heaven.'* You who will dispute against salvation by faith only, and who wish to have something of your own to found your hopes upon, do this. Bring forth some work, some *one* work at least, that shall stand the test of the divine law, and defy the scrutiny of the heart-searching God. But if you cannot find *one* such work, then see how unsuitable to your state is the doctrine for which you contend.

* Let not the reader suppose that any one is exhorted to go thus to almighty God. The whole passage is intended to show the horrible impiety of even entertaining such a thought. The scriptures frequently put such language into the *lips* of sinners, in order to show what is the real language of *their hearts*. See Rom. 3:5,7 and 9:19.

Charles Simeon, 1815 [143]

*
**

Our part consists in getting down into the death of Christ; his part is to live out his own life in us, just as the waters spring forth from the fountain. Then we shall know what the apostle meant when he said, 'Christ liveth in me'. Where Christ thus dwells in unhindered activity, there will be steady growth, perpetual freshness, and abundant fruitfulness; and the life will be marked by ease and spontaneity, because it will be natural.

From this we see that it is impossible to exaggerate the importance of understanding the meaning of his death. We must see that he not only died 'for sin' but 'unto sin'. In the first of these senses he died alone; we could not die with him. He trod the winepress alone; as the sin-offering he alone became the propitiation for our sins. But in the second we died *with* him. We must know what it is to be brought into sympathy with him in his death unto sin. Oneness with Christ in that sense is the means of becoming practically separated, not only from sinful desires, but also from the old self-life. And this assimilation to the dying Christ is not an isolated act, but a condition of mind ever to be maintained, and to go on deepening.

Evan Henry Hopkins, 1884 [144]

⁎
⁎⁎

It is quite true that we have not to propitiate an offended God: the very fact upon which the Gospel proceeds is that we *cannot* do any such thing. But it is not true that no propitiation is needed. As truly as guilt is a real thing, as truly as God's condemnation of sin is a real thing, a propitiation is needed. And it is here, I think, that those who make the objection referred to part company, not only with St. Paul, but with all the Apostles. God is love, they say, and therefore he does not require a propitiation. God is love, say the Apostles, and therefore he provides a propitiation. Which of these doctrines appeals best to the conscience? Which of them gives reality, and contents, and substance, to the love of God? Is it not the apostolic doctrine? Does not the other cut out and cast away that very thing which made the soul of God's love to Paul and John? 'Herein is love, not that we loved God, but that *he loved us, and sent his Son to be the propitiation for our sins.*' '*God commendeth his love toward us, in that, while we were yet sinners, Christ died for us . . . him that knew no sin he made to be sin on our behalf.*' That is how they spoke in the beginning of the Gospel, and so let us speak. Nobody has any right to borrow the words 'God is love' from an apostle, and then to put them in circulation after

carefully emptying them of their apostolic import. Still less
has any one a right to use them as an argument against the
very thing in which the Apostles placed their meaning. But
this is what they do who appeal to love against propitiation.
To take the condemnation out of the Cross is to take the
nerve out of the Gospel; it will cease to hold men's hearts
with its original power when the reconciliation which is
preached through it contains the mercy, but not the judgment of God. Its whole virtue, its consistency with God's
character, its aptness to man's need, its real dimensions as a
revelation of love, depend ultimately on this, that mercy
comes to us in it through judgment.

James Denney, 1894 [145]

*

The feeble gospel preaches 'God is ready to forgive'; the
mighty gospel preaches 'God has redeemed'. It works not
with forgiveness alone, which would be mere futile amnes-
ty, but with forgiveness in a moral way, with holy forgiveness, a forgiveness which not only restores the soul, but
restores it in the only final and eternal way, by restoring in
the same act the infinite moral order, and reconstructing
mankind from the foundation of a moral revolution. God
reconciles by making Christ to be sin, and not imputing it (2
Cor. 5:21). The Christian act of forgiveness at once regards
the whole wide moral order of things, and goes deep to the
springs of the human will for entire repentance and a new
order of obedience. This it does by the consummation of
God's judgment in the central act of mercy.

P.T. Forsyth, 1909 [146]

*

On June 7th, 1917, I was running to our lines half mad with
fright, though running in the right direction, thank God,
through what had been once a wooded copse. It was being

heavily shelled. As I ran I stumbled and fell over something. I stopped to see what it was. It was an undersized, underfed German boy, with a wound in his stomach and a hole in his head. I remember muttering, 'You poor little devil, what had you got to do with it? not much great blonde Prussian about you.' Then there came light. It may have been pure imagination, but that does not mean that it was not also reality, for what is called imagination is often the road to reality. It seemed to me that the boy disappeared and in his place there lay the Christ upon his cross, and cried, 'Inasmuch as ye have done it unto the least of these my little ones ye have done it unto me.' From that moment on I never saw a battlefield as anything but a crucifix. From that moment on I have never seen the world as anything but a crucifix.

G.A. Studdert Kennedy, 1917 [147]

*
**

The cross, conceived as the expiatory penal sacrifice of the Son of God, is the fulfilment of the scriptural revelation of God, in its most paradoxical incomprehensible guise. It is precisely in his revelation that the God of the Bible is incomprehensible, because in his nearness he reveals his distance, in his mercy his holiness, in his grace his judgment, in his personality his absoluteness; because in his revelation his glory and the salvation of man, his own will and his love for men, his majesty and his 'homeliness' cannot be separated from one another. It is thus that he is God, the One who comes, the One who comes to us in reality: who comes in the likeness of sinful flesh, the One who himself pays the price, himself bears the penalty, himself overcomes all that separates us from him – *really* overcomes it, does not merely declare that it does not exist. This real event is his real coming, and therefore it is both the revelation of that which *we* are and of that which *he* is.

Emil Brunner, 1927 [148]

When Christ calls a man, he bids him come and die.

Dietrich Bonhoeffer, 1937 [149]

*
**

If I cannot in honest happiness take the second place (or the twentieth); if I cannot take the first place without making a fuss about my unworthiness, then I know nothing of Calvary love.

If I say, 'Yes, I forgive, but I cannot forget', as though the God, who twice a day washes all the sands on all the shores of all the world, could not wash such memories from my mind, then I know nothing of Calvary love.

If I do not forget about such a trifle as personal success, so that it never crosses my mind, or if it does, is never given a moment's room there; if the cup of spiritual flattery tastes sweet to me, then I know nothing of Calvary love.

If I slip into the place that can be filled by Christ alone, making myself the first necessity to a soul instead of leading it to fasten upon him, then I know nothing of Calvary love.

If I covet any place on earth but the dust at the foot of the Cross, then I know nothing of Calvary love.

Amy Carmichael, 1938 [150]

*
**

Justification puts us in the right and truth of God and therefore tells us that we are in untruth. Now, let it be clear that justification by grace alone does not mean that there is no natural goodness in man, but that man with his natural goodness is called in question. Jesus Christ died for the whole man (with his good and his evil) not for part of him, the evil part, but for the whole man. He died for all men, the good and the bad, and all alike come under the total judgment of his Death and Resurrection; all alike have to be born again in him, and made new creatures. That is the radical nature of the Gospel, which becomes so clear to us when we communicate at the Holy Table in the Body and Blood of our Lord, for there we feel ashamed for our *whole being*, for our good as well as for our evil. But the same applies to our natural knowledge. Justification by the grace of Christ alone, does not mean that there is no natural knowledge — what natural man is there who does not know something of God even if he holds it down in unrighteousness or turns the truth into a lie? But it does mean that the whole of that natural knowledge is called in question by Christ who when he comes to us says: 'If any man will come after me, let him deny himself, take up his cross and follow me.' The whole man with his natural knowledge is there questioned down to the root of his being, for man is summoned to look away from all that he is and knows or thinks he knows to Christ who is the Way, the Truth and the Life; no one goes to the Father but by him.

T. F. Torrance, 1960 [151]

***

For the first time in my life I dared to demand an explanation. When none came, I was angrier than I ever remember being. I turned my eyes on the plain wooden cross and I remembered Calvary. I stood in the crowd which crucified him, hating and despising him. With my own hands I drove the nails into his hands and his feet, and with bursting energy I flogged him and reviled him and spat with nauseated loathing. Now *he* should know what it felt like – to live in the creation he had made. Every breath brought from me the words: 'Now you know! Now you know!'

And then I saw something which made my heart stand still. I saw his face, and on it twisted every familiar agony of my own soul. 'Now you know' became an awed whisper as I, motionless, watched his agony. 'Yes, now I know' was the passionate and pain-filled reply. 'Why else should I come?' Stunned, I watched his eyes search desperately for the tiniest flicker of love in mine, and as we faced one another in the bleak and the cold, forsaken by God, frightened and derelict, we loved one another and our pain became silent in the calm.

Nothing can bind us closer than common dereliction for nowhere else is companionship so longed for. From that moment I was tied on to Christ, knowing the rope would hold if I fell in the climb as he led me slowly and firmly out of hell, sometimes out of sight ahead of me, then dear and firm and calm as I scrambled up to his side.

Anonymous, quoted by Frank Lake 1966 [152]

*
**

His claim and our responsibility to respond lie in the fact that God set him forth as Saviour to bear for us and on our behalf the total consequences of the sin of the race, of the sin of the covenant people, of the parents whose sins are the evil of their children, of the fall of man out of relationship with God, of the ineradicable evils of soul and spirit, of the evil in which sin itself is posited, of the folly of the pride of self-sufficient man, and the thousand subsequent sins he commits as his contribution to the social and personal disruption about him. All these sins and evils, deprivations and depravities are laid on him. He bears the iniquity of us all. He carries this cross of his redemptive obedience over the peaks of pain and into the abyss of dread. He first makes the journey through the hell of alienation from God and from the source of being, in order to reach us. We are not first responsible to make the journey to him. We misconstrue the Gospel grievously and preach it fallaciously if we imply that what is required of man for his saving is more than the merest acceptance in gratitude of the fact that all that needed to be done has been done already by Christ. We do not begin, and are not required to begin, our journey into the wilderness of aridity or under the waters of affliction until we are already embodied 'in him'. It is in him that we are conveyed safe through the Valley of the Shadow of Death.

Frank Lake, 1966 [153]

***

The name of Christ can be used in two senses. It can mean both the historical person of two thousand years ago, and the mystical body of which the glorified Jesus is the head and we are all the body. This Christ bleeds continually. There has never been a day in history when at least one member of this mystical body has not bled. Their blood is the blood of Christ. Everything in them belongs to Christ. And they fill up in their flesh that which is behind of the afflictions of Christ. They perpetuate the sacrifice, and so it is his blood which continually cleanses.

We apply to events a false notion of time. When we travel in a train we have the impression that the villages and towns are passing us. We say that one station has passed and another follows. The truth is that all towns coexist at the same time. What we see is a delusion of our senses. So our mind, limited in time, sees some events of history as belonging to the past, and others as future. The reality is that there exists only an eternal 'now', in which the bleeding of Jesus on Calvary is as actual today as it was two thousand years ago. And the bleeding of martyrs from before the time of Jesus and those of all centuries all belong to the eternal now.

Richard Wurmbrand, 1969 [154]

***

It is understandable that a man should be fairly untroubled in mind and conscience when he has been living a fairly good life; but what happens when he falls into some grievous sin? A sudden temptation overtakes him and before he knows what has happened he has fallen . . .

I find that many are caught by the devil at that point. Because they have fallen into sin they query and question their salvation, they doubt their justification, they wonder whether they have ever been Christians at all. They lose their peace and they are in a torment and an agony. They have gone back, and have started doubting their whole standing in the presence of God because of that one sin.

Any man in that position is just betraying the fact that, for the time being at any rate, he is not clear about the doctrine of justification by faith only. Because if he believes that one sin can put a man out of the right relationship to God, then he has never seen clearly that hitherto he has been in that right relationship, not because of anything in himself, but because of the Lord Jesus Christ and his perfect work. When a man says, 'Because I have sinned I have lost it', what he is really saying on the other side is, 'I had it because I was good'. He is wrong in both respects. In other words, if we see that our justification is altogether and entirely in the 'Lord Jesus Christ and him crucified', we must see that, even though we fall into sin, that is still true.

Martyn Lloyd-Jones, 1971 [155]

*
**

And I wanted to say 'But it is Good Friday'

This morning I have had my annual, quite expected and yet still completely overwhelming dose of cultural shock. And so great has been the strain today of seeing everybody going about their ordinary everyday working affairs as if nothing had happened, that it is only with the greatest difficulty that I have smothered my impulse to say to everybody I meet: '*But today is Good Friday.*'

I wanted to say it to the local *maulvi* ranting away in his Friday sermon, amplified, and penetrating into our every room;

I wanted to say it to the cinema crowd turning up in high-spirited herds to see *Sin* and *My heart beats for you* at our local cinema;

I wanted to say it to the hungry group taking a snack of generously peppered vegetables and fruit off saucers from a stall outside our cathedral gate;

I wanted to say it to the policeman boxing the ears of some offending cyclist;

I wanted to say it to the slim girl in the black veil, deep black eyes peering modestly on a naughty world;

I wanted to say it to the hawker selling plastic syphons manifestly designed to enable those so minded to pinch petrol out of stationary vehicles;

I wanted to say it to the man rummaging around on the rubbish tip;

I wanted to say it to the youths riding three on a cycle from college;

I wanted to say it to the black-smocked Shia'h religious leader mourning his caliph these days;

I wanted them all to know the story which could alter the story of their lives.

To the man rummaging among the rubbish I wanted to say, 'Today, shalt thou be with me in paradise'. To the girl in the black veil I wanted to tell the story of the women at the Cross.

To the young men I wanted to repeat, 'Come, follow me'. To the Shia'h religious leader, 'Behold if there be any sorrow like unto my sorrow'. To the hungry crowd, 'My flesh is meat indeed . . .' To the policeman, 'This man was truly the son of God'.

And if not the story, at least the reality. I wanted to insert the reality of the Cross into the tissues of this life which goes on unhindered around.

And since this goodness is not the preserve of any single faith, I wanted to say:

Something good has happened today, something that cannot be confined to that little group of Christians who have taken off three hours to perform their religious observances. Something good has happened today which cannot be confined to churches and Christians, but must be out and about.

The goodness of forgiveness of sins;
the goodness of God's identification with men in their
    weakness and their suffering;
the goodness of the one perfect and sufficient sacrifice,
    oblation and satisfaction for the sins of the whole
    world;
the goodness of God's act of reconciliation in Christ.

But they see none of this. They see not the goodness, but the badness of this day. The badness of Christians in believing that Christ really died on the Cross. The badness of Christians in portraying the kind of God who would permit his holy prophet to suffer in this way. Their badness in sullying the doctrine of the unity of God. The badness of Christians in altering and perverting the gospel story.

Pity about all this, for I wanted so much to say '*But today is Good Friday*'.

Looks as though I can't say it, not like that anyway,
    but must pray it –
pray that the something good that has happened today
    may one day be known
in categories and experience understandable
by people who are not conscious of the great good
    they have missed

in Jesus crucified

today, on this ordinary working day,
which I just can't bear.

Lord Jesus
take my distress today,
and unite it with your own.

John Carden, 1971 [156]

∗∗∗

Because God 'does not spare' his Son, all the godless are
spared. Though they are godless, they are not godforsaken,
precisely because God has abandoned his own Son and has
delivered him up for them. Thus the delivering up of the
Son to godforsakenness is the ground for the justification of
the godless and the acceptance of enmity by God. It may
therefore be said that the Father delivers up his Son on the
cross in order to be the Father of those who are delivered up.
The Son is delivered up to this death in order to become the
Lord of both dead and living. And if Paul speaks emphati-
cally of God's 'own Son', the not-sparing and abandoning
also involves the Father himself. In the forsakenness of the
Son the Father also forsakes himself. In the surrender of the
Son the Father also surrenders himself, though not in the
same way. For Jesus suffers dying in forsakenness, but not
death itself; for men can no longer 'suffer' death, because
suffering presupposes life. But the Father who abandons
him and delivers him up suffers the death of the Son in the
infinite grief of love.

Jürgen Moltmann, 1974 [157]

∗∗∗

O Tree of Calvary,
send thy roots deep down
into my heart.

Gather together the soil of my heart,
the sands of my fickleness,
the stones of my stubbornness,
the mud of my desires,
bind them all together,
O Tree of Calvary,
interlace them with thy strong roots,
entwine them with the network
of thy love. .

Chandran Devanesen [158]

Life in the Spirit

Abbot Lot came to Abbot Joseph and said: Father, according as I am able, I keep my little rule, and my little fast, my prayer, meditation and contemplative silence; and according as I am able I strive to cleanse my heart of thoughts: now what more should I do? The elder rose up in reply and stretched out his hands to heaven, and his fingers became like ten lamps of fire. He said: Why not be totally changed into fire?

Abbot Lot, 4th cent. [159]

*
**

And why has he called the grace of the Spirit by the name of water? Because by water all things subsist; because of water are herbs and animals created; because the water of the showers comes down from heaven; because it comes down one in form, yet manifold in its working. For one fountain watered the whole of the Garden, and one and the same rain comes down upon all the world, yet it becomes white in the lily, and red in the rose, and purple in the violets and pansies, and different and varied in each several kind: so it is one in the palm tree, and another in the vine, and all in all things; being the while one in nature, not diverse from itself; for the rain does not change, when it comes down, first as one thing, then as another, but adapting itself to the nature of each thing which receives it, it becomes to each what is suitable. Thus also the Holy Ghost, being one, and of one nature, and undivided, divides to each his grace, according as he will: and as the dry tree, when it partakes of water, puts forth shoots, so also the soul in sin, when it has been through repentance made worthy of the Holy Ghost, brings forth clusters of righteousness.

Cyril of Jerusalem, 350 [160]

Those . . . who have within themselves Christ, illuminating and bringing them rest, are guided in many and various ways by the Spirit. . . .

Sometimes persons are guided by grace as persons who rejoice at a royal banquet. They are filled with joy and ineffable happiness. At other times they are like a spouse who enjoys conjugal union with her bridegroom in divine resting.

At other times they are like incorporeal angels, they are so light and transcendent, even in the body. Sometimes they are as if they have become intoxicated with a strong drink. They delight in the Spirit, being inebriated, namely, by the intoxication of the divine and spiritual mysteries.

Sometimes they find themselves immersed in weeping and, lamenting over the human race and in pouring out prayers on behalf of the whole human race of Adam, they shed tears and are overwhelmed by grief because they are consumed by the love of the Spirit towards mankind.

At another time they are so enflamed by the Spirit with such joy and love that, if it were possible, they could gather every human being into their very hearts, without distinguishing the bad and good. Again they are so filled with humility, regarding themselves below all men in the humility received from the Spirit, so they consider themselves as the least significant and worthless of all human beings.

Sometimes they are lifted up in 'joy unspeakable' (1 Peter 1:8). At other times they are like some powerful person who has donned the king's whole armour and has come down to do battle against the enemies. He fights courageously against them and conquers.

Similarly, the spiritual takes up the heavenly weapons of the Spirit and attacks the enemies and battles them and puts them under his feet.

Macarius, mid 4th cent. [161]

Holy Spirit, Lord of light!
From thy clear celestial height,
   Thy pure beaming radiance give:

Come, thou Father of the poor!
Come, with treasures which endure!
   Come, thou Light of all that live!

Thou, of all consolers best,
Visiting the troubled breast,
   Dost refreshing peace bestow;

Thou in toil art comfort sweet;
Pleasant coolness in the heat;
   Solace in the midst of woe.

Light immortal! light divine!
Visit thou these hearts of thine,
   And our inmost being fill:

If thou take thy grace away,
Nothing pure in man will stay;
   All his good is turn'd to ill.

Heal our wounds – our strength renew;
On our dryness pour thy dew;
   Wash the stains of guilt away:

Bend the stubborn heart and will;
Melt the frozen, warm the chill;
   Guide the steps that go astray.

Thou, on those who evermore
Thee confess and thee adore,
   In thy sevenfold gifts, descend:

Give them comfort when they die;
Give them life with thee on high;
   Give them joys which never end.

*Variously ascribed to Pope Innocent III or Archbishop Stephen Langton, c. 1215,
tr. Edward Caswall, 1849* [162]

Noah's dove was irrational and mortal; but this dove is rational and immortal. She even gives reason to the rational and life to the living. She flies without leaving her nest above, the church of the firstborn in heaven. She reaches all quarters without stirring from her place. All images are represented in her without her possessing colour herself. She abides in the East, yet the West is full of her. Her food is fire, and he who is crowned by her with wings will breathe forth flames from his mouth. All those who are burning from love and sick from affection reveal their secrets to her and she slakes their thirst. Her speech touches every ear, but few hear her voice.

Bar Hebraeus, c. 1278 [163]

*
**

By a kind of mutual bond the Lord has joined together the certainty of his Word and of his Spirit so that the perfect religion of the Word may abide in our minds when the Spirit, who causes us to contemplate God's face, shines; and that we in turn may embrace the Spirit with no fear of being deceived when we recognize him in his own image, namely, in the Word. So indeed it is. God did not bring forth his Word among men for the sake of a momentary display, intending at the coming of his Spirit to abolish it. Rather, he sent down the same Spirit by whose power he had dispensed the Word, to complete his work by the efficacious confirmation of the Word.

Jean Calvin, 1559 [164]

*
**

The Word of God is not received by faith if it flits about in the top of the brain, but when it takes root in the depth of the heart that it may be an invincible defence to withstand and drive off all the stratagems of temptation. But if it is true that the mind's real understanding is illumination by the Spirit of God, then in such confirmation of the heart his power is much more clearly manifested, to the extent that the heart's distrust is greater than the mind's blindness. It is harder for the heart to be furnished with assurance than for the mind to be endowed with thought. The Spirit accordingly serves as a seal, to seal up in our hearts those very promises the certainty of which it has previously impressed upon our minds; and takes the place of a guarantee to confirm and establish them. . . .

I have not forgotten what I have previously said, the memory of which is repeatedly renewed by experience: faith is tossed about by various doubts, so that the minds of the godly are rarely at peace – at least they do not always enjoy a peaceful state. But whatever siege engines may shake them, they either rise up out of the very gulf of temptations, or stand fast upon their watch. Indeed, this assurance alone nourishes and protects faith.

Jean Calvin, 1559 [165]

*
**

All the rest, all the feasts hitherto in the return of the year from his incarnation to the very last of his ascension, though all of them be great and worthy of all honour in themselves, yet to us they are as nothing, any of them or all of them, even all the feasts in the calendar, without this day, the feast which now we hold holy to the sending of the Holy Ghost.

Christ is the Word, and all of him but words spoken or words written, there is no seal put to till this day; the Holy Ghost is the seal or signature, *in Quo signati estis*. A testament we have and therein many fair legacies, but till this day nothing administered – 'The administrations are the Spirit's' . . .; for the Spirit is the *Arrha*, 'the earnest' or the investiture of all that Christ hath done for us.

These, if we should compare them, it would not be easy

to determine, whether the greater of these two: 1. That of the Prophet, *Filius datus est nobis*; 2. Or that of the Apostle, *Spiritus datus est nobis*; the ascending of our flesh, or the descending of his Spirit; *incarnatio Dei*, or *inspiratio hominis*; the mystery of his incarnation, or the mystery of our inspiration. For mysteries they are both, and 'great mysteries of godliness' both; and in both of them, 'God manifested in the flesh.' 1. In the former, by the union of his Son; 2. In the latter, by the communion of his blessed Spirit.

But we will not compare them, they are both above all comparison. Yet this we may safely say of them: without either of them we are not complete, we have not our accomplishment; but by both we have, and that fully, even by this day's royal exchange. Whereby, as before he of ours, so now we of his are made partakers. He clothed with our flesh, and we invested with his Spirit. The great promise of the Old Testament accomplished, that he should partake our human nature; and the great and precious promise of the New, that we should be *consortes divinæ naturæ*, 'partake his divine nature,' both are this day accomplished . . .

It is Tertullian; *Christus Legis, Spiritus Sanctus Evangelii complementum*; 'the coming of Christ was the fulfilling of the Law, the coming of the Holy Ghost is the fulfilling of the Gospel.'

Lancelot Andrewes, 1606 [166]

*

If you would not be taken with any of Satan's devices, then *labour to be filled with the Spirit*. The Spirit of the Lord is a Spirit of light and power; and what can a soul do without light and power 'against spiritual wickedness in high places'? Eph. 6:12. It is not enough that you have the Spirit, but you must be filled with the Spirit, or else Satan, that evil spirit, will be too hard for you, and his plots will prosper against you. That is a sweet word of the apostle, 'Be filled with the Spirit,' Eph. 5:18; i.e. labour for abundance of the Spirit. He that thinks he hath enough of the Holy Spirit, will quickly find himself vanquished by the evil spirit. Satan hath his snares to take you in prosperity and adversity, in health and sickness, in strength and weakness, when you are alone and when you are in company, when you come on to spiritual duties and when you come off from spiritual duties, and if you are not filled with the Spirit, Satan will be too hard and too crafty for you, and will easily and frequently take you in his snares, and make a prey of you in spite of your souls. Therefore labour more to have your hearts filled with the Spirit than to have your heads filled with notions, your shops with wares, your chests with silver, or your bags with gold; so shall you escape the snares of this fowler, and triumph over all his plots.

Thomas Brooks, 1652 [167]

*
**

There is a new edition of all a man's graces, when the Holy Ghost cometh as a sealer. Self-love bustleth before, and keepeth a coil to secure itself; but when once self-love is secure, and the love of God is shed abroad in a man's heart, it makes a man work for God ten times more than before, or else at least more kindly. I know there are ways wherein the soul can glorify God more, in a way of recumbency, when he hath not assurance, by submitting himself to God whatsoever becometh of him, and by pure trusting of God, though he know not whether he will save him or not, which is the greatest trust in the world. But yet in matter of holiness and obedience, the assurance of the love of God, when it is shed abroad in the heart, will constrain a man, as the apostle's phrase is . . .

I appeal to you, good souls, if Christ do but look toward you a little, how holy doth it make you! Much more, then, when the Holy Ghost is poured out upon you, and when you are baptized with the Holy Ghost as a Comforter. Look, as when the sun cometh near to the earth, then is the spring; it was winter before; so when the Holy Ghost cometh in this manner upon the heart, it was winter before, but it will be spring now.

Thomas Goodwin, d. 1680 [168]

***

The Holy Spirit supplies the bodily absence of Jesus Christ, and effects what he has to do and accomplish towards his people in the world; so that whatever is done by him, it is the same as if it were wrought immediately by the Lord Christ himself in his own person, whereby all his holy promises are fully accomplished towards them that believe.

John Owen, 1674 [169]

***

Let no one ever presume to rest in any supposed testimony of the Spirit, which is separate from the fruit of it. If the Spirit of God does really testify that we are children of God, the immediate consequence will be the fruit of the Spirit, even love, joy, peace, long-suffering, gentleness, goodness, fidelity, meekness, temperance. And however this fruit may be clouded for a while, during the time of strong temptation, while Satan is sifting him as wheat, yet the substantial part of it remains, even under the thickest cloud. It is true, joy in the Holy Ghost may be withdrawn, during the hour of trial. Yea, the soul may be exceeding sorrowful, while the hour and power of darkness continues. But even this is generally restored with increase, and he rejoices with joy unspeakable and full of glory.

John Wesley, 1788 [170]

I answered, 'I don't quite grasp how it is possible to be absolutely sure of living in God's Spirit. How can it be proved?' . . .

Then Father Seraphim gripped me firmly by the shoulders and said: 'My friend, both of us, at this moment, are in the Holy Spirit, you and I. Why won't you look at me?'

'I can't look at you, Father, because the light flashing from your eyes and face is brighter than the sun and I'm dazzled!'

'Don't be afraid, friend of God, you yourself are shining just like I am; you too are now in the fullness of the grace of the Holy Spirit, otherwise you wouldn't be able to see me as you do.'

Then I looked at the Staretz and was panic-stricken. Picture, in the sun's orb, in the most dazzling brightness of its noon-day shining, the face of a man who is talking to you. You see his lips moving, the expression in his eyes, you hear his voice, you feel his arms round your shoulders, and yet you see neither his arms, nor his body, nor his face, you lose all sense of yourself, you can see only the blinding light which spreads everywhere, lighting up the layer of snow covering the glade, and igniting the flakes that are falling on us both like white powder.

'What do you feel?' asked Father Seraphim.

'An amazing well-being!' I replied . . .

'I feel a great calm in my soul, a peace which no words can express . . . A strange, unknown delight . . . An amazing happiness . . . I'm amazingly warm . . . There's no scent in all the world like this one!'

'I know,' said Father Seraphim, smiling . . . 'This is as it should be, for divine grace comes to live in our hearts, within us. Didn't the Lord say: "The kingdom of God is within you" (Luke 17:21)? This kingdom is just the grace of the Holy Spirit, living in us, warming us, enlightening us, filling the air with his scent, delighting us with his fragrance and rejoicing our hearts with an ineffable gladness.'

Seraphim of Sarov, 1831 [171]

My dearly beloved flock, it is my heart's desire and prayer that this very day might be such a day among us – that God would indeed open the windows of heaven, as he has done in times past, and pour down a blessing, till there be no room to receive it.

Let us observe, then, how thanksgiving brings down the Spirit of God . . .

My dear flock, I am deeply persuaded that there will be no full, soul-filling, heart-ravishing, heart-satisfying, out-pouring of the Spirit of God, till there be more praise and thanking the Lord. Let me stir up your hearts to praise.

He is good. Believers should praise God for what he is in himself. Those that have never seen the Lord cannot praise him. Those that have not come to Christ, have never seen the King in his beauty. An unconverted man sees no loveliness in God. He sees a beauty in the blue sky – in the glorious sun – in the green earth – in the spangling stars – in the lily of the field; but he sees no beauty in God. He hath not seen him, neither known him; therefore there is no melody of praise in that heart. When a sinner is brought to Christ, he is brought to to the Father. Jesus gave himself for us, 'that he might bring us to God.' O! what a sight breaks in upon the soul – the infinite, eternal, unchangeable God! I know that some of you have been brought to see this sight. Oh! praise him, then, for what he is. Praise him for his *pure, lovely holiness*, that cannot bear any sin in his sight. Cry, like the angels, 'Holy, holy, holy, Lord God Almighty.' Praise him for his *infinite wisdom* – that he knows the end from the beginning. In him are hid all the treasures of wisdom and knowledge. Praise him for his *power* – that all matter, all mind, is in his hand. The heart of the king, the heart of saint and sinner, are all in his hand. Hallelujah! for the Lord God Omnipotent reigneth. Praise him for his *love*; for God is love. Some of you have been at sea. When far out of sight of land, you have stood high on the vessel's prow, and looked round and round – one vast circle of ocean without any bound. Oh! so it is to stand in Christ justified, and to behold the love of God – a vast ocean all around you, without a bottom and without a shore. Oh! praise him for what he is. Heaven will be all praise. If you cannot praise God, you never will be there.

Robert Murray M'Cheyne, 1839 [172]

*

[The apostles] did not begin their work under the direction of an intellectual theory, but under the impulse of the Spirit. This Spirit was in its nature world-wide, all-embracing. Consequently they did not gradually enlarge their sympathies, and extend their activities in obedience to the demands of an intellectual progress; the world-embracing spirit enlarged and expanded their sympathy, and intellectual illumination followed. They then perceived the wider and larger application of truths of which they had hitherto seen only the partial application. Study of the doctrine did not lead to the wider activity; enlarged activity led them to understand the doctrine . . .

They did not base their action upon any intellectual interpretation of the nature and work and command of Christ. Neither did they base their action upon any anticipation of results which might be expected to follow from it. They did not argue that the conversion of any particular class or race of men might be expected greatly to strengthen the Church for her work in the world and therefore they ought to make special efforts to win the adhesion of this class or race. They did not argue that the relaxation or abandonment of familiar rules would inevitably result in serious injury to the Church. They did not argue that any particular action of a missionary was to be condemned because, if it were approved, it would seem to undermine some generally accepted doctrine, or would greatly disturb the minds of a large body of Christians, or would lead to developments which might be undesirable. The apostles acted under the impulse of the Spirit; their action was not controlled by the exigencies of any intellectual theory . . .

The path by which the apostles reached the truth was submissive obedience in act to the impulse of the Holy Spirit. When the moment came, when the Spirit in them moved them to desire men's salvation, and to feel their need, they acted, they spoke, they expressed that Spirit of love and desire, not knowing what the result of their action might be, nor how to justify it intellectually, certain only that they were directed by the Holy Spirit.

Roland Allen, 1917 [173]

***

Pentecost is the crowning miracle and the abiding mystery of grace. It marks the beginning of the Christian dispensation. The tongues of fire sat upon each one of them. The word 'sat' in scripture marks an end and a beginning. The process of preparation is ended, and the established order has begun. It marks the end of creation, and the beginnng of normal forces. 'In six days the Lord made heaven and earth, the sea, and all that in them is, and rested the seventh day.' There is no weariness in God. He did not rest from fatigue. What it means is that all creative work was accomplished. The same figure of speech is used of the Redeemer. Of him it is said, 'When he had made purification of sins, (he) sat down on the right hand of the Majesty on high.' No other priest had sat down. The priests of the Temple ministered standing, because their ministry was provisional and preparatory, a parable and a prophecy. Christ's own ministry was part of the preparation for the coming of the Spirit. Until he 'sat down' in glory, there could be no dispensation of the Spirit. John says of our Lord's promise in the Temple, 'This spake he of the Spirit, which they that believed on him were to receive: for the Spirit was not yet given; because

Jesus was not yet glorified.' The descent of the One awaited the ascent of the Other. When the work of redemption was complete, the Spirit was given; and when he came he 'sat'. He reigns in the church, as Christ reigns in the heavens. This is the dispensation of the Spirit.

Samuel Chadwick, 1933 [174]

*
**

When we pray 'Come, Holy Ghost, our souls inspire', we had better know what we are about. He will not carry us to easy triumphs and gratifying successes; more probably he will set us to some task for God in the full intention that we shall fail, so that others, learning wisdom by our failure, may carry the good cause forward. He may take us through loneliness, desertion by friends, apparent desertion even by God; that was the way Christ went to the Father. He may drive us into the wilderness to be tempted of the devil. He may lead us from the Mount of Transfiguration (if he ever lets us climb it) to the hill that is called the Place of a Skull. For if we invoke him, it must be to help us in doing God's will, not ours. We cannot call upon the

> Creator Spirit, by whose aid
> The world's foundations first were laid

in order to use omnipotence for the supply of our futile pleasures or the success of our futile plans. If we invoke him, we must be ready for the glorious pain of being caught by his power out of our petty orbit into the eternal purposes of the Almighty, in whose onward sweep our lives are as a speck of dust. The soul that is filled with the Spirit must have become purged of all pride or love of ease, all self-complacence and self-reliance; but that soul has found the only real dignity, the only lasting joy. Come then, Great Spirit, come. Convict the world; and convict my timid soul.

William Temple, 1945 [175]

Christ is our sanctification and he becomes that through the Holy Spirit who, acting upon us, enables us to fight the fight with sin and to work out our own salvation with fear and trembling. The way of holiness, the method of sanctification, is to respond to all the promptings and leadings of the Spirit as he reveals things in our lives both within and without. We are to 'test the spirits' by reading the Scriptures regularly and prayerfully as opened by him. There, in the Scriptures, we are given all the reasons and the arguments which alone can stimulate within us the desire to become holy. There also we are shown what we have to do both negatively and positively. And as we come to know these things more and more we realize increasingly in experience the truth of our blessed Lord's words when he said, 'if ye know these things, happy are ye if ye do them'.

But what if we fail to do them? What if we are slack and indolent and lethargic? What if we do not obey the commands and respond to the appeals and the exhortations? Once more we are reminded that the work is finally God's and that 'he which hath begun a good work in you will perform it until the day of Jesus Christ'. If we are his in Christ, if it is true of us to say that 'of him are ye in Christ Jesus', then, if we do not respond to the appeals and exhortations and if we fail to apply the doctrine to our lives, God will employ another method to lead us to do so. Because we are his children, he will chastise us (see 1 Corinthians 11:30-32 and Hebrews 12). By illness and sickness, misfortune and apparent accidents, through what men call 'circumstance and chance', through business worries and losses and in numberless other ways. The method will still be mainly indirect and its object will be to bring us to a realization of the Truth.

But, however much we may respond and obey, something of the pollution of sin and of the old nature will still remain. But this shall not rob us of the vision of God. The Christ who died for us will cause it to slough away and will 'present us faultless before the presence of his glory with exceeding joy', and we shall be 'complete in him'. As in the salvation of the world and the perfecting of the Church, so here God, in his infinite grace, uses men and their powers, but himself guarantees, and is the guarantee of, the ultimate completion of the work.

Martyn Lloyd-Jones, 1948 [176]

**

The Holy Spirit is love, and love is properly a longing or *intention* towards someone. Thus when God sends his Spirit, when he directs towards some particular point this finger of the Father's right hand, he is sending a longing, an invitation to all things that exist to exist in relation to him and in dependence on him. It is this necessity and this need that is represented or released by the appearance of a dove above a baptistry, or the breath of the priest, or the tongue of fire, or a given sacred text which we inhale. I opened my mouth and drew forth the Spirit. The combined forces and faculties of our personality immediately conspire with this desire, as we have already read in the Canticle of Canticles: 'Let him kiss me with kisses of his mouth!'

He has ordered everything in me with respect to love. Thus when a vacuum is created in Mary by the words: 'Behold the handmaid of the Lord, be it done to me according to thy word!' it is the Holy Spirit mingled with that rush of air who fills her, who directs the charity that is in her and prepares all the forces of her body and soul for the realization of Jesus. She conspires with this inspiration: she conceives of the Holy Spirit.

Paul Claudel, 1948 [177]

**

Deity indwelling men! That, I say, is Christianity, and no man has experienced rightly the power of Christian belief until he has known this for himself as a living reality.

157

Everything else is preliminary to this. Incarnation, atonement, justification, regeneration; what are these but acts of God preparatory to the work of invading and the act of indwelling the redeemed human soul? Man who moved out of the heart of God by sin now moves back into the heart of God by redemption. God who moved out of the heart of man because of sin now enters again his ancient dwelling to drive out his enemies and once more make the place of his feet glorious.

A.W. Tozer, 1950 [178]

*
**

The Spirit is not the Word, and yet it also is the Spirit of the Word. But it does not proceed only from the Word but, simultaneously, also from the Father (Jn 15:26), who is God 'before' the Word. He is at once the Spirit of the Utterable and the Unutterable. He explains the Word by showing it as it proceeds from what is eternally beyond the Word. He transfigures both realities in their unity, since he is the unity of both and witnesses to this fact. Thus, he is at once the Spirit of form and formation and a Spirit of love and enthusiasm. In this incomprehensible unity he is the locus of the beauty of God. He is sober in order to show forth very precisely what is and to allow it to be seen; and he is intoxication and intoxicates because the raptures of love are the ultimate objectivity which must be seen and experienced. The Gospel and the Church are not Dionysian; they stand out for their soberness and banish the fanatical enthusiast to the sects. But an opponent of enthusiasm such as Ronald Knox has arguably more than a little underestimated the Song of Songs and its fulfilment in the New Testament and in every authentic Christian theology. How could Christianity have become such a universal power if it had always been as sullen as today's humourless and anguished Protestantism, or as grumpy as the super-organised and super-scholasticised Catholicism about us? If this were the face of Christ stamped by the Holy Spirit on Veronica's cloth, then we could really ask whether this is indeed the triune Spirit of God. The tension between precision and enthusiasm which is the Holy Spirit's must be accepted as he offers it; the saints were able to do it. Their enthusiasm is kindled, precisely, by the precision of the image of Jesus drawn by the Spirit, and this enthusiasm, in turn, expresses with precision, for all others to see, the fact of having been grasped by this image. It is not dry manuals (full as these may be of unquestionable truths) that express with plausibility for the world the truth of Christ's Gospel; it is the existence of the saints who have been grasped by Christ's Holy Spirit. And Christ himself foresaw no other kind of apologetics (Jn 13:35).

Hans Urs von Balthasar, 1961 [179]

*
**

There is no mechanical solution to true spirituality or the Christian life. Anything that has the mark of the mechanical upon it is a mistake. It is not possible to say, read so many chapters of the Bible every day, and you will have this much sanctification. It is not possible to say, pray so long every day, and you will have a certain amount of sanctification. It is not possible to add the two together and to say, you will have this big a piece of sanctification . . . The Christian life, true spirituality, can never have a mechanical solution. The real solution is being cast up into the moment by moment communion, personal communion, with God himself; and letting Christ's truth flow through me through the agency of the Holy Spirit.

Francis Schaeffer, 1971 [180]

What is this force which causes me to see in a way in which I have not seen? What makes a landscape or a person or an idea come to life for me and become a presence towards which I surrender myself? I recognise, I respond, I fall in love, I worship – yet it was not I who took the first step. In every such encounter there has been an anonymous third party who makes the introduction, acts as a go-between, makes two beings aware of each other, sets up a current of communication between them . . .

I have already started to talk about this force of influence in very personal terms. I am bound to do so because the effect of this power is always to bring a mere object into personal relationship with me, to turn an *It* into a *Thou*.

So Christians find it quite natural to give a personal name to this current of communication, this invisible go-between. They call him the Holy Spirit, the Spirit of God . . .

Ground of our Being has always seemed to me too static a concept of God. 'Ground of our Meeting' is nearer the mark, and I think of the Holy Spirit as the elemental energy of communion itself, within which all separate existences may be made present and personal to each other. The first essential activity of the Spirit is communication. It is always he who gives one to the other and makes each really see the other.

J.V. Taylor, 1972 [181]

*
**

Pentecost was the moment in which the new Breath which was breathed into them drove out all the poisonous fumes of negative self-images they had unwittingly inhaled from their milieu and each other . . . Henceforth, the beatitude will be: Blessed is the man who is poor in or free from the inhalations of false attitudes towards himself. Cursed is the man, on the other hand, who is rich in lies about his own identity. The joy of the Kingdom belongs to those to whom it has been given to inhale the truth about themselves. The limitations that are imposed by each baptised Christian on the power of the Spirit that would operate new Pentecosts in each of us come not so much from our own sinfulness, I suspect, as from our unwillingness to entertain the view of ourselves that God has of us. The Spirit's power in us is meant to provide an alternative to self-definitions that are fallacious, and, consequently, unfreeing.

John Haughey, 1973 [182]

**

Some time ago, Dr Michael Ramsey, the Archbishop of Canterbury, visited me at Malines. Before beginning our conversation, I suggested we should pray together. We opened the Bible at the words: 'Although the doors were locked, Jesus came and stood among them saying, "Peace be with you"' (Jn 20:26). It seemed to us that this was an invitation of the Lord to continue our dialogue despite closed doors, knowing in our hearts that the Lord was being true to his word; that he was present because we had come together in his name.

Cardinal Suenens, 1975 [183]

**

Creativity and spirituality are intimately related. One cannot do without the other. Traditional society has required certain of its members to behave spiritually without becoming at the same time creative . . . Liberation is a deeply spiritual matter. Basically, it is the interrelatedness between spirituality and creativity that poses a radical challenge to the institution called the church.

A church with true spirituality is a creative church. It is creative not only in matters strictly religious but must be creative also in all the areas and dimensions of human life. A truly creative spirituality is one that enables us to realize and experience the divine presence in all that we do, not only in religious worship, but also in all realms of our activities. It breaks down the barrier between the sacred and the profane, the religious and the nonreligious, the holy and the secular. To encounter other human beings in the rough and tumble of this world, to experience life in the midst of death, and to perceive meaning in the face of meaninglessness – this is spirituality.

Choan-Seng Song, 1979 [184]

***

The actual work of the Spirit in the mission of the Church often begins with a gestation period, a time of uncertainty, of unrest, of searching, more like the prelude to the emergence of a work of art or of a new scientific discovery than to the formulation of some secondary textbook. This is the dissatisfied questing and longing, half conscious sometimes, which characterises the early life of many a reformer or innovator. It can be a phase in the life of a Christian community. Then comes some fresh apprehension of Christ, breaking in upon the group or the individual with the force and often the form of a vision . . .

Often the confronting of the terrible reality of the Cross of Christ is the prelude to the receiving of his risen power. Many individuals and groups . . . (more and more I believe in recent years, particularly in Asia and Africa) have known a similar experience. They too have passed through the disclosure of the God who suffers, 'God with us', the Lamb who takes away the sin of the world, to the all–engulfing recognition of the victorious and exalted One, the Bestower of the Spirit. He summons them into the 'rivers of windfall light', releasing in them the spontaneous capacity to communicate, transforming them into channels of his love.

Simon Barrington-Ward, 1982 [185]

Spiritus

I used to think of you
as a symphony
neatly structured,
full of no surprises.
Now I see you as
a saxophone solo
blowing wildly
into the night,
a tongue of fire,
flicking in unrepeated
                    patterns.

Steve Turner, 1982 [186]

Being the Church

[The monthly gifts] are not taken thence and spent on feasts, and drinking-bouts, and eating-houses, but to support and bury poor people, to supply the wants of boys and girls desitute of means and parents, and of old persons confined now to the house; such, too, as have suffered shipwreck; and if there happen to be any in the mines, or banished to the islands, or shut up in the prisons, for nothing but their fidelity to the cause of God's Church, they become the nurslings of their confession. But it is mainly the deeds of a love so noble that lead many to put a brand upon us. *See,* they say, *how they love one another,* for themselves are animated by mutual hatred; *how they are ready even to die for one another,* for they themselves will sooner put to death. And they are wroth with us, too, because we call each other brethren; for no other reason, as I think, than because among themselves names of consanguinity are assumed in mere pretence of affection. . . .

One in mind and soul, we do not hesitate to share our earthly goods with one another. . . . What wonder if that great love of Christians towards one another is desecrated by you! For you abuse also our humble feasts, on the ground that they are extravagant as well as infamously wicked. . . . Yet about the modest supper-room of the Christians alone a great ado is made. Our feast explains itself by its name. The Greeks call it *agapè*, i.e., affection. Whatever it costs, our outlay in the name of piety is gain, since with the good things of the feast we benefit the needy; not as it is with you, do parasites aspire to the glory of satisfying their licentious propensities, selling themselves for a belly-feast to all disgraceful treatment, – but as it is with God himself, a peculiar respect is shown to the lowly.

Tertullian, 197 [187]

The difference between Christians and the rest of mankind is not a matter of nationally, or language, or customs. Christians do not live apart in separate cities of their own, speak any special dialect, nor practise any eccentric way of life. The doctrine they profess is not the invention of busy human minds and brains, nor are they, like some, adherents of this or that school of human thought. They pass their lives in whatever township – Greek or foreign – each man's lot has determined; and conform to ordinary local usage in their clothing, diet, and other habits. Nevertheless, the organization of their community does exhibit some features that are remarkable, and even surprising. For instance, though they are residents at home in their own countries, their behaviour there is more like that of transients; they take their full part as citizens, but they also submit to anything and everything as if they were aliens. For them, any foreign country is a motherland, and any motherland is a foreign country. Like other men, they marry and beget children, though they do not expose their infants. Any Christian is free to share his neighbour's table, but never his marriage-bed. Though destiny has placed them here in the flesh, they do not live after the flesh; their days are passed on the earth, but their citizenship is above in the heavens. They obey the prescribed laws, but in their own private lives they transcend the laws. They show love to all men – and all men persecute them. They are misunderstood, and condemned; yet by suffering death they are quickened into life. They are poor, yet making many rich; lacking all things, yet having all things in abundance. They are dishonoured, yet made glorious in their very dishonour; slandered, yet vindicated. They repay calumny with blessings, and abuse with courtesy. For the good they do, they suffer stripes as evil-doers; and under the strokes they rejoice like men given new life. Jews assail them as heretics, and Greeks harass them with persecutions; and yet of all their ill-wishers there is not one who can produce good grounds for his hostility.

Epistle to Diognetus, early 3rd cent. [188]

The stimulus of friendship was brought to bear upon us . . . the argument of a kind and affectionate disposition . . . [Origen's] desire was, with a benignant, and affectionate, and most benevolent mind, to save us, and make us partakers in the blessings that flow from philosophy, and most especially also in those other gifts which the Deity has bestowed on him above most men, or, as we may perhaps say, above all men of our own time. I mean the power that teaches us piety, the word of salvation, that comes to many, and subdues to itself all whom it visits . . . And thus, like some spark lighting upon our inmost soul, love was kindled and burst into flame within us, – a love at once to the Holy Word, the most lovely object of all, who attracts all irresistibly toward himself by his unutterable beauty, and to this man, his friend and advocate. . . .

'And the soul of Jonathan was knit with David.'

Gregory Thaumaturgus, c. 238 [189]

**
*

Many things can be done that look well, yet do not issue from the root of charity. Thorns too have their flowers. Some actions seem harsh or savage, but are performed for our discipline at the dictate of charity. Thus a short and simple precept is given you once for all: Love, and do what you will. Whether you keep silence, keep silence in love; whether you exclaim, exclaim in love; whether you correct, correct in love; whether you forbear, forbear in love. Let love's root be within you, and from that root nothing but good can spring.

Augustine, 416 [190]

**
*

It is evident that Christ meant by footwashing a perfect love which causes us gladly to serve all the needs of our brothers. It is this that makes us truly blessed and immortal, as John says: 'We know that we have passed out of death into life, because we love the brethren' (1 John 3:14).

Wherever men are so minded that they humble themselves, hold others in higher esteem than themselves, and therefore gladly serve them in the way we have described, there all wars, quarrels, strife and disharmony must cease, and peace, unity, and all good works will rule and flourish. There then would be no room for the daughters of self-love, such as envy, egotism, and ambition, from which grow greed, arrogance, and contempt of the neighbour.

Christopher Ostorodt, 1604 [191]

**

Weak Christians are like glasses which are hurt with the least violent usage, otherwise if gently handled will continue a long time . . . The ambassadors of so gentle a Saviour should not be over-masterly, setting up themselves in the hearts of people where Christ alone should sit as in his own temple.

Richard Sibbes, 1630 [192]

**

If you had a friend with whom you might now and then spend a little time, in conferring together, in opening your hearts, and presenting your unutterable groanings before God, it would be of excellent use . . . And be much in quickening conference, giving and taking mutual encouragements and directions in the matters of Heaven . . . Be open hearted to one another, and stand for one another against the devil and all his angels. Make it thus your business in these and such like ways, to provide for eternity.

Jonathan Mitchel, c. 1720 [193]

Friday, April 26. Conversed with a Christian friend with some warmth; felt a spirit of mortification to the world in a very great degree. Afterwards was enabled to pray fervently, and to rely on God sweetly for 'all things pertaining to life and godliness.' Just in the evening was visited by a dear Christian friend, with whom I spent an hour or two in conversation, on the very soul of religion. There are many with whom I can talk *about religion*; but alas! I find few with whom I can talk *religion itself*. But, blessed be the Lord, there are some that love to feed on the kernel, rather than the shell.

David Brainerd, 1745 [194]

*
**

To a Roman Catholic

If God still loveth us, we ought also to love one another. We ought, without this endless jangling about opinions, to provoke one another to love and to good works. Let the points whereon we differ stand aside: here are enough wherein we agree, enough to be the ground of every Christian temper and every Christian action. . . .

In the name then, and in the strength of God, let us resolve, first, not to hurt one another; to do nothing unkind or unfriendly to each other, nothing we would not have done to ourselves. Rather let us endeavour after every instance of a kind, friendly, and Christian behaviour towards each other.

Let us resolve, secondly, God being our helper, to speak nothing harsh or unkind of each other. The sure way to avoid this is to say all the good we can both of and to one another; in all our conversation, either with or concerning each other to use only the language of love, to speak with all softness and tenderness, with the most endearing expression which is consistent with truth and sincerity.

Let us, thirdly, resolve to harbour no unkind thought, no unfriendly temper towards each other. Let us lay the axe to the root of the tree; let us examine all that rises in our heart, and suffer no disposition there which is contrary to tender affection. Then we shall easily refrain from unkind actions and words, when the very root of bitterness is cut up.

Let us, fourthly, endeavour to help each other on in whatever we are agreed leads to the kingdom. So far as we can let us always rejoice to strengthen each other's hands in God. Above all, let us each take heed to himself . . . that he fall not short of the religion of love . . .

John Wesley, 1749 [195]

*
**

The longer I live, the more I see of the vanity and the sinfulness of our unchristian disputes: they eat up the very vitals of religion . . . I allow that every branch of gospel truth is precious, that errors are abounding, and that it is our duty to bear an honest testimony to what the Lord has enabled us to find comfort in, and to instruct with meekness such as are willing to be instructed; but I cannot see it my duty, nay, I believe it would be my sin, to attempt to beat my notions into other people's heads. Too often I have attempted it in times past; but now I judge, that both my zeal and my weapons were carnal. When our dear Lord questioned Peter, after his fall and recovery, he said not, Art thou wise, learned, and eloquent? nay, he said not, Art thou clear and sound, and orthodox? But this only, 'Lovest thou me?'

John Newton, 1757 [196]

*
**

Christianity is essentially a social religion, and to turn it into a solitary religion is indeed to destroy it.

John Wesley, 1771 [197]

What would be wrong in one person, would not be so in another; and what would be wrong under some circumstances, would not be so under other circumstances. What would be wrong if done from choice, might not be wrong if done for fear of offending others, or of casting a stumbling-block before them, or with a view to win them. The whole College of Apostles advised St Paul to purify himself with those who had on them the vows of Nazarites. And, though I doubt not but that there are Christians of a high stamp, who would condemn them all, and call it a sinful conformity, I am not prepared to do so. I suspect my own judgment rather than that of the Apostles. Christians of this high cast will bend to no one either in sentiment or in conduct; but will inflexibly adhere to their own way: but I feel inclined rather to become (as far as God's word will admit) 'all things to all men,' not through *fear* of their destroying me; but from *love*, that I may save them. I would eat or not eat meat, according to circumstances; and act differently towards Timothy and Titus, according as I thought I should promote or obstruct the welfare of others. I know I should be called inconsistent, and unstable, and be represented as conceding too much to the opinions and prejudices of men. But I should account it a small matter to be judged of man's judgment, if only I approved myself to God and my own conscience.

Charles Simeon, 1823 [198]

*
**

My beloved Mary,

 . . . That we may show our love improperly, I readily grant; but that we can love one another too much, I utterly deny, provided only it be in subserviency to the love of God. I think I have explained to you that word *fervently* ('see that ye love one another with a pure heart *fervently*'): its precise meaning is *intensely*. No two words in any two languages more exactly agree than 'intensely' does with the original. If then our love be with a pure heart, this alone were sufficient to establish the point. But I am anxious to convey to you more fully my views of this matter, because as God himself is love, I think that the more intensely I love those who are beloved of him, the more I think I resemble him. The proper model for our love to each other is Christ's love to us. If you will not fall short of that, I have no fear of your exceeding it. We are required to lay down our lives for the brethren. We shall not readily exceed that. The union that should subsist between the saints should resemble, as far as possible, the love that subsists between God the Father and his Son Jesus Christ. How then can we fear excess?. . .

Perhaps you will say, my grief is, that my love generates disquietude when those who are dear to me are ill; and this is an evidence that my love is idolatrous, and not truly Christian. Then what will you say to Paul, who confesses, 'he had no rest in his Spirit because he found not Titus his brother?' Christianity does not encourage apathy: it is to regulate, not to eradicate, our affections. It admits to their full operation, but tempers them as to their measure, and sanctifies them to the Lord.

But I will not delay this, that I may shew at least, that if love be a crime, there are few more guilty than your friend
C. Simeon.

Charles Simeon, 1835 [199]

*
**

One tribe of these Ishmaelites is made up of highflying ignoramuses who are very mighty about the doctrine of a sermon – here they are as decisive as sledge-hammers and as certain as death. He who knows nothing is confident in everything; hence they are bullheaded beyond measure. Every clock, and even the sundial must be set according to their watches; and the slightest difference from their opinion, proves a man to be rotten at heart. Venture to argue with them, and their little pot boils over in quick style; ask them for reason, and you might as well go to a sand-pit for sugar. They have bottled up the sea of truth, and carry it in their waistcoat pockets; they have measured heaven's line of grace, and have tied a knot in a string at the exact length of electing love; and as for the things which angels long to know, they have seen them all as boys see sights in a peepshow at our fair. Having sold their modesty and become wiser than their teachers, they ride a very high horse, and jump over all five-barred gates of Bible-texts which teach doctrines contrary to their notions. When this mischief happens to good men, it is a great pity for such sweet pots of ointment to be spoiled by flies, yet one learns to bear with them just as I do with old Violet, for he is a rare horse, though he does set his ears back and throw out his leg at times. But there is a black bragging lot about, who are all sting and no honey; all whip and no hay; all grunt and no bacon. These do nothing but rail from morning to night at all who cannot see through their spectacles. If they would but mix up a handful of good living with all their bushels of bounce, it would be more bearable; but no, they don't care for such legality; men so sound as they are can't be expected to be good at anything else; they are the heavenly watchdogs to guard the house of the Lord from those thieves and robbers who don't preach sound doctrine, and if they do worry the sheep, or steal a rabbit or two by the sly, who would have the heart to blame them? The Lord's *dear* people, as they call themselves, have enough to do to keep their doctrine sound; and if their manners are cracked, who can wonder! no man can see to everything at once. These are the moles that want catching in many of our pastures, not for their own sakes, for there is not a sweet mouthful in them, but for the sake of the meadows which they spoil. I would not find half a fault with their doctrine, if it were not for their spirit, but vinegar is sweet to it, and crabs are figs in comparison. It must be very high doctrine that is too high for me, but I must have high experience and high practice with it, or it turns my stomach.

C. H. Spurgeon, 1868 [200]

***

Let him who cannot be alone beware of community.
Let him who is not in community beware of being
    alone.

Dietrich Bonhoeffer, 1939 [201]

***

Well, Whitsuntide is here, and we are still separated; but it is in a special way a feast of fellowship. When the bells rang this morning, I longed to go to church, but instead I did as John did on the island of Patmos, and had such a splendid service of my own, that I did not feel lonely at all, for you were all with me, every one of you, and so were the congregations in whose company I have kept Whitsuntide. Every hour or so since yesterday evening I've been repeating to my own comfort Paul Gerhardt's Whitsun hymn with the lovely lines 'Thou art a Spirit of joy' and 'Grant us joyfulness and strength', and besides that, the words 'If you faint in the day of adversity, your strength is small' (Prov. 24), and 'God did not give us a spirit of timidity but a spirit of power and love and self-control' (2 Tim. 1). I have also been considering again the strange story of the gift of tongues. That the confusion of tongues at the Tower of Babel, as a result of which people can no longer understand each other, because everyone speaks a different language, should at last be brought to an end and overcome by the language of God, which everyone understands and through which alone people can understand each other again, and that the church should be the place where that happens –

173

these are great momentous thoughts. Leibniz grappled all his life with the idea of a universal script consisting, not of words, but of self-evident signs representing every possible idea. It was an expression of his wish to heal the world, which was then so torn to pieces, a philosophical reflection on the Pentecost story.

Dietrich Bonhoeffer, 1943 [202]

*
**

I take my help where I find it and set my heart to graze where the pastures are greenest. Only one stipulation do I make: my teacher must know God, as Carlyle said, 'otherwise than by hearsay', and Christ must be all in all to him. If a man have only correct doctrine to offer me I am sure to slip out at the first intermission to seek the company of someone who has seen for himself how lovely is the face of him who is the Rose of Sharon and the Lily of the Valleys. Such a man can help me and no one else can.

A. W. Tozer, 1950 [203]

*
**

A girl in a gentian blue frock broke away from the rest and came across the path towards my hut. I bent over the shirt on the table and a moment later there was a shy tap on the open door. During the exchange of salutations at the threshold she remained half hidden behind the doorpost, but when I had invited her to come in, she slipped past me and in one flowing, silent movement was seated on the mat in the corner of the little room, her legs tucked sideways out of sight under the blue dress. As I gave her the formal indoor greeting, cool fingertips brushed mine and for one instant she looked up and around with the devouring curiosity of a child. Then the eyes were downcast, the slender hands lay still in her lap, and she leaned one shoulder against the lime-washed wall, as relaxed as a young antelope asleep in the sun.

She looked about twelve years old. . . .

I went on with my ironing.

It was one of those models which work with paraffin and a pressure pump. It makes a continuous small hiss, a comfortable purring sound, and after a few minutes I noticed that my visitor's eyes were following my hand to and fro with puzzled fascination. Then she caught sight of the little blue flame of burning vapour inside the shoe of the iron, leant forward to make certain she had seen aright, and a longdrawn *Haa* of wonderment escaped her lips. She glanced up, saw that I was watching her, and embarrassment wrestled with curiosity across her face. 'Do you see the fire?' I asked.

'Yes. It is a marvel.'

'It burns with paraffin like a small primus stove.'

Her face lit up and she laughed for the joy of comprehension. Then she relaxed again into her former position, no longer shy but quiescent and companionable. It is an unfailing wonder and delight, this tranquillity of human relationships in Africa. Whether it be child or adult makes no difference; one can enjoy the other's presence without fuss or pressure, in conversation or in silence as the mood dictates. Whether the task in hand may be continued or must be left depends upon a score of fine distinctions which the stranger must slowly learn; but one thing is certain – a visitor is never an interruption.

J. V. Taylor, 1963[204]

*
**

An optimistic and idealistic view of the Church and of history would see a Church in constant development, unfolding and becoming more perfect, constantly making progress and improving itself. But this is not a view the New Testament allows us to hold, still less Church history.

Given that Christ is the head of the Church and hence the origin and goal of its growth, growth is only possible in *obedience* to its head. If the Church is disobedient to its head and his word, it cannot grow, however busy and active it may seem to be, it can only wither. Its development, no matter how spectacular, will prove basically misdirected; its progress, no matter how grandiose, will prove ultimately a disastrous retrogression. The valid movements in the Church are those that are set in motion by God's grace. The Church does not grow automatically and ontologically, but only historically. Real growth in the Church occurs when Christ penetrates the world by the activity of his Church in history, whether outwards, through missions to the pagans which reveal the mystery of Christ and the election of all mankind in him, or inwards through men of faith and love in whom Christ established his reign over the world, who act in faith and love in every sphere of their everyday life and reveal the world as the kingdom of Christ from which all demons have been banished, and as the creation of God.

Hans Küng, 1968 [205]

*
**

Christianity is an individual thing, but it is not *only* an individual thing. There is to be true community, offering true spiritual and material help to each other. . . .

The local church or Christian group should be right, but it should also be beautiful. The local group should be the example of the supernatural, of the substantially healed relationship in this present life between men and men.

Francis Schaeffer, 1971 [206]

*
**

I vividly remember the day on which a man who had been a student in one of my courses came back to the school and entered my room with the disarming remark: 'I have no problems this time, no questions to ask you. I do not need counsel or advice, but I simply want to celebrate some time with you.' We sat on the ground facing each other and talked a little about what life had been for us in the last year, about our work, our common friends, and about the restlessness of our hearts. Then slowly as the minutes passed by we became silent. Not an embarrassing silence but a silence that could bring us closer together than the many small and big events of the last year. We would hear a few cars pass and the noise of someone who was emptying a trash can somewhere. But that did not hurt. The silence which grew between us was warm, gentle and vibrant. Once in a while we looked at each other with the beginning of a smile pushing away the last remnants of fear and suspicion. It seemed that while the silence grew deeper around us we became more and more aware of a presence embracing both of us. Then he said, 'It is good to be here' and I said, 'Yes, it is good to be together again,' and after that we were silent again for a long period. And as a deep peace filled the empty space between us he said hesitantly, 'When I look at you it is as if I am in the presence of Christ.' I did not feel startled, surprised or in need of protesting, but I could only say, 'It is the Christ in you, who recognizes the Christ in me.' 'Yes,' he said, 'he indeed is in our midst,' and then he spoke the words which entered into my soul as the most healing words I had heard in many years. 'From now on, wherever you go, or wherever I go, all the ground between us will be holy ground.' And when he left I knew that he had revealed to me what community really means.

Henri Nouwen, 1975 [207]

*
**

All I want to say is this: it is by sharing the earthly goods that we come to have an idea of what it is like to share the life of God. As long as we do not know how to share earthly goods, as God would have us do, it is an illusion to imagine that we know what it is to share the life of the Trinity which is our destiny. If you cannot manage with toys, nobody is going to entrust you with the real thing.

The question is: Have we imitated the Holy Trinity in sharing earthly goods? Have Christians tried to do this in all earnest? Could I truthfully say: 'All mine are thine and thine are mine' to each and all? This is what we are supposed to imitate (John 17:10). Then in what sense can we be said to be practising to live the life of God? How can we dare to profess the religion of the Trinity?

Christopher Mwoleka, 1975 [208]

*
**

Though for us knowledge of the life of Trinity is indeed little, yet we can say that the most perfect community or *ujamaa* is the Trinity. The Trinity establishes God as community. Jesus Christ revealed the Trinity to us. God wished to share with humanity and the entire creation his own community life in the person of Jesus Christ who became consubstantial with us. Our life is a shared life in the Trinity.

Camillus Lyimo, 1976 [209]

*
**

As I was nearing the end of the evangelization of the first six Masai communities, I began looking towards baptism. So I went to the old man Ndangoya's community to prepare them for the final step.

I told them I had finished the imparting of the Christian message inasmuch as I could. I had taught them everything I knew about Christianity. Now it was up to them. They could reject it or accept it. I could do no more. If they did accept it, of course, it required public baptism. So I would

178

go away for a week or so and give them the opportunity to make their judgment on the gospel of Jesus Christ. If they did accept it, then there would be baptism. However, baptism wasn't automatic. Over the course of the year it had taken me to instruct them, I had gotten to know them very well indeed.

So I stood in front of the assembled community and began: 'This old man sitting here has missed too many of our instruction meetings. He was always out herding cattle. He will not be baptized with the rest. These two on this side will be baptized because they always attended, and understood very well what we talked about. So did this young mother. She will be baptized. But that man there has obviously not understood the instructions. And that lady there has scarcely believed the gospel message. They cannot be baptized. And this warrior has not shown enough effort . . .'

The old man, Ndangoya, stopped me politely but firmly, 'Padri, why are you trying to break us up and separate us? During this whole year that you have been teaching us, we have talked about these things when you were not here, at night around the fire. Yes, there have been lazy ones in this community. But they have been helped by those with much energy. There are stupid ones in the community, but they have been helped by those who are intelligent. Yes, there are ones with little faith in this village, but they have been helped by those with much faith. Would you turn out and drive off the lazy ones and the ones with little faith and the stupid ones? From the first day I have spoken for these people. And I speak for them now. Now, on this day one year later, I can declare for them and for all this community, that we have reached the step in our lives where we can say, "We believe".'

We believe. Communal faith. Until that day I had never heard of such a concept, certainly had never been taught it in a classroom. But I did remember the old ritual for baptism

179

of children, the first question in that ceremony. 'What do you ask of the church of God?' we inquired of the infant. Of course, he couldn't answer for himself. He couldn't speak for himself. He couldn't even think for himself. He certainly could not believe. And there is no such thing as a valid baptism without belief. Such an act would be magic, witchcraft.

The answer to that question, supplied by sponsors, was not 'baptism' or 'salvation'. It was, 'faith'. That is what the child asked of the church of God, of the community of believers – faith, their faith, to become his, to make baptism possible.

I looked at the old man, Ndangoya. 'Excuse me, old man,' I said. 'Sometimes, my head is hard and I learn slowly. "We believe," you said. Of course you do. Everyone in the community will be baptized.'

Vincent Donovan, 1978 [210]

*
* *

But how can one live this Christian community if the option of l'Arche is to welcome handicapped people because they are in need and in distress, and not because they are Christian? Our aim is not just to have Christian assistants bound together in Christian love to 'look after' the weak and the poor. Our goal is to live community *with* handicapped men and women, to create bonds with them and thus to discover their prophetic call. It is to create a community where handicapped people are fully members. It is to enter into deep relationships that are healing for them and hence for the assistants as well. Handicapped people are so frequently closer to living the Beatitudes than the assistants; to live with them can only constitute a real gain from a spiritual point of view. This unity in community between assistants and handicapped people is the heart and essence of l'Arche.

If one day it disappears so that assistants can live a 'deeper' spiritual life together, or so that they can have a more reasonable private life, less harrassed, less stressful, then l'Arche will no longer be. Our therapy and our call are based on this 'family living' together, where we share, work, pray, suffer, and celebrate together; where we grow together in love, in hope and in freedom of heart.

Jean Vanier, 1982 [211]

***
****

Peace between neighbours,
Peace between kindred,
Peace between lovers,
   In love of the King of Life.

Peace between person and person,
Peace between wife and husband,
Peace between woman and children,
   The peace of Christ above all peace.

Bless, O Christ, my face,
   Let my face bless every thing;
Bless, O Christ, mine eye,
   Let mine eye bless all it sees.

Scots Gaelic blessing [212]

3
Food and Drink

We begin with Scripture – it couldn't be otherwise in a collection with evangelical roots. But it is a little misleading to start with Luther and the great discovery of Scripture in the sixteenth century. Unfortunately, the Church Fathers who exhorted their flock to read and absorb Scripture – John Chrysostom is one example – did not do so in easily extractable form! None the less, it is true to say that the sixteenth century reopened what had become a closed book.

The Reformation material emphasises the richness and the joy to be found in Scripture. Latimer strikes the note of Scripture as nourishment, to be taken on a daily basis; centuries later Tozer castigates those whose reading is swift and superficial. But all these exhortations would be so much hot air were it not for the simplicity and clarity of those crucial Scriptures which deal with the life and death issues. The Scriptures do contain their mysteries, but they are also life-giving and authoritative for the church and the believer. Jesus himself used the scripture to repel the devil; and indeed began by quoting from Deuteronomy, 'Man does not live on bread alone, but on every word that comes from the mouth of God.'

The sacrament of Communion – often known as an ordinance in deference to Christ's command to eat and drink in remembrance and proclamation of him – is also an important part of the Christian pilgrim's nourishment, and, as the *Didache* extract shows, part of the devotion in the early church. It is noticeable, too, how high a view of it was taken by those who sought to reform our understanding of it in the sixteenth and seventeenth centuries. The extract from Bayly's *Practice of Piety*, the most popular devotional book of the period in England, shows how imaginative the response sometimes was. More than a century later, Charles Wesley's *Hymns on the Lord's Supper* draw out the multiple significance of the celebration – memorial and thanksgiving in our two examples. Later discussions extend our understanding of the nature of Christ's presence and the expression of our communion with each other in this meal.

Prayer is properly thought of as one of the resources of the pilgrim; but it would also be quite accurate to characterise the whole of spirituality as the life of prayer in its broadest sense. We can talk of the kinds of prayer that we pray as thanksgiving, praise, confession, petition, and intercession; or we can go further, perhaps in obedient exploration of the command to pray constantly (1 Thessalonians 5:17), to consider how a prayer can intervene in the middle of a busy day (the 'arrow prayer') or how our whole life can develop into a continual contemplation of, or keeping company with God. Here, too, we find the Orthodox 'Prayer of Jesus', a constant prayer of the heart, a resource. It may be that some will find this section intimidating – some of these passages go very deep – when the need is to find something simple that will bring one's prayer life out of the doldrums. So here, also, is advice on how to begin, on how to deal with distractions, on recognising how the Spirit helps us with our prayers when we don't know how to pray.

Scripture

In order that those who are not more familiar with it may have instruction and guidance for reading the Old Testament with profit, I have prepared this preface to the best of the ability God has given me. I beg and really caution every pious Christian not to be offended by the simplicity of the language and stories frequently encountered there, but fully realize that, however simple they may seem, these are the very words, works, judgments, and deeds of the majesty, power, and wisdom of the most high God. For these are the Scriptures which make fools of all the wise and understanding, and are open only to the small and simple, as Christ says in Matthew 11:25. Therefore dismiss your own opinions and feelings, and think of the Scriptures as the loftiest and noblest of holy things, as the richest of mines which can never be sufficiently explored, in order that you may find that divine wisdom which God here lays before you in such simple guise as to quench all pride. Here you will find the swaddling cloths and the manger in which Christ lies, and to which the angel points the shepherds (Luke 2:12). Simple and lowly are these swaddling cloths, but dear is the treasure, Christ, who lies in them.

Martin Luther, 1523 [213]

**
**

Evangelion (that we call the gospel) is a Greek word; and signifieth good, merry, glad and joyful tidings, that maketh a man's heart glad, and maketh him sing, dance, and leap for joy: as when David had killed Goliath the giant, came glad tidings unto the Jews, that their fearful and cruel enemy was slain, and they delivered out of all danger: for gladness whereof, they sung, danced, and were joyful. In like manner is the Evangelion of God (which we call gospel, and the New Testament) joyful tidings; and, as some say, a good hearing published by the apostles throughout all the world, of Christ the right David; how that he hath fought with sin, with death, and the devil, and overcome them: whereby all men that were in bondage to sin, wounded with death, overcome of the devil, are, without their own merits or deservings, loosed, justified, restored to life and saved, brought to liberty and reconciled unto the favour of God, and set at one with him again: which tidings as many as believe laud, praise, and thank God; are glad, sing and dance for joy.

This Evangelion or gospel (that is to say, such joyful tidings) is called the New Testament; because that as a man, when he shall die, appointeth his goods to be dealt and distributed after his death among them which he nameth to be his heirs; even so Christ before his death commanded and appointed that such Evangelion, gospel, or tidings should be declared throughout all the world, and therewith to give unto all that repent, and believe, all his goods: that is to say, his life, wherewith he swallowed and devoured up death; his righteousness, wherewith he banished sin; his salvation, wherewith he overcame eternal damnation. Now can the wretched man (that knoweth himself to be wrapped in sin, and in danger to death and hell) hear no more joyous a thing, than such glad and comfortable tidings of Christ; so that he cannot but be glad, and laugh from the low bottom of his heart, if he believe that the tidings are true.

William Tyndale, c.1525 [214]

*
**

These books, therefore, ought to be much in our hands, in our eyes, in our ears, in our mouths, but most of all in our hearts. For the Scripture of God is the heavenly meat of our souls: the hearing and keeping of it maketh us blessed, sanctifieth us, and maketh us holy; it turneth our souls; it is a light lantern to our feet; it is a sure, stedfast, and everlasting instrument of salvation; it giveth wisdom to the humble and lowly hearts, it comforteth, maketh glad, cheereth, and cherisheth our conscience; it is a more excellent jewel, or treasure, than any gold or precious stone; it is more sweet than honey or honeycomb; it is called *the best part*, which Mary did choose, for it hath in it everlasting comfort. The words of holy Scripture be called words of *everlasting life*; for they be God's instrument, ordained for the same purpose . . .

Let us hear, read, and know these holy rules, injunctions, and statutes of our christian religion, and upon that we have made profession to God at our baptism. Let us with fear and reverence lay up, in the chest of our hearts, these necessary and fruitful lessons. Let us night and day muse, and have meditation and contemplation in them. Let us ruminate, and, as it were, chew the cud, that we may have the sweet juice, spiritual effect, marrow, honey, kernel, taste, comfort, and consolation of them. Let us stay, quiet, and certify our consciences with the most infallible certainty, truth, and perpetual assurance of them. Let us pray to God, the only author of these heavenly studies, that we may speak, think, believe, live, and depart hence, according to the wholesome doctrine and verities of them. And, by that means, in this world we shall have God's defence, favour, and grace, with the unspeakable solace of peace, and quietness of conscience; and, after this miserable life, we shall enjoy the endless bliss and glory of heaven: which he grant us all, that died for us all, Jesus Christ: to whom, with the Father and the Holy Ghost, be all honour and glory, both now and everlastingly. *Amen.*

Thomas Cranmer, 1547 [215]

The preaching of the word of God unto the people is called meat. Scripture calleth it meat; not strawberries, that come but once a year, and tarry not long, but are soon gone; but it is meat, it is no dainties. The people must have meat that must be familiar and continual, and daily given them to feed upon. Many make a strawberry of it, ministering it but once a year; but such do not the office of good prelates.

Hugh Latimer, 1548 [216]

*
**

Let this point therefore stand: that those whom the Holy Spirit has inwardly taught truly rest upon Scripture, and that Scripture indeed is self-authenticated; hence, it is not right to subject it to proof and reasoning. And the certainty it deserves with us, it attains by the testimony of the Spirit. For even if it wins reverence for itself by its own majesty, it seriously affects us only when it is sealed upon our hearts through the Spirit. Therefore, illumined by his power, we believe neither by our own nor by anyone else's judgment that Scripture is from God; but above human judgment we affirm with utter certainty (just as if we were gazing upon the majesty of God himself) that it has flowed to us from the very mouth of God by the ministry of men. We seek no proofs, no marks of genuineness upon which our judgment may lean; but we subject our judgment and wit to it as to a thing far beyond any guesswork! This we do, not as persons accustomed to seize upon some unknown thing, which, under closer scrutiny, displeases them, but fully conscious that we hold the unassailable truth! Nor do we do this as those miserable men who habitually bind over their minds to the thralldom of superstition; but we feel that the undoubted power of his divine majesty lives and breathes there. By this power we are drawn and inflamed, knowingly and willingly, to obey him, yet also more vitally and more effectively than by mere human willing or knowing!

Jean Calvin, 1559 [217]

[John Robinson] charged us before God and his blessed angels, to follow him no further than he followed Christ; and if God should reveal anything to us by any other instrument of his, to be as ready to receive it as ever we were to receive any truth by his ministry; for he was very confident the Lord had more truth and light yet to break forth out of his holy Word. He took occasion also miserably to bewail the state and condition of the reformed churches, who were come to a period in religion, and would go no further than the instruments of their reformation. As, for example, the Lutherans, they could not be drawn to go beyond what Luther saw; for whatever part of God's will he had further imparted and revealed to Calvin, they will rather die than embrace it. And so also, saith he, you see the Calvinists, they stick where he left them; a misery much to be lamented; for though they were precious shining lights in their times, yet God had not revealed his whole will to them; and were they now living, saith he, they would be as ready and willing to embrace further light, as that they had received. Here also he put us in mind of our church covenant, at least that part of it whereby we promise and covenant with God and one with another, to receive whatsoever light or truth shall be made known to us from his written Word; but withal exhorted us to take heed what we received for truth, and well to examine and compare it and weigh it with other scriptures of truth before we received it.

Memoir of John Robinson, 1620 [218]

**
*

All things in Scripture are not alike plain in themselves, nor alike clear to all: yet those things which are necessary to be known, believed, and observed for salvation, are so clearly propounded, and opened in some place of Scripture or other, that not only the learned, but the unlearned, in a due use of the ordinary means, may attain unto a sufficient understanding of them.

Westminster Assembly, 1644 [219]

*
**

Oftentimes (as cows afford both milk and beef) the same texts that babes may suck milk from, strong men may find strong meat in; the Scripture itself in some sense fulfilling the promise made to us in it, that *to him that hath shall be given*, and being like a fire that serves most men but to warm, and dry themselves, and dress their meat, but serves the skilful chemist to draw quintessences and make extracts.

Robert Boyle, 1661 [220]

*
**

Lord, I have made thy word my choice,
    my lasting heritage:
there shall my noblest powers rejoice,
    my warmest thoughts engage.

Isaac Watts, 1719 [221]

*
**

Scripture can be savingly understood only in and by the inward illumination of the Holy Ghost. The gospel is a picture of God's free grace to sinners. Were we in a room, hung with the finest paintings, and adorned with the most exquisite statues, we could not see one of them, if all light was excluded. Now, the blessed Spirit's irradiation is the same to the mind, that outward light is to the bodily eyes.

Augustus Toplady, before 1779 [222]

If people will be governed by the occurrence of a single text of Scripture, without regarding the context, or duly comparing it with the general tenor of the word of God, and with their own circumstances, they may commit the greatest extravagances, expect the greatest impossibilities, and contradict the plainest dictates of common sense, while they think they have the word of God on their side . . .

The word of God is not to be used as a lottery; nor is it designed to instruct us by shreds and scraps, which, detached from their proper places, have no determinate import; but it is to furnish us with just principles, right apprehensions to regulate our judgments and affections, and thereby to influence and direct our conduct.

John Newton, 1785 [223]

*
**

There are indeed a considerable number of persons, who avowedly disparage all commentators and their labours, and profess to read the Scriptures alone. But if knowledge, in a variety of things, be useful, (not to say absolutely needful,) in order to understand the Scriptures, and to make the best application of them to practical purposes; and if these persons have not that knowledge, and despise the labours of those who have; it is not likely that they should make much proficiency, even in understanding the book to which they exclusively confine themselves. And surely, a man, who has daily and for a long course of years been traversing an intricate path through a forest, may, without arrogance, propose to give some useful directions and cautions, to those who are beginning to explore the same path. Nor would it savour either of wisdom or humility, if such persons should contemptuously refuse to avail themselves of the experience and observation of him, who had long traced and retraced the way; and determine to proceed on their journey, without a guide, or a chart of the road.

Thomas Scott, 1788 [224]

The Author is no friend to systematizers in Theology.

He is disposed to think that the Scripture system, be it what it may, is of a broader and more comprehensive character than some very exact and dogmatical theologians are inclined to allow: and that as wheels in a complicated machine may move in opposite directions and yet subserve one common end, so may truths *apparently opposite* be perfectly reconcileable with each other, and equally subserve the purposes of God in the accomplishment of man's salvation. . . . But he feels it impossible to repeat too often, or avow too distinctly, that it is an invariable rule with him to endeavour to give to every portion of the Word of God its full and proper force, without considering one moment what scheme it favours, or whose system it is likely to advance. Of this he is sure, that there is not a decided Calvinist or Arminian in the world, who equally approves of the whole of Scripture. He apprehends that there is not a determined votary of either system, who, if he had been in the company of St. Paul whilst he was writing his different epistles, would not have recommended him to alter one or other of his expressions.

But the Author would not wish one of them altered: he finds as much satisfaction in one class of passages as in another; and employs the one, he believes, as often and as freely as the other. Where the inspired writers speak in unqualified terms, he thinks himself at liberty to do the same; judging that they needed no instruction from *him* how to propagate the truth. He is content to sit as a *learner* at the feet of the holy Apostles, and has no ambition to teach them how they ought to have spoken.

Charles Simeon, 1832 [225]

*
**

It is upon the *broad grand principles* of the Gospel that I repose – it is not upon any particular promise here or there – any little portions of the word, which some people seem to take comfort from; but I wish to look at the *grand whole* – at the vast scheme of redemption as from eternity to eternity.

Charles Simeon, 1836 [226]

**

We wait for no new truth: we believe in no development of old truths. The truths of Holy Scripture, by its very faculty of life (Heb. 4:12) adapt themselves to each succeeding age, and portions long neglected, or but partially understood, break forth often with new energy when circumstances call for their application. Of others it is only by careful study and diligent and oft-repeated examination, that the Church at length attains to their full meaning, and due relation to other truths. But a new article of the faith, by its very novelty, stands self-condemned. The Church's duty is, not to invent, but to defend and maintain in its integrity the whole truth entrusted to its charge. Our duty is to study the inspired records, so carefully and with prayer, that by the Holy Spirit's aid we may comprehend, as adequately as our limited powers will permit, the unsearchable riches of the truth as revealed in Jesus Christ our Lord.

Robert Payne Smith, 1869 [227]

**

The promises of God's word, what power they give a man. To get ahold of a 'shall' and 'will' in the time of trouble is a heavenly safeguard. 'My God will hear me.' 'I will not fail thee nor forsake thee.' These are divine holdfasts. Oh, how strong a man is for overcoming the wicked one when he has such a promise to hand! Do not trust yourself out of a morning in the street till you have laid a promise under your tongue!

C. H. Spurgeon, 1883 [228]

I want to see a new translation of the Bible into the hearts and conduct of living men and women. I want an improved translation – or transference it might be called – of the commandments and promises and teachings and influences of this Book to the minds and feelings and words and activities of the men and women who hold on to it and swear by it and declare it to be an inspired Book and the only authorized rule of life.

That seems to me to be the only translation, after all, that will in the long run prove to be of any value. It is the reproduction of the scriptures in men and women that makes their worth. The Bible is a book intended to make Bible-men – that is, good men. If the end is not gained, where is the value of the means? What will be the value of the Bible in the day of judgment apart from transformations of character it has produced? It is of no use making correct translations of words, if we cannot get the *words translated into life*.

William Booth, 1885 [229]

*
**

Consecutive reading of biblical books forces everyone who wants to hear to put himself, or to allow himself to be found, where God has acted once and for all for the salvation of men. We become part of what once took place for our salvation. Forgetting and losing ourselves, we, too, pass through the Red Sea, through the desert, across the Jordan into the promised land. With Israel we fall into doubt and unbelief and through punishment and repentance experience again God's help and faithfulness. All this is not mere reverie but holy, godly reality. We are torn out of our own existence and set down in the midst of the holy history of God on earth. There God dealt with us; and there he still deals with us, our needs and our sins, in judgment and grace. It is not that God is the spectator and sharer of our present life, howsoever important that is; but rather that we are the reverent listeners and participants in God's action in the sacred story, the history of the Christ on earth. And only in so far as we are *there*, is God with us today also.

A complete reversal occurs. It is not in our life that God's help and presence must still be proved, but rather God's presence and help have been demonstrated for us in the life of Jesus Christ. It is in fact more important for us to know what God did to Israel, to his Son Jesus Christ, than to seek what God intends for us today. The fact that Jesus Christ died is more important than the fact that *I* shall die, and the fact that Jesus Christ rose from the dead is the sole ground of my hope that I, too, shall be raised on the Last Day. Our salvation is 'external to ourselves'. I find no salvation in my life history, but only in the history of Jesus Christ. Only he who allows himself to be found in Jesus Christ, in his incarnation, his Cross, and his resurrection, is with God and God with him . . .

We must learn to know the Scriptures again, as the Reformers and our fathers knew them. We must not grudge the time and the work that it takes. We must know the Scriptures first and foremost for the sake of our salvation. But besides this, there are ample reasons that make this requirement exceedingly urgent. How, for example, shall we ever attain certainty and confidence in our personal and church activity if we do not stand on solid biblical ground? It is not our heart that determines our course, but God's Word. But who in this day has any proper understanding of the need for scriptural proof? How often we hear innumerable arguments 'from life' and 'from experience' put forward as the basis for most crucial decisions, but the argument of Scripture is missing. And this authority would perhaps point in exactly the opposite direction. It is not surprising, of course, that the person who attempts to cast discredit upon their wisdom should be the one who himself does not seriously read, know, and study the scriptures. But one who will not learn to handle the Bible for himself is not an evangelical Christian.

Dietrich Bonhoeffer, 1939 [230]

* *

No doubt the inspiration of the Scriptures will seem to many people a topic so old and so wearisome that it can be no longer endured. But if so, it will either be because they have no interest in the Scriptures themselves, or because they have not discovered what the Scriptures are good for. Anyone who has felt, even in the least degree, the power of these texts to enliven the soul and to open the gates of heaven must have some curiosity about the manner in which the miracle is worked. And, looking about him, he will quickly realize that interests more vital than those of curiosity are at stake. The prevalent doctrine about scriptural inspiration largely determines the use men make of the Scriptures. When verbal inspiration was held, men nourished their souls on the Scriptures, and knew that they were fed. Liberal enlightenment claims to have opened the scriptural casket, but there appears now to be nothing inside – nothing, anyhow, which ordinary people feel moved to seek through the forbidding discipline of spiritual reading.

Austin Farrer, 1948 [231]

* *

The idea of cultivation and exercise, so dear to the saints of old, has now no place in our total religious picture. It is too slow, too common. We now demand glamour and fast flowing dramatic action . . .

We read our chapter, have our short devotions and rush away, hoping to make up for our deep inward bankruptcy by attending another gospel meeting or listening to another thrilling story told by a religious adventurer lately returned from afar.

The tragic results of this spirit are all about us. Shallow lives, hollow religious philosophies, the preponderance of the element of fun in gospel meetings, the glorification of men, trust in religious externalities . . .

A. W. Tozer, 1948 [232]

**

We can no more speak of dictation in the doctrine of the Scripture than we can speak of the life of Christ as dictated by the Father. Just as we speak of his life in terms of obedience, so we must speak of the Bible as obedience to the Divine self-revelation, in which the human word of Holy Scripture bows under the divine judgment just because it is part of his redemptive and reconciling work. In the Bible, therefore, the Word of God is not given to us ready-made. We see it growing in wisdom and grace before God and before man. We see it in the midst of our God-forsakenness and darkness, struggling with our temptations and our rebellious will. The Word of God comes to us in the midst of our sin and darkness at once revealing and reconciling, but it comes with strong crying and tears, pressing its way through the speech of our fallen flesh, graciously assuming it in spite of all its inadequacy and faultiness and imperfection, and giving it a holy perfection in the Word of God. The doctrine of verbal inspiration does not, therefore, mean the inerrancy and infallibility of the biblical word in its linguistic and historical and other characteristics as human word. It means that the errant and fallible human word is, as such, used by God and has to be received and heard in spite of its human weakness and imperfection . . .

Although we cannot speak of a direct identity between the human word of Scripture and the Word that was made flesh in Jesus Christ resting in the essence either of the divine

Word or the human word, we must speak of an identity
between the word of man and the Word of God in the Bible
which rests upon the gracious decision of God to unite it
with his own Word, and so to give it a divine perfection in
spite of its human imperfection. Therefore the Bible has to
be heard as the very Word of God in which we acknowledge
that, although in itself, in its human expression, it is involved in the limitation and imperfection of human flesh
under judgment, it is so inseparably conjoined with the
divine Word as to be the written Word of God to man, and is
brought into such a faithful correspondence with the divine
revelation that it mediates to us in and through itself the
exemplary obedience of Christ as the authoritative pattern
and norm for the obedience of the Church in all its thinking
and speaking. It is because the humanity of the apostolic
Scriptures is already incorporated in the revelation and
already enclosed within the reconciliation of Christ that
these Scriptures are both the organ through which Jesus
Christ from age to age conveys his Word to men with
saving power and the canon by which he rules his Church,
shaping its mind and forming it to be his Body.

T. F. Torrance, 1956 [233]

*
**

Scripture is not the Word itself, but rather the Spirit's
testimony concerning the Word, which springs from an
indissoluble bond and marriage between the Spirit and
those eye-witnesses who were originally invited and admitted to the vision. With such an understanding of Scripture,
we can say further that its testimony possesses an inner form
which is canonical simply by being such a form, and for this
reason we can 'go behind' this form only at the risk of losing
both image and Spirit conjointly. Only the final result of the
historical developments which lie behind a text – a history
never to be adequately reconstructed – may be said to be

inspired, not the bits and scraps which philological analysis thinks it can tear loose from the finished totality in order, as it were, to steal up to the form from behind in the hope of enticing it to betray its mystery by exposing its development. Does it not make one suspicious when Biblical philology's first move in its search for an 'understanding' of its texts is to dissect their form into sources, psychological motivations, and the sociological effects of milieu, even before the form has been really contemplated and read for its meaning *as form*? For we can be sure of one thing: we can never again recapture the living totality of form once it has been dissected and sawed into pieces, no matter how informative the conclusions which this anatomy may bring to light. Anatomy can be practised only on a dead body.

Hans Urs von Balthasar, 1961 [234]

Sacrament

At the Eucharist, offer the eucharistic prayer in this way. Begin with the chalice: 'We give thanks to thee, our Father, for the holy Vine of thy servant David, which thou hast made known to us through thy servant Jesus.'

'Glory be to thee, world without end.'

Then over the particles of bread: 'We give thanks to thee, our Father, for the life and knowledge thou hast made known to us through thy servant Jesus.'

'Glory be to thee, world without end.'

'As this broken bread, once dispersed over the hills, was brought together and became one loaf, so may thy Church be brought together from the ends of the earth into thy kingdom.' . . .

When all have partaken sufficiently, give thanks in these words:

'Thou, O Almighty Lord, hast created all things for thine own Name's sake; to all men thou hast given meat and drink to enjoy, that they may give thanks to thee, but to us thou hast graciously given spiritual meat and drink, together with life eternal, through thy Servant. Especially, and above all, do we give thanks to thee for the mightiness of thy power.'

'Glory be to thee for ever and ever.'

'Be mindful of thy Church, O Lord; deliver it from all evil, perfect it in thy love, sanctify it, and gather it from the four winds into the kingdom which thou hast prepared for it.'

'Thine is the power and the glory for ever and ever.'

'Let his Grace draw near, and let this present world pass away.'

The Didache, before 150 [235]

The proof that a man has eaten and drunk is this, if he abides and is abode in, if he dwells and is dwelt in, if he adheres so as not to be deserted . . . But we abide in him when we are his members, and he abides in us when we are his temple . . . Let all this, then, avail us to this end, most beloved, that we eat not the flesh and blood of Christ merely in the sacrament . . . but that we eat and drink to the participation of the Spirit, that we abide as members in the Lord's Body, to be quickened by his Spirit.

Augustine, 416 [236]

*
**

In the Supper there is a twofold analogy. The first is to Christ. For as the bread supports and sustains human life, and wine makes glad the heart of man, so Christ alone sustains and supports and rejoices the soul when it has no other hope. For who is the man who can yield to despair when he sees that the Son of God is his, and he guards him in his soul like a treasure, and for his sake he can ask anything of the Father? The second analogy is to ourselves. For as bread is made up of many grains and wine of many grapes, so by a common trust in Christ which proceeds from the one Spirit the body of the Church is constituted and built up out of many members a single body, to be the true temple and body of the indwelling Spirit . . .

With the sight we see the bread and wine which in Christ's stead signify his goodness and favourable disposition. Is it not therefore the handmaid of faith? For it sees Christ before it as it were, and the soul is enflamed by his beauty and loves him most dearly. With the sense of touch we take the bread into our hands and in signification it is no longer bread but Christ. And there is also a place for taste and smell in order that we may taste and see how good the Lord is and how blessed is the man that trusts in him: for just as these senses take pleasure in food and are stimulated by it, so the soul exults and rejoices when it tastes the sweet savour of heavenly hope.

Huldreich Zwingli, 1531 [237]

*
**

The Lord instituted this communion of himself, this sharing of his body and blood, as the Holy Spirit calls it (1 Cor. 10), so that we may receive *them*, not simply bread and wine. Otherwise we should have had to call it a communion of bread and wine and not a communion of the body and blood of the Lord; and there would have been no reason for the Lord when he distributed the bread and wine to the disciples, and said 'Take, eat, drink,' to have added 'This is my body, This is my blood.' And so in this sacrament we receive not only bread and wine but at the same time his body and blood, and indeed not these only but with them the whole Christ, both God and man.

Because we receive him who is truly man, and at the same time truly God, we therefore receive his flesh and blood. And because this flesh, and likewise this blood, is that of the Son of God, it is 'life-giving'.

Martin Bucer, 1551 [238]

*
**

It has come about that almost all, when they have taken communion once, as though they have beautifully done their duty for the rest of the year, go about unconcerned. It should have been done far differently: the Lord's Table should have been spread at least once a week for the assembly of Christians, and the promises declared in it should feed us spiritually . . . None is indeed to be forcibly compelled, but all are to be urged and aroused . . . All, like hungry men, should flock to such a bounteous repast.

Jean Calvin, 1559 [239]

We affirm that bread and wine are holy and heavenly mysteries of the body and blood of Christ, and that by them Christ himself, being the true bread of eternal life, is so presently given unto us, as that by faith we verily receive his body and his blood. Yet say we not this so, as though we thought that the nature of bread and wine is clearly changed and goeth to nothing; as many have dreamed in these later times, which yet could never agree among themself of this their dream. For that was not Christ's meaning, that the wheaten bread should lay apart his own nature, and receive a certain new divinity; but that he might rather change us, and (to use Theophylactus' words) might transform us into his body. . . .

For we affirm that Christ doth truly and presently give his own self in his sacraments; in baptism, that we may put him on; and in his supper, that we may eat him by faith and spirit, and may have everlasting life by his cross and blood. And we say not, this is done slightly and coldly, but effectually and truly. For, although we do not touch the body of Christ with teeth and mouth, yet we hold him fast, and eat him by faith, by understanding, and by the spirit. And this is no vain faith which doth comprehend Christ; and that is not received with cold devotion, which is received with understanding, with faith, and with spirit. For Christ himself altogether is so offered and given us in these mysteries, that we may certainly know we be flesh of his flesh, and bone of his bones; and that Christ continueth in us, and we in him.

John Jewel, 1560 [240]

***

If thou comest humbly, in faith, repentance and charity, abhorring thy sins past, and purposing unfeignedly to amend thy life henceforth; let not thy former sins affright thee; for they shall never be laid to thy charge: and this sacrament shall seal unto thy soul, that all thy sins, and the judgement due to them, are fully pardoned, and clean washed away by the blood of Christ. For, this sacrament was not ordained for them who are perfect; but to help penitent sinners unto perfection.

When thou eatest the bread, imagine that thou seest Christ hanging upon the cross, and by his unspeakable torments, fully satisfying God's justice for thy sins; and strive to be as verily partaker of the spiritual grace, as of the elemental signs . . .

When thou seest the wine brought to thee apart from the bread: then remember that the blood of Jesus Christ was as verily separated from his body upon the cross for the remission of thy sins. And that this is the seal of that new covenant which God hath made to forgive all the sins of all penitent sinners that believe the merits of his blood-letting . . .

As thou drinkest the wine, and pourest it out of the cup into thy stomach; meditate and believe that by the merits of that blood which Christ shed upon the cross, all thy sins are as verily forgiven, as thou hast now drunk this sacramental wine, and hast it in thy stomach . . .

As thou feelest the sacramental wine which thou has drunk, warming thy cold stomach: so endeavour to feel the Holy Ghost cherishing thy soul in the joyful assurance of the forgiveness of all thy sins . . . And so lift up thy mind from the contemplation of Christ, as he was crucified on the cross: to consider how he now sits in glory at the right hand of his Father, making intercession for thee.

Lewis Bayly, 1613 [241]

*
**

If this sacrament could be spared, that a man might keep the strength of the inward man without it, the Lord would not have put you to this trouble, but he seeth it necessary and therefore he hath appointed it to be received, and that often, that you might feed upon the body and blood of Christ, that you might eat his flesh and drink his blood, and gather strength from it, that when there is decay of grace in your hearts, you may go to this fountain and fill the cisterns again to renew your strength; for when a man comes to the sacrament as he ought, he gathers a new strength, as a man from a feast, his heart is cheered up as it is with flagons of wine, he is refreshed, his hunger and thirst is satisfied, that is the desires of his soul that long after Christ, and after righteousness, and assurance.

John Preston, 1631 [242]

*
**

Deck thyself, my soul, with gladness,
Leave the gloomy haunts of sadness,
Come into the daylight's splendour,
There with joy thy praises render
Unto him, whose boundless grace
Grants thee at his feast a place;
He whom all the heavens obey
Deigns to dwell in thee today.

Hasten as a bride to meet him,
And with loving reverence greet him,
Who with words of life immortal
Now is knocking at thy portal;
Haste to make for him a way,
Cast thee at his feet, and say:
Since, oh Lord, thou com'st to me,
Never will I turn from thee.

Ah how hungers all my spirit,
For the love I do not merit!
Ah how oft with sighs fast thronging
For this food have I been longing!
How have thirsted in the strife
For this draught, O Prince of Life,
Wish'd, O Friend of man, to be
Ever one with God through thee!

Here I sink before thee lowly,
Fill'd with joy most deep and holy,
As with trembling awe and wonder
On thy mighty works I ponder;
On this banquet's mystery,
On the depths we cannot see;
Far beyond all mortal flight
Lie the secrets of thy might.

Sun, who all my life dost brighten,
Light, who dost my soul enlighten,
Joy, the sweetest man e'er knoweth,
Fount, whence all my being floweth,
Here I fall before thy feet,
Grant me worthily to eat
Of this blessed heavenly food,
To thy praise, and to my good.

Jesus, Bread of Life from heaven,
Never be thou vainly given,
Nor I to my hurt invited;
Be thy love with love requited;
Let me learn its depths indeed,
While on thee my soul doth feed;
Let me here so richly blest,
Be hereafter too thy guest.

Johann Frank, 1653 tr. Catherine Winkworth, 1858 [243]

*
**

Meditation: John 6:51. I am the Living Bread

I kenning through astronomy divine
   The world's bright battlement, wherein I spy
A golden path my pencil cannot line,
   From that bright throne unto my threshold lie
   And while my puzzled thoughts about it pore
   I find the bread of life in't at my door.

When that this bird of paradise put in
   This wicker cage (my corpse) to tweedle praise
Had pecked the fruit forbad; and so did fling
   Away its food; and lost its golden days;
     It fell into celestial famine sore:
     And never could obtain a morsel more.

Alas! alas! Poor bird, what wilt thou do?
   The creatures' field no food for souls e'er gave.
And if thou knock at angels' doors they show
   An empty barrel: they no soul bread have.
     Alas! Poor bird, the world's white loaf is done.
     And cannot yield thee here the smallest crumb.

In this sad state, God's tender bowels run
   Out streams of grace: and he to end all strife
The purest wheat in heaven, his dear-dear son
   Grinds, and kneads up into this bread of life.
     Which bread of life from heaven down came and
      stands
     Dished on thy table up by angels' hands.

Did God mould up this bread in heaven, and bake,
   Which from his table came, and to thine goeth?
Did he bespeak thee thus, 'This soul bread take.
   Come eat thy fill of this thy God's white loaf?
     It's food too fine for angels, yet come, take
     And eat thy fill. It's heaven's sugar cake.'

What grace is this knead in this loaf? This thing
   Souls are but petty things it to admire.
Ye angels, help; this fill would to the brim
   Heaven's whelmed-down crystal meal-bowl, yea and
     higher:
     This bread of life dropped in thy mouth, doth cry
     'Eat, eat me, soul, and thou shalt never die.'

Edward Taylor, 1684 [244]

Here is a feast that's a feast indeed. It excels the most sumptuous and magnificent feast of the most magnificent monarch that ever breathed on earth. The guests are saints sparklingly adorned in the vestments of glorifying grace. The waiters are the all gloriously holy angels of light. The authors, the everlasting King of Glory. The occasion, the wedding and marriage of his only Son, to his bride the souls of his elect, the church of the first born whose names are written in heaven. And the entertainment itself, and this is most rich and royal, the manna of heaven, angels' bread, the bread of life, the water of life, the fruits of 'the Tree of Life in the middest of the paradise of God' (Rev. 2:7). Spiritual dainties: Oh! the sweet heart-ravishing melodies, musics, and songs of a spiritual nature with which Christ entertains souls hereat, what tongue of man or angel is able to relate? It is as it were the very suburbs of glory.

Edward Taylor, late 17th cent. [245]

Come, thou everlasting Spirit,
    Bring to every thankful mind
All the Saviour's dying merit,
    All his sufferings for mankind;
True Recorder of his passion,
    Now the living faith impart,
Now reveal his great salvation,
    Preach his gospel to our heart.

Come, thou Witness of his dying,
    Come, Remembrancer Divine,
Let us feel thy power applying
    Christ to every soul and mine;
Let us groan thine inward groaning,
    Look on him we pierced and grieve,
All receive the grace atoning,
    All the sprinkled blood receive.

Charles Wesley, 1745 [246]

After the sacrament

Sons of God, triumphant rise,
Shout th' accomplish'd sacrifice!
Shout your sins in Christ forgiven,
Sons of God, and heirs of heaven!

Ye that round our altars throng,
Listening angels, join the song:
Sing with us, ye heavenly powers,
Pardon, grace, and glory ours!

Love's mysterious work is done!
Greet we now th' accepted Son,
Heal'd and quicken'd by his blood,
Join'd to Christ, and one with God.

Christ, of all our hopes the seal;
Peace divine in Christ we feel,
Pardon to our souls applied:
Dead for all, for me he died!

Sin shall tyrannize no more,
Purged its guilt, dissolved its power;
Jesus makes our hearts his throne,
There he lives, and reigns alone.

Grace our every thought controls,
Heaven is open'd in our souls,
Everlasting life is won,
Glory is on earth begun.

Christ in us; in him we see
Fulness of the Deity.
Beam of the eternal beam;
Life divine we taste in him!

Him we only taste below;
Mightier joys ordain'd to know,
Him when fully ours we prove,
Ours the heaven of perfect love!

Charles Wesley, 1745 [247]

My God, and is thy table spread?
And does thy cup with love o'erflow?
Thither be all thy children led,
And let them all its sweetness know.

Hail, sacred feast, which Jesus makes!
Rich banquet of his flesh and blood!
Thrice happy he, who here partakes
That sacred stream, that heavenly food!

Why are its dainties all in vain
Before unwilling hearts displayed?
Was not for you the victim slain?
Are you forbid the children's bread?

O let thy table honoured be,
And furnished well with joyful guests;
And may each soul salvation see,
That here its sacred pledges taste.

Let crowds approach with hearts prepared;
With hearts inflamed let all attend;
Nor, when we leave our Father's board,
The pleasure or the profit end.

Revive thy dying churches, Lord,
And bid our drooping graces live;
And more that energy afford,
A Saviour's blood alone can give.

Philip Doddridge, 1755 [248]

*
**

That sacrament of the Word is what gives value to all other
sacraments. They are not ends, they are but means to that
grace. They are but visible, tangible modes of conveying
the same gospel which is audible in the Word. In the
sacrament of the Word the ministers are themselves the

living elements in Christ's hands – broken and poured out in soul, even unto death; so that they may not only witness Christ, or symbolise him, but by the sacrament of personality actually convey him crucified and risen. This cannot be done officially. It cannot be done without travail. A mother church must die daily in bringing the gospel into the world – and especially in her ministry must she die. There is indeed a real change in these true elements. Their transubstantiation is a constantly renewed conversion. It is the passage of the preacher's soul from death to life incessantly. The apostles were greater sacraments than those they administered, as man is more than the Sabbath, Christ than the temple.

For the true sacrament is holy personality.

P. T. Forsyth, 1947 [249]

***

The question arises whether one can speak of a special presence of Christ in the Lord's Supper. Is there a separate, special presence of Christ in the Supper which cannot be enjoyed apart from that Supper? The New Testament makes it clear that believers do not stand in true communion with Christ only in the Lord's Supper. We hear of his promise to be with us until the end of the world, and of his being in the midst of us even though only two or three are gathered together in his name. Furthermore, many references are made to our communion with Christ. To be sure, it is a communion with Christ through the Holy Spirit, but this does not at all minimize the reality of our communion with Christ of which we read that Christ dwells in the hearts of men through faith (Eph. 3:17) and that nothing can separate the believers from the love of Christ (Rom. 8:35) . . .

The celebration of the Lord's Supper is a matter of the strengthening of faith through the signs of bread and wine, and every Supper is precisely oriented toward continuous communion with the living Lord, the crucified, resurrected, and glorified Redeemer.

The Lord's Supper does not stand as a meeting isolated from normal life, separated from it by sharp boundaries such as fulfilment and enjoyment versus poverty and privation. The contrary is the case: the Lord's Supper is oriented toward that normal life and toward the communion which Christ promised to us all the days until the end of the world. The crux of the matter is, as Paul says: so that Christ may dwell in our hearts through faith.

G. C. Berkouwer, 1954 [250]

**
*

So many of our Eucharists fall short of the glory of God because, while purporting to concentrate on the Real Presence of Christ, they seem to be oblivious to the real presence of men, either in the worshipping family or the world around. To present oneself to God means to expose oneself, in an intense and vulnerable awareness, not only to him but to all that is.

J. V. Taylor, 1963 [251]

**
*

This characteristic Christian attitude to life is set forth whenever the Eucharist is celebrated – the sacrament in which all is offered to God, to be taken out of our dream or terror and made part of his kingdom. And it is just the case that a fantastic number of Christians have prayed in this way down the centuries of the human experiment. They have taken the particular gloom or sorrow or fear into which life has plunged them and gone to some place where the Church was doing the Eucharist. There, in the setting forth of the only truly offered being that ever lived, they have tried to offer up this situation (whatever it was) that terrified them or made them furious with God. They have tried to separate *themselves* from it, to offer up not only it but their ridiculous wishes concerning it or their desire to escape from it. They have sought to see it within the purpose of God, within the great image of that purpose truly fulfilled in a human life which is the sacrifice of Christ. They have been ready to bring their particular pain into vital relation with all that God wills for man, all that they have believed through Christ about God's ways of working with man and through man. And again and again the certain grace has come. Their desires and fears have changed out of all recognition, and have become first an acceptance, then a wish to do what the situation requires rather than to be relieved of its burden, a wish to make their distress a creative part of God's presence in life, and finally a fresh appetite for their difficult world.

Neville Ward, 1967 [252]

***

The basis of the entire eucharistic event is Christ's personal gift of himself to his fellow-men and, within this, to the Father. . . .

The Eucharist is the sacramental form of this event, Christ's giving of himself to the Father and to men. It takes the form of a commemorative meal in which the usual secular significance of the bread and wine is withdrawn and these become bearers of Christ's gift of himself – 'Take and eat, this is my body.' Christ's gift of himself, however, is not ultimately directed towards bread and wine, but towards the faithful. The real presence is intended for believers, but through the medium of and *in* this gift of bread and wine. In other words, the Lord who gives himself thus is *sacramentally* present. In this commemorative meal, bread and wine become the subject of a new *establishment of meaning*, not by men, but by the living Lord *in* the Church, through which they become the *sign* of the real presence of Christ giving himself to us.

Edward Schillebeeckx, 1967 [253]

On 6 April (1971), exactly fifty years after Kimbangu had performed his first healing in answer to prayer, the first celebration of Holy Communion was held . . . During the special service Joseph Diangienda announced the nature of the elements to be used in the communion, namely bread baked from a mixture of potatoes, maize and bananas (in which the latter served as 'yeast') and 'wine' made of honey and water.

L. Luntadila wrote an explanation of this . . . under the title *Reflexions sur la Sainte-Cène* ('Thoughts on the Lord's Supper'). In it he says that 'The foods used to make the elements are found in Zaire and the neighbouring countries. In order to be obedient to the spirit of the Gospel our church has chosen African foods, just as Christ in his day used bread and wine, the daily foods of Palestine . . . Just as pollen is transformed by bees into honey, so we too should be inwardly transformed by the Holy Spirit so that we can be witnesses to the risen Christ . . . Just as the body which was given for us saves us, so maize and potatoes have saved millions in the world. Just as the ingredients maize, potatoes, and bananas are mixed, so the body of Christ is formed of men and women of all races and lands . . .'

Marie-Louise Martin, 1971 [254]

*
**

We must consider more carefully the *real presence of Christ*, the *eucharistic parousia*. . . .

It is the whole Jesus Christ who makes himself specifically and intensely present to us in this eucharistic form in his oneness as Gift and Giver, the whole Jesus Christ in the fulness of his deity and in the fulness of his humanity, crucified and risen, not a bare or naked Christ, far less only his body and blood, but Jesus Christ clothed with his Gospel and clothed with the power of his Spirit, who cannot be separated from what he did or taught or was in the whole course of his historical existence in the flesh. What he has done once and for all in history has the power of permanent presence in him. He is present in the unique reality of his incarnate Person, in whom Word and Work and Person are indissolubly one, personally present therefore in such a way that he creatively effects what he declares, and what he promises actually takes place: 'This is my body broken for you', 'This is my blood shed for many for the remission of sins'. The real presence is the presence of the Saviour in his personal being and atoning self-sacrifice, who once and for all gave himself up on the Cross for our sakes but who is risen from the dead as the Lamb who has been slain but is alive for ever more, and now appears for us in the presence of the Father as himself prevalent eternally propitiation.

T. F. Torrance, 1975 [255]

*
**

I came across another extraordinary custom of the Masai. Sometimes the sin occurs, not between individuals, but among groups in the same community. One family might offend another family, and disruption sets in on the whole community. This can be disastrous to a nomadic type community who must have unity above all else for the sake of their herding together and moving together and for their common defence against enemies. A disruption like this can rupture the whole agreement or pact or covenant on which the community first came together and on which it remains together. If at all possible, both the offending and the offended family must be brought back together by an act of forgiveness sought and bestowed. So at the behest of the total community both families prepare food. The word for food in Masai is *endaa*. But this will be a special kind of food called the *endaa sinyati*, meaning *holy food*. This holy food is brought to the centre of the village by the two families accompanied by the rest of the community, encouraging both families all along the way. There in the centre of the village the food is exchanged between the two families, each family accepting the food prepared by the other family. Then the holy food is eaten by both families, and when it is, forgiveness comes, and the people say that a new *osotua* has begun. *Osotua* is the word for covenant or pact or testament.

A new testament of forgiveness is brought about by the exchange of holy food. What can one say?

Vincent Donovan, 1978 [256]

Prayer

A theologian is one whose prayer is true. If you truly pray, you are a theologian.

Evagrius of Pontus, 4th cent. [257]

*
**

It is thy heart's desire that is thy prayer; and if thy desire continues uninterrupted, thy prayer continueth also . . . There is another inward kind of prayer without ceasing, which is the desire of the heart. Whatever else you are doing, if you do but long for that Sabbath, you do not cease to pray. If you would never cease to pray, never cease to long after it. The continuance of thy longing is the continuance of thy prayer.

Augustine, 420 [258]

*
**

When you face God in prayer, become in your thought like a speechless babe. Do not utter before God anything which comes from knowledge, but approach him with childlike thoughts, and so walk before him as to be granted that fatherly care, which fathers give their children in their infancy.

Isaac of Nineveh, 7th cent. [259]

*
**

When the Apostle commanded us to 'Pray without ceasing' (1 Thess. 5:17), he meant that we must pray inwardly with our mind: and this is something that we can do always. For when we are engaged in manual labour and when we walk or sit down, when we eat or when we drink, we can always pray inwardly and practise prayer of the mind, true prayer, pleasing to God. Let us work with our body and pray with our soul. Let our outer man perform physical work, and let the inner man be consecrated wholly and completely to the service of God and never flag in the spiritual work of inner prayer.

Gregory Palamas, 14th cent. [260]

*
**

For in the beginning it is usual to feel nothing but a kind of darkness about your mind, or as it were, a *cloud of unknowing*. You will seem to know nothing and to feel nothing except a naked intent toward God in the depths of your being. Try as you might, this darkness and this cloud will remain between you and your God. You will feel frustrated, for your mind will be unable to grasp him, and your heart will not relish the delight of his love. But learn to be at home in this darkness. Return to it as often as you can, letting your spirit cry out to him whom you love. For if, in this life, you hope to feel and see God as he is in himself, it must be within this darkness and this cloud. But if you strive to fix your love on him forgetting all else, which is the work of contemplation I have urged you to begin, I am confident that God in his goodness will bring you to a deep experience of himself.

The Cloud of Unknowing, c. 1370 [261]

*
**

To this day I suckle at the Lord's Prayer like a child, and as an old man eat and drink from it and never get my fill. It is the very best prayer, even better than the psalter, which is so very dear to me. It is surely evident that a real master composed and taught it. What a great pity that the prayer of such a master is prattled and chattered so irreverently all over the world! How many pray the Lord's Prayer several thousand times in the course of a year, and if they were to keep on doing so for a thousand years they would not have tasted nor prayed one iota, one dot, of it! In a word, the Lord's Prayer is the greatest martyr on earth (as are the name and word of God). Everybody tortures and abuses it; few take comfort and joy in its proper use. . .

A good and attentive barber keeps his thoughts, attention, and eyes on the razor and hair and does not forget how far he has gotten with his shaving or cutting. If he wants to engage in too much conversation or let his mind wander or look somewhere else he is likely to cut his customer's mouth, nose, or even his throat. Thus if anything is to be done well, it requires the full attention of all one's senses and members, as the proverb says, *Pluribus intentus, minor est ad singula sensus* – 'He who thinks of many things, thinks of nothing and does nothing right.' How much more does prayer call for concentration and singleness of heart if it is to be a good prayer! . . .

It may happen occasionally that I may get lost among so many ideas in one petition that I forego the other six. If such an abundance of good thoughts comes to us we ought to disregard the other petitions, make room for such thoughts, listen in silence, and under no circumstances obstruct them. The Holy Spirit himself preaches here, and one word of his sermon is far better than a thousand of our prayers. Many times I have learned more from one prayer than I might have learned from much reading and speculation.

Martin Luther, 1535 [262]

*
**

But when we consider with a religious seriousness the manifold weakness of the strongest devotions in time of prayer, it is a sad consideration. I throw myself down in my

218

chamber, and I call in and invite God and his angels thither, and when they are there, I neglect God and his angels for the noise of a fly, for the rattling of a coach, for the whining of a door; I talk on, in the same posture of praying, eyes lifted up, knees bowed down, as though I prayed to God; and if God or his angels should ask me when I thought last of God in that prayer, I cannot tell: sometimes I find that I had forgot what I was about, but when I began to forget it, I cannot tell. A memory of yesterday's pleasures, a fear of tomorrow's dangers, a straw under my knee, a noise in mine ear, a light in mine eye, an anything, a nothing, a fancy, a chimera in my brain troubles me in my prayer. So certainly there is nothing, nothing in spiritual things, perfect in this world.

John Donne, 1626 [263]

***

A Christian complaineth he cannot pray. O I am troubled with so many distracting thoughts, and never more than now. But hath he put into thine heart a desire to pray? He will hear the desires of his own Spirit in thee, Rom. 8:26, which are not hid from God. 'My groanings are not hid from thee,' Ps. 38:9. God can pick sense out of a confused prayer. These desires cry louder in his ears than thy sins. Sometimes a Christian hath such confused thoughts, he can say nothing, but as a child crieth, O Father, not able to shew what it needs, as Moses at the Red Sea.

These stirrings of spirit touch the bowels of God, and melt him into compassion towards us, when they come from the spirit of adoption, and from a striving to be better . . .

There is never a holy sigh, never a tear we shed, lost. And as every grace increaseth by exercise of itself, so doth the grace of prayer. By prayer we learn to pray. So, likewise, we should take heed of a spirit of discouragement in all other holy duties, since we have so gracious a Saviour. Pray as we are able, hear as we are able, strive as we are able, do as we are able, according to the measure of grace received. God in Christ will cast a gracious eye upon that which is his own . . .

Let us not be cruel to ourselves when Christ is thus gracious.

Richard Sibbes, 1630 [264]

**
*

If a King of the earth say to a man, 'I will be ready to do thee a good turn, make use of me when thou hast occasion,' he would be ready enough to do it. Now when the Lord of heaven saith, 'Ask what you will at my hands and I will do it'; shall we not seek to him, and make use of such a promise as this? Beloved, we are too backwards in this.

John Preston, 1631 [265]

**
*

The directions how to examine thyself are such as these:– Empty thy mind of all other cares and thoughts, that they may not distract or divide thy mind. This work will be enough at once, without joining others with it. Then fall down before God in hearty prayer, desiring the assistance of his Spirit, to discover to thee the plain truth of thy condition, and to enlighten thee in the whole progress of this work. Make choice of the most convenient time and place. Let the place be the most private; and the time, when you have nothing to interrupt you; and, if possible, let it be the present time. Have in readiness, either in memory or writing, some Scriptures, containing the descriptions of the saints, and the gospel terms of salvation; and convince thyself thoroughly of their infallible truth. Proceed then to put the question to thyself. Let it not be whether there be any good in thee at all? nor, whether thou hast such and such a degree and measure of grace? But, whether such and such a saving grace be in thee, in sincerity or not? If thy heart draw back from the work, force it on. Lay thy command upon it, let reason interpose, and use its authority. Yea, lay the command of God upon it, and charge it to obey upon pain of his displeasure. Let conscience also do its office, till thy heart be excited to the work. Nor let thy heart trifle away the time, when it should be diligently at the work. Do as the psalmist: 'My spirit made diligent search.' He that can prevail with his own heart, shall also prevail with God.

If, after all thy pains, thou are not resolved, then seek out for help. Go to one that is godly, experienced, able, and faithful, and tell him thy case and desire his best advice. Use the judgment of such a one, as that of a physician for thy body; though this can afford thee no full certainty, yet it may be a great help to stay and direct thee. But do not make it a pretence to put off thy own self-examination: only use it as one of the last remedies, when thy own endeavours will not serve. When thou hast discovered thy true state, pass sentence on thyself accordingly; either that thou art a true Christian, or that thou are not. Pass not this sentence rashly, nor with self-flattery, nor from melancholy terrors; but deliberately, truly, and according to thy conscience, convinced by Scripture and reason. Labour to get thy heart affected with its condition, according to the sentence passed on it. If graceless, think of thy misery. If renewed and sanctified, think what a blessed state the Lord hath brought thee into. Pursue these thoughts till they have left their impression on thy heart. Write this sentence at least in thy memory: 'At such a time, upon thorough examination, I found my state to be thus, or thus.' Such a record will be very useful to thee hereafter. Trust not to this one discovery, so as to try no more; nor let it hinder thee in the daily search of thy ways; neither be discouraged if the trial must be often repeated. Especially take heed, if unregenerate, not to conclude of thy future state by the present. Do not say, 'Because I am ungodly, I shall die so; because I am a hypocrite, I shall continue so.' Do not despair. Nothing but thy willingness can keep thee from Christ, though thou hast hitherto abused him, and dissembled with him.

Richard Baxter, 1649 [266]

***

Prayer is a shelter to the soul, a sacrifice to God and a scourge to the devil.

Thomas Brooks, 1652 [267]

***

I have abandoned all my own forms of worship, and those prayers which are not obligatory, and I do nothing else but abide in his holy presence, and I do this by simple attentiveness and an habitual, loving turning of my eyes on him. This I should call the actual presence of God, or to put it better, a wordless and secret conversation between the soul and God which no longer ends. It often gives me such deep feelings of inner (even outer) contentment and joy, that to restrain them and prevent their visible manifestation, I am induced to act childishly in a manner which smacks more of folly than of worship.

Indeed, my Reverend Father, I can in no way doubt that my soul has been with God these past thirty years. I omit many matters lest I should weary you, but I think however, it is appropriate to set out for you how I look upon myself before God whom I regard as my king.

I regard myself as the most wretched of all men, ragged with sores, full of malodorous things and guilty of all manner of crimes against his king. Touched by a live repentance, I confess all my evil deeds to him, I implore his pardon, and give myself over into his hands to do with me as he will. This king, full of goodness and mercy, far from chastising me, embraces me lovingly, makes me eat at his table, serves me with his own hands, gives me the keys to his treasures, and treats me just as if I were his favourite. He talks with me and has ceaseless pleasure in my company in a thousand thousand ways. He does not speak of my pardon or taking away my one-time way of life, though I beseech him to do with me according to his heart, and see myself as ever more weak and wretched, yet more cherished by God. That is how I sometimes think of myself in his holy presence.

My commonest attitude is this simple attentiveness, an habitual, loving turning of my eyes to God . . .

Brother Lawrence, 1680s [268]

*
**

For Believers Praying

Jesu, my strength, my hope,
On thee I cast my care,
With humble confidence look up,
And know thou hears't my prayer.
Give me on thee to wait,
Till I can all things do,
On thee almighty to create,
Almighty to renew.

I want a sober mind,
A self-renouncing will
That tramples down and casts behind
The baits of pleasing ill:
A soul inured to pain,
To hardship, grief, and loss,
Bold to take up, firm to sustain
The consecrated cross.

I want a godly fear,
A quick-discerning eye,
That looks to thee when sin is near
And sees the tempter fly;
A spirit still prepared
And armed with jealous care,
Forever standing on its guard,
And watching unto prayer.

I want a heart to pray,
To pray and never cease,
Never to murmur at thy stay,
Or wish my sufferings less.
This blessing above all,
Always to pray I want,
Out of the deep on thee to call,
And never, never faint.

I want a true regard,
A single, steady aim,
Unmoved to threat'ning or reward,
To thee and thy great name;
A jealous, just concern
For thine immortal praise;
A pure desire that all may learn
And glorify thy grace.

I rest upon thy Word,
The promise is for me;
My succour, and salvation, Lord,
Shall surely come from thee.
But let me still abide,
Nor from thy hope remove,
Till thou my patient spirit guide
Into thy perfect love.

Charles Wesley, 1742 [269]

It may be your prayer is like a ship, which, when it goes on a very long voyage, does not come home laden so soon; but when it does come home, it has a richer freight. Mere 'coasters' will bring you coals, or such like ordinary things; but they that go afar to Tarshish return with gold and ivory. Coasting prayers, such as we pray every day, bring us many necessaries, but there are great prayers, which, like the old Spanish galleons, cross the main ocean, and are longer out of sight, but come home deep laden with a golden freight.

C. H. Spurgeon, 19th cent. [270]

**\
* ***

Prayer is the test of everything; prayer is also the source of everything; prayer is the driving force of everything; prayer is also the director of everything. If prayer is right, everything is right. For prayer will not allow anything to go wrong.

Theophan the Recluse, 19th cent. [271]

**\
* ***

The practice of the Jesus Prayer is simple. Stand before the Lord with the attention in the heart, and call to him: 'Lord Jesus Christ, Son of God, have mercy on me!' The essential part of this is not in the words, but in faith, contrition, and self-surrender to the Lord. With these feelings one can stand before the Lord even without any words, and it will still be prayer.

Theophan the Recluse, 19th cent. [272]

**\
* ***

So I began by searching out my heart in the way Simeon the New Theologian teaches. With my eyes shut I gazed in thought, i.e., in imagination, upon my heart. I tried to picture it there in the left side of my breast and to listen carefully to its beating. I started doing this several times a day, for half an hour at a time, and at first I felt nothing but a sense of darkness. But little by little after a fairly short time I was able to picture my heart and to note its movement, and further with the help of my breathing I could put into it and draw from it the Prayer of Jesus in the manner taught by the saints, Gregory of Sinai, Callistus and Ignatius. When drawing the air in I looked in spirit into my heart and said, 'Lord Jesus Christ,' and when breathing out again, I said, 'Have mercy on me.' I did this at first for an hour at a time, then for two hours, then for as long as I could, and in the end almost all day long. If any difficulty arose, if sloth or doubt came upon me, I hastened to take up *The Philokalia* and read again those parts which dealt with the work of the heart, and then once more I felt ardour and zeal for the Prayer.

When about three weeks had passed I felt a pain in my heart, and then a most delightful warmth, as well as consolation and peace. This aroused me still more and spurred me on more and more to give great care to the saying of the Prayer so that all my thoughts were taken up with it and I felt a very great joy. From this time I began to have from time to time a number of different feelings in my heart and mind. Sometimes my heart would feel as though it were bubbling with joy, such lightness, freedom and consolation were in it. Sometimes I felt a burning love for Jesus Christ and for all God's creatures. Sometimes my eyes brimmed over with tears of thankfulness to God, who was so merciful to me, a wretched sinner. Sometimes my understanding, which had been so stupid before, was given so much light that I could easily grasp and dwell upon matters of which up to now I had not been able even to think at all. Sometimes that sense of a warm gladness in my heart spread throughout my whole being and I was deeply moved as the fact of the presence of God everywhere was brought home to me. Sometimes by calling upon the Name of Jesus I was overwhelmed with bliss, and now I knew the meaning of the words '*The Kingdom of God is within you.*'

Russian, 19th cent. [273]

**

My prayers, my God, flow from what I am not;
I think thy answers make me what I am.
Like weary waves thought follows upon thought,
But the still depth beneath is all thine own,
And there thou mov'st in paths to us unknown.
Out of strange strife thy peace is strangely wrought;
If the lion in us pray – thou answerest the lamb.

George Macdonald, 1880 [274]

**

It does not follow that because a thing is the will of God, he will necessarily lead *you* to pray for it. He may have other burdens for you. We must *get our prayers from God*, and pray to know his will. It may take time. God was dealing with Hudson Taylor for fifteen years before he laid upon him the burden of definite prayer for the foundation of the China Inland Mission. God is not in a hurry. He cannot do things with us until we are trained and ready for them . . . It is a solemn thing to enter into a faith covenant with God. It is binding on both parties. You lift up your hand to God, you definitely ask for and definitely receive his proffered gift – then do not go back on your faith, even if you live to be a hundred.

J. O. Fraser, 1915 [275]

**

I believe in the sun even when it is not shining.
I believe in love even when I cannot feel it.
I believe in God, even when he is silent.

Jewish Prisoner, 1940s [276]

Hearts that are 'fit to break' with love for the Godhead are those who have been in the Presence and have looked with opened eye upon the majesty of Deity. Men of the breaking hearts had a quality about them not known to or understood by common men. They habitually spoke with spiritual authority. They had been in the Presence of God and they reported what they saw there. They were prophets, not scribes, for the scribe tells us what he has read, and the prophet tells us what he has seen.

The distinction is not an imaginary one. Between the scribe who has read and the prophet who has seen there is a difference as wide as the sea. We are today overrun with orthodox scribes, but the prophets, where are they? The hard voice of the scribe sounds over evangelicalism, but the Church waits for the tender voice of the saint who has penetrated the veil and has gazed with inward eye upon the Wonder that is God. And yet, thus to penetrate, to push in sensitive living experience into the holy Presence, is a privilege open to every child of God.

A. W. Tozer, 1948 [277]

*
**

The greatest miracle of all is prayer. I only have to turn my thoughts to God, and I suddenly feel a force bursting into me; there is a new strength in my soul, in my entire being . . . The basis of my whole spiritual life is the Orthodox liturgy, so while I was in prison I attended it every day in my imagination. At 8 in the morning I would begin walking around my cell, repeating its words to myself. I was then inseparably linked to the whole Christian world . . . At the central point in the Liturgy . . . I felt myself standing before the face of the Lord, sensing almost physically his wounded bleeding body. I would begin praying in my own words, remembering all those near to me, those in prison and those who were free, those still alive and those who had died.

More and more names welled up from my memory . . .
The prison walls moved apart and the whole universe
became my residence, visible and invisible, the universe for
which that wounded, pierced body offered itself as a sacrifice . . . After this I experienced an exaltation of spirit all day
– I felt purified within. Not only my own prayer helped me
but even more the prayer of many other faithful Christians.
I felt it continually, working from a distance, lifting me up
as though on wings, giving me living water and the bread of
life, peace of soul, rest and love.

Anatoly Levitin, 1950s [278]

*
**

If we must therefore conceive of a privileged period for
prayer, it can not be after the manner of 'a spiritual capital'
which, acquired in the morning, for example, will be
slowly spent throughout the course of the day under the
corrosive and disintegrating effect of the manifold tasks
which duty imposes. Far from destroying the work of
prayer, activity ought to awaken a fresh prayer suitable to
the very conditions in which it unfolds, which causes us 'to
find God' in all things.

Maurice Giuliani, 1958 [279]

*
**

Some years ago I received a letter from a missionary in a
rather desolate area of Nigeria. She wrote both from a sense
of shame at the ineffectualness of her intercession, and also
to share a basic query. 'Let me give an example,' she said.
'There were five boys weighing on my mind at the end of
last term as I knew their fees for this year were just hopelessly inadequate. They were pretty constantly in my mind, yet
I do not recall that I formulated any prayer for them.
However, within a month four of them had adequate

financial assistance. A week later came a Christmas gift from my sister and her husband for any student needing help; so that was the fifth! I quite simply regard this as miraculous – the result of God's concern – and I do not see that formal intercession would have made any difference one way or the other.' When someone whose life is simply and sacrificially dedicated to God has any fellow man 'pretty constantly in mind' to the extent that the feeling of concern leads to responsible action, that, surely, is the whole of intercession. For a timeless moment it makes one totally present with the other person or persons across the intervening distances, without words and in a manner that goes beyond thought. It is simply a matter of 'being there for them' in a concentration upon the other which obliterates all awareness of self and yet is not strung up but totally relaxed. In that stillness which lies beyond thought we are to let the presence of that other person impinge upon our spirit across the distance, with all his rich reality and all his need and burden. His presence matters more than our own.

So is it also when the other on whom our silent regard is concentrated is once again God himself. For in this prayer of awareness we swing from intercession to worship and back again, we alternate between communion with fellow men and with God, the image of the symbol merges into the image of Christ, without any break in the stillness. This is the gift of the Spirit, the beloved Go-Between, the opener of eyes and giver of life.

J. V. Taylor, 1972 [280]

*
**

I have said that Christ was at a certain point of the storm which we should reach in order to be with God in the storm; that Peter nearly drowned because he did not reach it. Where is this point? This point of the storm is not a point where there is no storm, it is what one calls the eye of the hurricane, it is the point where all conflicting forces meet and where an equipoise is reached not because there is no violence – not because there is no tension, not because there is no tragedy, but because the tragedy and the tension have come to such a pitch that they meet so forcibly as to balance each other; they are at the point of breaking. This is the point where God stands, and when we think of God, the God of history, the God of human life, the God whom we accuse all the time, to whom we give from time to time a chance by saying 'he must be right because he is God' – this is the God who has chosen to stand at the breaking point of things, and this is why he can be respected, why we can trust him with consideration, why we can believe in him and not despise him . . .

This is what we truly mean by Intercession. This God is the one who stands at the middle of history. He is the one who stands at the breaking point of the storm, and he calls us to stand where he stands, to be involved, to be committed, to be committed to life and death within the storm, and yet neither to accept this fallacy of a ghost in the storm instead of God, or to turn to God and say 'If you can do nothing more, at least be together with us, in anguish and in despair.' He wants us to take a step, to be *in* the world at the point which I called 'the eye of the hurricane', but not *of* the world, because we are free from the uncertainty, from the fear, from the self-centredness of Peter, remembering himself at a moment when the whole sea was death and danger for the other disciples, for all the other boats around, and when God stood there as the key of harmony, but was not the harmony that he expected.

I should like to give you one example of what it means both to make an act of intercession and to stand in the place which is ours. It is the story of a woman of whom we know nothing except the name. She was called Natalie. The story was told me by the other people involved in it. In 1919 at a moment when the Civil War was raging like a storm over

Russia, when our cities were falling prey to one army after the other, a woman with two young children was trapped in a city which had fallen into the hands of the Red Army, while her husband was an officer of the White Army. To save her life and theirs, she hid in a small cabin on the outskirts of the city. She wanted to wait until the first assaults were over and try to escape afterwards. On the second day someone knocked at her door towards the evening. She opened it in fear and she was confronted with a young woman of her own age. The woman said 'You must flee at once because you have been discovered and betrayed; you will be shot tonight.' The other woman, showing her children that stood there, said, 'How could we do that? We would be recognised at once, and they can't walk far.' The young woman who so far had been nothing but a neighbour, someone living next door, became that great thing which one calls a neighbour in the Gospel. She grew to the full stature of the Gospel of God, of the good news of the dignity and greatness of man, and she said 'They won't look for you, I shall stay behind.' And the mother said 'But they will kill you.' 'Yes,' said the woman, 'but I have no children, you must go.' And the mother went.

Metropolitan Anthony, 1971 [281]

*

Liturgy is essentially something given, and in this it expresses a fundamental feature of all prayer. Its sublime lack of concern for our personal moods is a forcible reminder that when we come to God, it is not to force our moods or our interests on to him, but to receive his interests and to let him, in a sense, share his moods with us.

If our primary model of prayer is that we should be allowed to express ourselves to God, then we shall probably remain terribly imprisoned within ourselves and our prayer will become hopelessly stuck at a very elementary stage.

It is far more central to prayer that we should let ourselves become involved in God, in his great enterprise of giving himself, and all the various interests and concerns that form part of this.

It is therefore a positive advantage that the liturgy does not just reflect our own concerns and interests, but confronts us with definite moods of its own.

We may come along feeling right down in the dumps and the liturgy will present us with praising psalms and alleluias. Or we may be as high as kites only to find ourselves obliged to recite penitential psalms. The prayers will in all probability have no relevance to the particular issues weighing on our minds at the moment, and may expect us to intercede for matters that do not interest us in the slightest.

All this is a challenge to us to become free enough and generous enough to be able, for the moment, to leave behind our moods and whims and even our most pressing concerns, and to engage ourselves in other moods, other interests. As long as we approach it wondering what we are going to get out of it, we are likely to remain discontented and bored. The question is much rather how far we are free enough from ourselves and in ourselves to be able to give ourselves, to put something into it. Then we shall find that it is in giving that we receive . . .

The liturgy, faithfully celebrated, should be a long term course in heart-expansion, making us more and more capable of the totality of love that there is in the heart of Christ.

It is not the immediate feeling that is important; that may or may not come. What matters is that we should be, slowly and quietly, moulded by this rehearsal for an anticipation of the worship of heaven. It is a schooling for paradise . . .

In our earthly liturgy we are, in a way, only eavesdropping, listening in on the liturgy of the saints. It is with the whole company of heaven that we worship, and it is their perfect worship which sustains and enfolds our prayer.

Simon Tugwell, 1974 [282]

But through the grace of God, contemplation – true contemplation – does not depend on you. You are not the dawn, you are the land that awaits the dawn.

Your God is the dawn, and later he is full daylight, and later still high noon.

You are the land that waits for the light, the blackboard that waits for the white chalk of the draughtsman who walks towards you with that chalk in his hand. Sit down and try to be still; sit still and try to hope. Leave behind you time, space, number, thought, reason, culture, and look ahead.

Look beyond yourself, beyond your helplessness and your limitations, and wait.

Your heart has been tried by suffering and darkness; now allow it to stop relying on the earth it is leaving.

Let your tears flow, to water the arid land of your faith. Persevere.

Do not think of anything else. God is before you.

God is coming to you.

Contemplation is not a matter of watching, but of being watched, and he is there watching you.

And if he is watching you, he loves you, and in loving you, he gives you what you are looking for: himself.

What other gift could there be for one who had searched so hard.

Our heart is so hard to satisfy.

God alone can fill it.

Things never can.

Carlo Carretto, 1975 [283]

*
**

Half the time I find my prayers are wholly wordless. It consists in a sort of feeling of spiritual sunbathing, turning myself towards the spiritual light and allowing it to revive the spirit, like the sunlight on a flower, or a mother's smile on the child. Of course, this does not happen every time. There are terrible periods of emptiness and darkness. But it happens sufficiently often and it is sufficiently real to be infinitely worthwhile. There are moments of simple adoration and thankfulness for all the beauty and glory in the world.

Lord Hailsham, 1975 [284]

*
**

Contemplation belongs to prayer, but it is not exhausted by it nor identical with it. In contemplation, complaining ceases. The heart opens itself for reception. We become free from our self-serving desires and also from the ideals that we have for others, for our children, or for society. We listen and wait for the voice of God. Prayers without hearing and speaking with God, without waiting for God, do not lead very far. For this reason contemplation is important. It is not in itself practical, it is utterly 'impractical.' Yet our meditation on Christ's passion and our contemplation of his spiritual presence can alter our praxis more radically than all the other alternatives which even the most active among us can conceive. In contemplation we ourselves become another. We experience the conversion of our life and live the pains and joys of our rebirth.

A 'transcendental meditation' without an object can only lead to flight from life, if not to a psychiatric clinic. *Christian* meditation is not transcendental; it is at the core always meditation on the crucified Christ in light of his resurrection. It has Christ as its 'object'; it encounters him as one who stands over against the meditator. What kind of knowledge do we gain through meditation? When we wish to know something with modern scientific method we know in order to dominate or control, that is, we appropriate the object. In meditation exactly the reverse occurs: We do not appropriate Christ for our use, but we give ourselves over to Christ for his kingdom. We do not change him, but he changes us. We do not 'grasp' him, but he grasps us.

Jürgen Moltmann, 1978 [285]

*
**

Distractions in prayer play an important role in Christian life. They show me where healing is needed in my life. I am not referring so much to minor distractions like a fly buzzing as to preoccupations. I can be praying and find my mind on another matter, on work to be done, on my brother who is seriously ill, on someone who has hurt me, on a problem coming up. This kind of distraction indicates what is on my mind that is not integrated into my personal relationship with Jesus Christ. It shows up what is not under his Lordship, what I have not yet consciously and fully brought into the zone of the power of his love for me. If it is a distraction, falling outside my relationship with the Lord in prayer, then it is – in my life as a whole – not yet in his hands. In my prayer, I can put the matter into his hands, turning the distraction into a prayer. In this way, I co-operate with him in his work of reconciling the various things on my mind by bringing them into a unity in him; I let him integrate me, pull me together, become more the centre of my life . . .

Robert Faricy, 1979 [286]

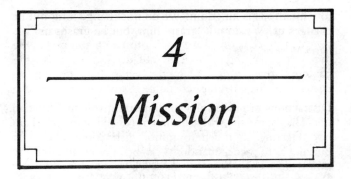

4

Mission

We have been learning this century that mission derives from God and not from the church. There are a number of contributory factors. Lesslie Newbigin has reminded us of the Trinitarian basis of mission; the growth of the church in China has been infinitely greater in the thirty years since the ejection of missionaries than in the hundred years before; the decline of the British Empire, and (to an extent) of Western Christianity has meant that Europe can no longer think of itself simply as a mission-exporter; the arrival of many thousands of peoples from other cultures and religions in our own country has brought 'the mission field' from 'abroad' to 'home'; and the tremendous growth of Christianity in other continents without any help from Western Christians has led to a growing sense that God's mission everywhere requires much more of a humble, listening response to the work of the Sovereign Spirit. We are becoming aware of the need for shared partnership world-wide.

The possibility of bearing witness by silence is a valuable counter to over-talkativeness; mission through presence counter-balances over-aggressive interference; mission through community (like the previous two) also has clear New Testament roots, and all need to be given full play as

237

the church learns again God's inventiveness in mission. The heritage of Columba, Boniface, Aidan, Lull and Xavier has been continued in the history of Protestant missions; but the dynamic out-going mission of Paul looks for the balancing contemplative strength of John. And all have to come to terms with the extreme resistance to the Gospel of all the other faiths.

The relationship between witness to the world and service in the world has continually exercised the Protestant mind. Today, following a period of retreat from involvement in social concerns, Evangelicals are seeing that evangelism and radical social commitment are an inextricable pair. Conversion is seen to be a complex experience, a socio-political reality needed within the church as much as outside, as it faces the iniquitous and grinding facts of poverty, and as it confronts demonic nuclear power in the power of the Spirit. The radical commitment which, in some ways, has always constituted Evangelicalism at its best, has again caught hold of the mighty Old Testament prophetic consciousness, lived out in Christ himself, and begun to echo Amos' call to 'let justice roll on like a river, and righteousness like an everlasting stream' as the 'politics of God' and the 'politics of repentance' (C.S. Song).

Mission has come full circle: those to whom we once took the Gospel now bring it back to us – with their challenge; and the Gospel we thought was ours to manage we learn is God's to direct. Extravagance is more God's way than efficiency. We must learn to walk at the pace of the Three-Mile-an-Hour God (Koyama) – apparently slow, but Lord of all speeds because it is the pace of love.

The Gospel

Our Saviour and Lord Jesus Christ was silent when false witnesses spoke against him, and answered nothing when he was accused; he was convinced that all his life and actions among the Jews were better than any speech in refutation of the false witness and superior to any words that he might say in reply to the accusations.

Origen, 246–8 [287]

*
**

It seems to me that the conquest of the Holy Land ought not to be attempted except in the way in which thou and thine apostles acquired it, namely, by love and prayers, and the pouring out of tears and of blood.

Ramon Lull, 1270s [288]

*
**

Everlasting God! how much ground there is in the world where the seed of the Gospel has never yet been sown, or where there is a greater crop of tares than of wheat! . . .

Regions hitherto unknown are being daily discovered, and more there are, as we are told, into which the Gospel has never yet been carried. . . . Travellers bring home from distant lands gold and gems; but it is worthier to carry hence the wisdom of Christ, more precious than gold, and the pearl of the Gospel, which would put to shame all earthly riches. Christ orders us to pray the Lord of the harvest to send forth labourers, because the harvest is plenteous and the labourers are few. Must we not then pray God to thrust forth labourers into such vast tracts? . . . Bestir yourselves,

then, ye heroic and illustrious leaders of the army of Christ.
. . . Address yourselves with fearless minds to such a
glorious work. . . . It is a hard work I call you to, but it is the
noblest and highest of all. Would that God had accounted
me worthy to die in so holy a work!

Desiderius Erasmus, 1534 [289]

***

There is now in these parts a very large number of persons
who have only one reason for not becoming Christian, and
that is that there is no one to make them Christians. It often
comes into my mind to go round all the Universities of
Europe, and especially that of Paris, crying out everywhere
like a madman, and saying to all the learned men there
whose learning is so much greater than their charity, *'Ah!
what a multitude of souls is through your fault shut out of heaven
and falling into hell!'* Would to God that these men who
labour so much in gaining knowledge would give as much
thought to the account they must one day give to God of the
use they have made of their learning and of the talents
entrusted to them! I am sure that many of them would be
moved by such considerations, would exercise themselves
in fitting meditations on divine truths, so as to hear what
God might say to them, and then, renouncing their ambi-
tions and desires, and all the things of the world, they would
form themselves wholly according to God's desire and
choice for them. They would exclaim from the bottom of
their hearts: *'Lord, here am I; send me whithersoever it shall
please Thee, even to India!'*

Francis Xavier, 1543 [290]

***

I preached, as never sure to preach again
And as a dying man to dying men.

Richard Baxter, 1681 [291]

At the Nottingham meeting in June, 1792 Mr. Carey preached from Isaiah 54:2,3. 'Enlarge the place of thy tent, and let them stretch forth the curtains of thine habitations: spare not, lengthen thy cords, and strengthen thy stakes; for thou shalt break forth on the right hand and on the left; and thy seed shall inherit the Gentiles, and make the desolate cities to be inhabited.' After observing, by way of introduction, that the church was here compared to a poor desolate widow, who lived alone in a small tent; that she who had thus lived in a manner childless, was told to expect an increase in her family, such as would require a much larger dwelling; and this because her Maker was her husband, whose name was not only the Lord of Hosts, the Holy One of Israel, but the God of the whole earth; he proceeded to take up the spirit of the passage in two exhortations, which he addressed to his brethren. 1. Expect great things from God; 2. Attempt great things for God. The discourse was very animated and impressive. After it was concluded, the ministers resolved, that at the next Kettering ministers' meeting, on the first of October of the same year, the plan of a society should be brought forward, and, if found practicable, a society formed.

William Carey, 1792 [292]

*
**

He is one who, like Enoch, walks with God, and derives from constant communion with him a portion of the divine likeness. Dead to the usual pursuits of the world, his affections are fixed upon things above, where Christ sitteth at the right hand of God. He is not influenced, therefore, by the love of fame and distinction, the desire of wealth, or the love of ease and self-indulgence. Deeply affected by the sinful and ruined state of mankind, especially of the heathen, he devotes his life, with all its faculties, to promote their salvation. Undaunted by dangers, unmoved by sufferings and pain, he considers not his life dear, so that he may

glorify God. With the world under his feet, with heaven in
his eye, with the Gospel in his hand, and Christ in his heart,
he pleads as an ambassador for God, knowing nothing but
Jesus Christ, enjoying nothing but the promotion of the
Kingdom of Christ, and glorying in nothing but in the cross
of Christ Jesus, by which he is crucified to the world and the
world to him. Daily studying the word of life, and transformed himself more and more into the image which it sets
before him, he holds it forth to others as a light to illuminate
the darkness of the world around him, as an exhibition of
the light and glory of a purer and higher world above.

John Venn, 1806 [293]

*
**

A feeble, nominal Christianity is the great obstacle to the
conversion of the world.

Henry Venn, 1865 [294]

*
**

'Do you believe that each unit of these millions has an
immortal soul,' he questioned searchingly, 'and that there is
"none other name under heaven given among men" save the
precious name of Jesus "whereby we must be saved"? Do
you believe that he and he alone is "the way, the truth, and
the life", and that "no man cometh unto the Father" but by
him? If so, think of the condition of these unsaved souls, and
examine yourself in the sight of God to see whether you are
doing your utmost to make him known to them or not.

'It will not do to say that you have no special call to go to
China. With these facts before you, you need rather to
ascertain whether you have a special call to stay at home. If
in the sight of God you cannot say you are sure that you
have a special call to stay at home, why are you disobeying

the Saviour's plain command to go? Why are you refusing to come to the help of the Lord against the mighty? If, however, it is perfectly clear that duty – not inclination, not pleasure, not business – detains you at home, are you labouring in prayer for these needy ones as you might? Is your influence used to advance the cause of God among them? Are your means as largely employed as they should be in helping forward their salvation?'

Hudson Taylor, 1865 [295]

*
**

To get a man soundly saved it is not enough to put on him a pair of new breeches, to give him regular work, or even to give him a university education. These things are all outside a man, and if the inside remains unchanged you have wasted your labour. You must some way or other graft upon the man's nature a new nature, which has in it the element of the divine. All that I propose in this book is governed by that principle.

The difference between the method which seeks to re-generate the man by ameliorating his circumstances and that which ameliorates his circumstances in order to get at the regeneration of his heart, is the difference between the method of the gardener who grafts a Ribstone Pippin on a crab-apple tree and one who merely ties apples with string upon the branches of the crab. To change the nature of the individual, to get at the heart, to save his soul is the only real, lasting method of doing him any good. In many modern schemes of social regeneration it is forgotten that 'it takes a soul to move a body, e'en to a cleaner sty,' and at the risk of being misunderstood and misrepresented, I must assert in the most unqualified way that it is primarily and mainly for the sake of saving these souls that I seek the salvation of the body.

But what is the use of preaching the Gospel to men whose

whole attention is concentrated upon a mad, desperate struggle to keep themselves alive? You might as well give a tract to a shipwrecked sailor who is battling with the surf which has drowned his comrades and threatens to drown him. He will not listen to you. Nay, he cannot hear you any more than a man whose head is under water can listen to a sermon. The first thing to do is to get him at least a footing on firm ground, and to give him room to live. Then you may have a chance. At present you have none. And you will have all the better opportunity to find a way to his heart, if he comes to know that it was you who pulled him out of the horrible pit and the miry clay in which he was sinking to perdition.

William Booth, 1890 [296]

*
**

We have allowed racial and religious pride to direct our attitude towards those whom we have been wont to call 'poor heathen'. We have approached them as superior beings, moved by charity to impart of our wealth to destitute and perishing souls. We have used that argument at home to wring grudging and pitiful doles for the propagation of our faith, and abroad we have adopted that attitude as missionaries of a superior religion. We have not learnt the lesson that it is not for our righteousness that we have been entrusted with the Gospel, but that we may be instruments in God's hands for revealing the universal salvation of his Son in all the world. We have not learnt that as Christians we exist by the Spirit of him who gave up the glory of heaven in order to pour out his life for the redemption of the world. We have not learnt the lesson that our own hope, our own salvation, our own glory, lies in the completion of the Temple of the Lord. We have not understood that the members of the Body of Christ are scattered in all lands, and that we, without them, are not made perfect.

Roland Allen, 1912 [297]

It is in the revelation of the Holy Spirit as a missionary Spirit that the Acts stands alone in the New Testament. The nature of the Spirit as missionary can indeed be observed in the teaching of the gospels and the epistles; but there it is hinted rather than asserted. In the Acts it is the one prominent feature. It is asserted, it is taken for granted, from the first page to the last. Directly and indirectly it is made all-important. To treat it as secondary destroys the whole character and purpose of the book. It is necessary to any true apprehension of the Holy Spirit and his work that we should understand it and realize it.

Roland Allen, 1917 [298]

*
**

Most futile, most disappointing, and most foolish of all quests would be that which were only to seek to substitute for one ritual another, for one system another system, for devotion to one series of ordinances another series. Christianity has always cut its most pitiful figure when seen trying to meet Islam with Islam's weapons, or competing with it on its own ground. Nothing but the Spirit can bind and free Islam. Let the Church that does not believe in the Holy Ghost save herself the trouble of attempting the conversion of Islam. The Spirit of the Father in Jesus Christ – we have nothing else to give Islam: no, NOTHING! We owe to that great host that follows the great Mohammed the realization, final and definitive, that *the Spirit of Jesus is the only asset of the Church.*

Temple Gairdner, 1920 [299]

*
**

On the human side, evangelistic work on the mission field is like a man going about in a dark, damp valley with a lighted match in his hand, seeking to ignite anything inflammable. But things are damp through and through, and will not burn however much he tries. In other cases, God's wind and sunshine have prepared the tinder beforehand. The valley is dry in places, and when the lighted match is applied – here a shrub, there a tree, here a few sticks, there a heap of leaves take fire and give light and warmth long after the kindling match and its bearer have passed on. And this is what God wants to see, and what he will be inquired of us for: little patches of fire burning all over the world.

J. O. Fraser, 1922 [300]

*
**

Our message is Jesus Christ; we dare not give less, and we cannot give more.

William Temple, 1928 [301]

*
**

The retrieval is not territorial. Christianity is not a territorial expression. The retrieval is spiritual. It aims not to have the map more Christian but Christ more widely known. We are not concerned with the comparative strength of Islam and 'Christendom' but the absolute loss of Christ. The retrieval to which we are called does not mean taking back cathedrals from mosques, but giving back the Christ. The external tokens of his displacement are important only because of the displacement they symbolize. To restore Christ transcends all else.

Kenneth Cragg, 1956 [302]

*
**

No Christian mission is constituted in its success, and none, therefore, is invalidated by numerical failure . . . There is a Christian obligation to Islam which neither begins nor ends in how Muslims respond. It is rooted in the nature of Christ and of his Gospel . . . If Christ is what Christ is, he must be uttered. If Islam is what Islam is, that 'must' is irresistible. Wherever there is misconception, witness must penetrate: wherever there is the obscuring of the beauty of the Cross it must be unveiled: wherever men have missed God in Christ he must be brought to them again. This book has failed in its purpose if it is not undubitably clear that in such a situation as Islam presents the Church has no option but to present Christ.

This is a categorical imperative . . . The mission is not a calculus of success, but an obligation in love . . .

We present Christ for the sole, sufficient reason that he deserves to be presented.

Kenneth Cragg, 1956 [303]

*
**

I have heard it asserted that we must not attach any significance to the numerical factor, or to the idea that the number of nominal Christians in a country like Britain could prove that it was really more Christian than any other. With this point of view I have great sympathy. Numbers can be extremely misleading. And yet they cannot be altogether disregarded. Medical provision in a country which has one qualified doctor per 10,000 of the population is not as adequate as that in a country which has one doctor for every thousand of the population – a simple truth which no member of the World Health Organization is likely to deny. It just is not the case that the provision for Christian witness in the State of Rewa in Central India, with an area equal to that of Holland and a population of two million, and scarcely any regular and organized witness for Christ, is as adequate as that in Protestant Switzerland with a smaller area and a similar population. It is just the fact that four years ago the Church of Geneva arranged to visit within fifteen days every single family in the Canton that was not known to be Roman Catholic. This effort could be repeated every year, if it was thought to be desirable, and thus the Gospel in some form brought near to 'every creature' in the area. The same plan could easily be adopted in Bradford or Plymouth, if the Church approved of this method of evangelism. It cannot be done in Karachi or Baghdad. Unless we are prepared to face such facts as these and to take them seriously, 'the whole Church bringing the whole Gospel to the whole world' is just a mockery, or worse still, an evasion, the sign of our refusal in our day to face the challenge of 'the evangelization of the world in this generation'.

Stephen Neill, 1957 [304]

*
**

I was young, inexperienced, and the words *red-hot soul-winning campaign* thrilled my soul. To give up a salary and live like Hudson Taylor would be heroic – just the strongest kind of appeal to me at that period. It was many years yet before a quiet article in the C.I.M.'s private *News Bulletin* alerted me to the danger of *missionary heroics*. That article pointed out that just because a line of action is difficult, painful or dangerous does not necessarily prove that it is the will of God.

Isobel Kuhn, 1957 [305]

*
**

Our first task in approaching another people, another culture, another religion, is to take off our shoes, for the place we are approaching is holy. Else we may find ourselves treading on men's dreams. More serious still, we may forget that God was here before our arrival.

Max Warren, 1959 [306]

Probably the hardest thought of all for our natural egotism to entertain is that God does not need our help. We commonly represent him as a busy, eager, somewhat frustrated Father hurrying about seeking help to carry out his benevolent plan to bring peace and salvation to the world; but, as said the Lady Julian, 'I saw truly that God doeth all-thing, be it never so little.' The God who worketh all things surely needs no help and no helpers.

Too many missionary appeals are based upon this fancied frustration of Almighty God. An effective speaker can easily excite pity in his hearers, not only for the heathen but for the God who has tried so hard and so long to save them and has failed for want of support. I fear that thousands of young persons enter Christian service from no higher motive than to help deliver God from the embarrassing situation his love has gotten him into and his limited abilities seem unable to get him out of. Add to this a certain degree of commendable idealism and a fair amount of compassion for the underprivileged and you have the true drive behind much Christian activity today.

A. W. Tozer, 1961 [307]

*
**

Dialogue challenges both partners, takes them out of the security of their own prisons their philosophy and theology have built for them, confronts them with reality, with truth: a truth that cannot be carried home black on white, a truth that cannot be left to gather dust in libraries, a truth that demands all. Truth was there in so many a true dialogue; never before had he felt so small, so helpless, so inadequate. All of a sudden the shallowness of all religious routine was laid bare, the compromise with the world, that which is essentially un-Christian in so many things that bear Christ's name. Suddenly he became aware of the fact that he, too, had to be 'converted', that he could not confront his neighbour as one who demands, but that they both jointly would have to ask God for his grace. If dialogue is taken seriously, Christianity must be deeply sincere and upright – different from what it is now. He understood that the lack of 'conversion' of the nations was not due to their obduracy but to the lack of conversion among those who had sent themselves.

Klaus Klostermaier, 1969 [308]

**
*

'Aya-chan! Don't do that! You'll die if you go on as you are,' he almost shouted. He heaved a great sigh and then as if he'd suddenly thought of something he picked up a nearby stone and began to hammer his foot with it.

Of course I was taken by surprise, but when I tried to stop him he firmly seized my hand.

'Aya-chan! I don't know how often I've been praying that you will get better and live. I don't mind dying if it means you will live, but I'm such a poor Christian, I've come to see that I have no power to save you. That's why I'm striking myself, as a punishment for being so useless.'

I gazed at him, speechless with amazement. Before I knew what was happening I was in tears, and there was something human in those tears as they flowed. I felt I was being deceived, but I wondered if I should try following his way of life. I felt his love for me penetrating my whole being. And I knew it was not just the love of a man for a woman. He did not want me for himself, he wanted me to discover the real meaning of life.

Behind his self-condemnation and punishment I felt I had seen a light I had not known before. What was that strange light within him? Was it Christianity? He loved me not as a woman but as a human being and an individual, and I decided, just as I was, to seek the Christ in whom this man believed.

'During the war you believed and you were wrong, weren't you? In spite of this, won't you try and believe in something again?'

If the end of man's existence was death, it seemed foolish to try and believe in anything again, but I decided bravely that it didn't matter if I was foolish. I could only believe in Tadashi Maekawa's love for me as he beat himself on that hill. And if I could not believe, that would be the end of me.

Ayako Miura, 1969 [309]

* **

It is almost impossible for me to enter into simple, honest, open, and friendly communication with another person as long as I have at the back of my mind the feeling that I am one of the saved and he is one of the lost. Such a gulf is too vast to be bridged by any ordinary human communication. But the problem is not really solved if I decide from my side of the abyss that he also is saved. In either case the assumption is that I have access to the secret of his ultimate destiny. If I were a Hindu, I do not think that even a decision by an ecumenical Christian council that good Hindus can be saved would enable me to join in ordinary human conversation with a Christian about our ultimate beliefs. All such pronouncements go beyond our authority and destroy the possibility of a real meeting. The truth is that my meeting with a person of another religion is on a much humbler basis. I do not claim to know in advance his ultimate destiny. I meet him simply as a witness, as one who has been laid hold of by Another and placed in a position where I can only point to Jesus as the one who can make sense of the whole human situation which my partner and I share as fellow human beings. This is the basis of our meeting.

Lesslie Newbigin, 1978 [310]

Our Saviour is our Elder Brother who has participated with us in our African experience in every respect, except in our sin and alienation from God; an alienation with which our myths of origins make us only too familiar. Being our true Elder Brother now in the presence of God, his Father and our Father, he displaces the mediatorial function of our natural 'spirit fathers'. For these latter themselves need saving, since they originated from among us. It is known from African missionary history that sometimes one of the first actions of new converts was to pray for their ancestors, who had passed on before the Gospel was proclaimed. The Christological point is that their action is an important testimony to the depth of their perception of Jesus as sole Lord and Saviour.

Kwame Bediako, 1983 [311]

In Society

A Christian is a perfectly free lord of all, subject to none.
A Christian is a perfectly dutiful servant of all, subject to all.

Martin Luther, 1520 [312]

**
*

Although the Christian is free from all works, he ought in this liberty to empty himself, take upon himself the form of a servant, be made in the likeness of men, be found in human form, and to serve, help, and in every way deal with his neighbour as he sees that God through Christ has dealt and still deals with him. . . . As our heavenly Father has in Christ freely come to our aid, we also ought freely to help our neighbour through our body and its works, and each should become as it were a Christ to the other that we may be Christs to one another and Christ may be the same in all. . . . We are named after Christ, not because he is absent from us, but because he dwells in us, that is, because we believe in him and are Christs to one another and do to our neighbours as Christ does to us.

Martin Luther, 1520 [313]

**
*

Now, since all God's gifts – not only spiritual, but also material things – are given to man, not that he should have them for himself or alone but with all his fellows, therefore the communion of saints itself must show itself not only in spiritual but also in temporal things (Acts 2:42–47, 4:32–37); that as Paul said, one might not have abundance and another suffer want, but that there may be equality (2 Cor. 8:7–15). This he showed from the law touching manna, in that he who gathered little had no less, since each was given what he needed according to the measure (Ex. 16:16–18).

Furthermore, one sees in all things created, which testify to us still today, that God from the beginning ordained nothing private for man, but all things to be common (Gen. 1:26–29). But through wrong-taking, since man took what he should not and forsook what he should take (Gen. 3:2–12), he drew such things to himself and made them his property, and so grew and became hardened therein. Through such wrong-taking and collecting of created things he has been led so far from God that he has even forgotten the creator (Rom. 1:18–25), and has even raised up and honoured as god the created things which had been put under and made subject to him (Wisd. 13:1–3, 15:14–19). And such is still the case if one steps out of God's order and forsakes the same.

Peter Riedemann, 1540 [314]

*
**

But what meaneth God by this inequality, that he giveth to some an hundred pound; unto this man five thousand pound; unto this man in a manner nothing at all? What meaneth he by this inequality? Here he meaneth, that the rich ought to distribute his riches abroad amongst the poor: for the rich man is but God's officer, God's treasurer: he ought to distribute them according unto his Lord God's commandment. If every man were rich, then no man would do anything: therefore God maketh some rich and some poor. Again; that the rich may have where to exercise his charity, God made some rich and some poor: the poor he sendeth unto the rich to desire of him in God's name help and aid. Therefore, you rich men, when there cometh a poor man unto you, desiring your help, think none other-

wise but that God hath sent him unto you; and remember
that thy riches be not thy own but thou art but a steward
over them . . .

Hugh Latimer, 1552 [315]

*
**

A Christian is the freest of all men in the world. For in that
respect he is the child of God in Christ, he is truly freed from
death and condemnation; yea, and in part from sin and
Satan, and that in this life: and yet for all this, he must be a
servant unto every man. But how? by all the duties of love,
as occasion shall be offered, and that for the common good
of all men.

William Perkins, 1602 [316]

*
**

And is it nothing for a man to be employed in comforting,
relieving and supporting others! This is so great a service
that the very angels are employed therein, as in a work most
suitable to them . . . If you look into the New Testament,
you will find that when Christ was on Mount Tabor, in his
transfiguration then the angels are not said to attend upon
him; but when he was sweating in the garden, then an angel
came and comforted and ministered to him. Why? Because
this is angelical work, to comfort, relieve, and support
others in the time of distress. Now are you not trusted with
this work? How many poor, drooping, tempted, and deserted souls are there whom you may go and minister to!

William Bridge, 1648 [317]

*
**

God loves a cheerful giver, for God gives cheerfully and
freely and liberally. 'He that gives to the poor, lends to the
Lord, for the Lord restores him double again' (Prov. 19:17).

But people's hearts are hardened, and they mind not to disgrace the truth; and the custom of the cries of the blind, the lame, the widows, and the fatherless have taken away the sense of compassion. Therefore, let there be a storehouse where all may be relieved, and let none want, that all may have enough. The Lord can take away from you as much in a week that would (it may be) serve thousands of the poor, and cross you by sea and by land for your hardheartedness; which otherwise you would see as a blessing and feel as a blessing both within and without, in store, in field, by sea and land.

As you come into the wisdom of God, and stand in it, and are preservers of the creation, then God will bless you, and what you take in hand will prosper. A preserver of the creation visits the sick and the fatherless, and causes not the blind to wander. Cannot God bring the proudest of you all down, and make you as poor as them that wander in the streets, because you do not do good in your life time? Therefore, come to work, and do the work of the Lord while you have poor, you great ones; and come to the feeling of these things, you magistrates, that none of these may lie up and down your streets, while it is in your power to do good.

George Fox, 1657 [318]

*
**

An oppressor is an antichrist and an antigod; he is contrary to God, who delighteth to do good, and whose bounty maintaineth all the world; who is kind to his enemies, and causeth his sun to shine, and his rain to fall on the just and on the unjust: and even when he afflicteth doth it as unwillingly, delighting not to grieve the sons of men. He is contrary to Jesus Christ, who gave himself a ransom for his enemies, and made himself a curse to redeem them from the curse, and condescended in his incarnation to the nature of man, and in his passion to the cross and suffering which they deserved; and being rich and Lord of all, yet made himself poor, that we by his poverty might be made rich. He endured the cross and despised the shame, and made himself as of no reputation, accounting it his honour and joy to be the Saviour of men's souls, even of the poor and despised of the world. And these oppressors live as if they were made to afflict the just, and to rob them of God's mercies, and to make crosses for other men to bear, and to tread on their brethren as stepping stones of their own advancement. The Holy Ghost is the Comforter of the just and faithful. And these men live as if it were their calling to deprive men of their comfort.

Richard Baxter, 1665 [319]

*
**

The nature and effects of that unhappy and disgraceful branch of commerce, which has long been maintained on the coast of Africa, with the sole and professed design of purchasing our fellow creatures, in order to supply our West India islands and the American colonies, when they were ours, with slaves, is now generally understood . . .

I hope it will always be a subject of humiliating reflection to me, that I was once an active instrument in a business at which my heart now shudders . . .

Every plan, which aims at the welfare of a nation, in defiance of [God's] authority and laws, however apparently wise, will prove to be essentially defective, and, if persisted in, ruinous. The righteous Lord loveth righteousness, and he has engaged to plead the cause and vindicate the wrongs of the oppressed. It is righteousness that exalteth a nation; and wickedness is the present reproach, and will, sooner or later, unless repentance intervene, prove the ruin of any people . . .

Though I were even sure that a principal branch of the

public revenue depended upon the African trade (which I apprehend is far from being the case), if I had access and influence, I should think myself bound to say to Government, to Parliament, and to the nation, 'It is not lawful to put it into the treasury, because it is the price of blood' (Matt 27:6) . . .

God forbid that any supposed profit or advantage which we can derive from the groans, and agonies, and blood of the poor Africans, should draw down his heavy curse upon all that we might, otherwise, honourably and comfortably possess.

John Newton, 1788 [320]

**

About the close of the year 1788 during the great scarcity of bread, a subscription was raised in the University, and by the inhabitants of the town, to which Mr. Simeon very largely contributed, to enable the poor in Cambridge to obtain bread at half-price. It occurred to Mr. S., who was a well acquainted with the state of the villages in the neighbourhood, that they must be equally distressed with the town: 'What is to become of them?' he asked. 'That is more than we can undertake to answer for,' was the reply. 'Then,' said Mr. Simeon, 'that shall be my business.' Accordingly, he set on foot a plan, by which they too might be included in the benefit; and taking himself a large share of the expense and most of the trouble, he set about it with all his wonted energy – inspired others with the same desire to extend more widely the circle of relief – and every Monday rode himself to the villages within his reach, to see that the bakers performed their duty in selling to the poor at half-price.

Charles Simeon, 1788 [321]

**

Dear Sir,–Unless the divine power has raised you up to be as *Athanasius contra mundum*, (Athanasius against the world), I see not how you can go through your glorious enterprise in opposing that execrable villainy, which is the scandal of religion, of England, and of human nature. Unless God has raised you up for this very thing, you will be worn out by the opposition of men and devils. But if God be for you, who can be against you? Are all of them together stronger than God? O be not weary of well doing! Go on, in the name of God and in the power of his might, till even American slavery (the vilest that ever saw the sun) shall vanish away before it. . . .

That he who has guided you from youth up may continue to strengthen you in this and all things is the prayer of, dear sir, Your affectionate servant

John Wesley, 1791 [322]

*
**

Many persons have of late left off the use of West-India sugar on account of the iniquitous manner in which it is obtained. Those families who have done so, and have not substituted any thing else in its place, have not only cleansed their hands of blood, but have made a saving to their families, some of six pence and some of a shilling a week. If this, or a part of this were appropriated to the uses before-mentioned, it would abundantly suffice. We have only to keep the end in view, and have our hearts thoroughly engaged in the pursuit of it, and means will not be very difficult.

William Carey, 1792 [323]

*
**

Christianity assumes her true character, no less than she performs her natural and proper office, when she takes under her protection those poor degraded beings, on whom philosophy looks down with disdain, or perhaps with contemptuous condescension. On the very first promulgation of Christianity, it was declared by its great Author, as 'glad tidings to the poor'; and, ever faithful to her character, Christianity still delights to instruct the ignorant, to succour the needy, to comfort the sorrowful, to visit the forsaken.

William Wilberforce, 1813 [324]

*
**

How many Christians, who, acting as individuals, would be filled with horror at the thought of taking away the life of a man of another country for any provocation which could be given, – can, when acting as members of the commonwealth, put to death men of other lands without remorse, and even glory in the deed, as conferring a title to honour and renown. The obligation on the followers of Jesus to the exercise of universal love and of good will to mankind, will be both clearly understood and deeply felt. It will be ascertained, that individual accountableness runs through every relation in which man can be placed; – that a Christian cannot lend his influence or his energies to execute the designs of caprice, avarice, ambition, or revenge; – and that when mixed with a hundred thousand of his species, he is no more justified in taking away the life of a man of another country for those ends, than if he acted by himself alone.

David Bogue, 1813 [325]

*
**

This, then, was the primary reason for establishing the Orphan-House. I certainly did from my heart desire to be used by God to benefit the bodies of poor children, bereaved of both parents, and seek, in other respects, with the help of God, to do them good for this life; – I also particularly longed to be used by God in getting the dear orphans trained up in the fear of God; – but still the first and primary object of the work was (and still is), that God might be magnified by the fact, that the orphans under my care are provided with all they need, only *by prayer and faith*, without any one being asked by me or my fellow-labourers, whereby it may be seen, that God is *faithful still* and *hears prayer still*.

George Mueller, 1835 [326]

*
**

Religion consists, not so much in doing spiritual or sacred acts, as in doing secular acts from a sacred or spiritual motive . . . A life spent amidst holy things may be intensely secular; a life the most of which is passed in the thick and throng of the world, may be holy and divine. A minister, for instance, preaching, praying, ever speaking holy words and performing sacred acts, may be all the while doing actions no more holy than those of the printer who prints Bibles, or the bookseller who sells them; for, in both cases alike, the whole affair may be nothing more than a trade. Nay, the comparison tells worse for the former, for the secular trade is innocent and commendable, but the trade which traffics and tampers with holy things is, beneath all its mock solemnity, 'earthly, sensual, devilish.' . . . To spiritualise what is material, to Christianise what is secular – that is the noble achievement of Christian principle . . . It is a great thing to love Christ so dearly as to be 'ready to be bound and to die' for him; but it is often a thing not less great to be ready to take up our daily cross, and to live for him . . . Live for Christ in common things, and all your work will become priestly work . . .

John Caird, 1855 [327]

*
**

The Christian Gospel does not exist to keep men comfortable in their contradictions, or to avert the consequences of them. It exists as a perpetual witness against those contradictions, and a perpetual prophecy of the result which must come from them. A society which has reached the point of confessing no principle but that of rivalry, no maxim but that of 'Every man for himself', may in its dying agonies ask help of the Gospel – but assuredly too late. What can it do to save a community which has been deliberately, systematically, setting aside its first and most notorious precepts – which has pronounced the principle, my text announces, to be no foundation of human life at all, but only an excuse for pretty sentences in commendation of charity and gentleness such as preachers deliver, and which it is respectable to listen to for a few minutes on a Sunday? No! religion, or the religious principle, if it is worth anything – if it is not another name for the worship of the God of this world, of the Evil Spirit – cannot be the instrument of preventing or even delaying that destruction which the righteous and true God has pronounced against all unrighteousness and untruth.

Either the Gospel declares what society is, and what it is not; what binds men together, what separates them, or it has no significance at all.

. . . A Christian man must believe that the law of Christ is applicable to all persons and all cases, or he will very soon apply it really and practically to no persons and in no cases. He must acknowledge it as the human law, or it certainly will not be the law of his church, or circle, or caste; he must believe that it lies at the root of all politics and of all daily business, or he will not make it the guide of his individual conduct, not even of his most sacred and solemn transactions.

There is another way in which this general application of the principle is often evaded by good men: they think that Christ is to come some day to restore the world and set all right, but that in the meantime society is to be left to take its course, and to follow what evil maxims it chooses for itself. That Christ will one day be the acknowledged Ruler of this earth, and of all that dwell on it, no one who calls him Lord and Master can bear to doubt. 'I should utterly have fainted,' says the Psalmist, 'if I had not verily believed to see the goodness of God in the land of the living.' No man who feels the oppressions of the world, and tries to bear up against them, can help utterly fainting, if he does not verily believe that this earth shall not always be a den of robbers, but that its true Saviour and Helper shall himself purge it and restore it. But the men of old were able verily to believe this truth; because they verily believed, in their own day, that the universe was not the devil's but God's, and because they set themselves manfully to fight in that conviction against those who said it was the devil's, and tried to make it so, we must do the same.

F. D. Maurice, 1858 [328]

**

What the church and the world both need is this: men and women full of the Holy Ghost and of love, who, as the living embodiments of the grace and power of Christ, witness for him, and for his power on behalf of those who believe in him. Living so, with our hearts longing to have Jesus glorified in the soul he is seeking after, let us offer ourselves to him for direct work. There is work in our own homes. There is work among the sick, the poor, and the outcast. There is work in a hundred different paths which the Spirit of Christ opens up through those who allow themselves to be led by him. There is work perhaps for us in ways that have not yet been opened up by others. Abiding in Christ, let us work. Let us work, not like those who are content if they now follow the fashion, and take some share in religious work. No; let us work as those who are growing liker to Christ because they are abiding in him, and who, like him, count the work of winning souls to the Father the very joy and glory of heaven begun on earth.

Andrew Murray, c. 1882 [329]

What a satire it is upon our Christianity and our civilisation that the existence of these colonies of heathens and savages in the heart of our capital should attract so little attention! It is no better than a ghastly mockery – theologians might use a stronger word – to call by the name of One who came to seek and to save that which was lost those Churches which in the midst of lost multitudes either sleep in apathy or display a fitful interest in a chasuble. Why all this apparatus of temples and meeting-houses to save men from perdition in a world which is to come, while never a helping hand is stretched out to save them from the inferno of their present life? Is it not time that, forgetting for a moment their wranglings about the infinitely little or infinitely obscure, they should concentrate all their energies on a united effort to break this terrible perpetuity of perdition, and to rescue some at least of those for whom they profess to believe their Founder came to die?

William Booth, 1890 [330]

*
**

In view of the destructive errors of the German Christians and the present national church government, we pledge ourselves to the following evangelical truths:

1   'I am the way and the truth and the life: no man cometh unto the Father, but by me' (John 14:6).

'Verily, verily, I say unto you, he that entereth not by the door into the sheepfold, but climbeth up some other way, the same is a thief and robber . . . I am the door: by me if any man enter in, he shall be saved' (John 10:1, 9)

Jesus Christ, as he is testified to us in Holy Scripture, is the one Word of God, which we are to hear, which we are to trust and obey in life and in death.

We repudiate the false teaching that the Church can and must recognize yet other happenings and powers, personalities and truths as divine revelation alongside this one Word of God, as a source of her preaching . . .

2 . . . We repudiate the false teaching that there are areas of our life in which we belong not to Jesus Christ but another lord, areas in which we do not need justification and sanctification through him.

3 . . . We repudiate the false teaching that the Church can turn over the form of her message and ordinances at will or according to some dominant ideological and political convictions.

4 . . . We repudiate the false teaching that the Church can and may set up or accept special leaders (*Führer*) equipped with powers to rule.

5   'Fear God, honour the king!' (I Peter 2:17).

The Bible tells us that according to divine arrangement the State has the responsibility to provide for justice and peace in the yet unredeemed world, in which the Church also stands, according to the measure of human insight and human possibility, by the threat and use of force.

The Church recognizes with thanks and reverence toward God the benevolence of this, his provision. She reminds men of God's kingdom, God's commandment and righteousness, and thereby the responsibility of rulers and ruled. She trusts and obeys the power of the Word, through which God maintains all things.

We repudiate the false teaching that the State can and should expand beyond its special responsibility to become the single and total order of human life, and also thereby fulfil the commission of the Church.

We repudiate the false teaching that the Church can and should expand beyond its special responsibility to take on the characteristics, functions and dignities of the State, and thereby become itself an organ of the State.

6 . . . We repudiate the false teaching that the Church, in human self-esteem, can put the word and work of the Lord

in the service of some wishes, purposes and plans or other, chosen according to desire. . . .

The Barmen Declaration, 1934 [331]

**
*

Our charity must be a real and costly love, with deep feeling for the sins in spite of which we love the sinner – no mere tolerance or indulgence which parodies love as flippancy parodies merriment. Next to the Blessed Sacrament itself, your neighbour is the holiest object presented to your senses. If he is your Christian neighbour he is holy in almost the same way, for in him also Christ *vere latitat* – the glorifier and the glorified, Glory himself, is truly hidden.

C. S. Lewis, 1941 [332]

**
*

During the last year or so I've come to know and understand more and more the profound this-worldliness of Christianity. The Christian is not a *homo religiosus*, but simply a man, as Jesus was a man – in contrast, shall we say, to John the Baptist. I don't mean the shallow and banal this-worldliness of the enlightened, the busy, the comfortable, or the lascivious, but the profound this-worldliness, characterized by discipline and the constant knowledge of death and resurrection. I think Luther lived a this-worldly life in this sense.

I discovered later, and I'm still discovering right up to this moment, that it is only by living completely in this world that one learns to have faith. One must completely abandon any attempt to make something of oneself, whether it be a saint, or a converted sinner, or a churchman (a so-called priestly type!), a righteous man or an unrighteous one, a sick man or a healthy one. By this-worldliness I mean living unreservedly in life's duties, problems, successes and failures, experiences and perplexities. In so doing we throw ourselves completely into the arms of God, taking seriously, not our own sufferings, but those of God in the world – watching with Christ in Gethsemane. That, I think, is faith; that is *metanoia*; and that is how one becomes a man and a Christian (cf. Jer. 45!). How can success make us arrogant, or failure lead us astray, when we share in God's sufferings through a life of this kind?

Dietrich Bonhoeffer, 1944 [333]

*

He who is devoid of the power to forgive is devoid of the power to love. . . . Forgiveness is a catalyst creating the atmosphere necessary for a fresh start and a new beginning. It is the lifting of a burden or the cancelling of a debt. The words 'I will forgive you, but I'll never forget what you've done' never explain the real nature of forgiveness. Certainly one can never forget, if that means erasing it totally from his mind. But when we forgive, we forget in the sense that the evil deed is no longer a mental block impeding a new relationship. Likewise, we can never say, 'I will forgive you, but I won't have anything further to do with you.' Forgiveness means reconciliation, a coming together again. Without this, no man can love his enemies. The degree to which we are able to forgive determines the degree to which we are able to love our enemies.

Martin Luther King, 1963 [334]

*

'I say to you today, my friends, that in spite of the difficulties and frustrations of the moment I still have a dream. It is a dream deeply rooted in the American dream. I have a dream that one day this nation will rise up and live out the true meaning of its creed: "We hold these truths to be self-evident – that all men are created equal." I have a dream that one day on the red hills of Georgia the sons of former slaves and the sons of former slaveowners will be able to sit down together at the table of brotherhood. I have a dream that one day even the state of Mississippi, a desert state sweltering with the heat of injustice and oppression, will be transformed into an oasis of freedom and justice. I have a dream that my four little children will one day live in a nation where they will not be judged by the colour of their skin but by the content of their character.

'I have a dream today.

'I have a dream that one day the state of Alabama, whose governor's lips are presently dripping with the words of interposition and nullification, will be transformed into a situation where little black boys and black girls will be able to join hands with little white boys and white girls and walk together as sisters and brothers.

'I have a dream today.' Below him, people had joined hands and were swaying back and forth, crying out to him, 'Dream some more.'

'I have a dream that one day every valley shall be exalted, every hill and mountain shall be made low, the rough places will be made plains, and the crooked places will be made straight, and the glory of the Lord shall be revealed, and all flesh shall see it together.

'This is our hope. This is the faith I shall return to the South with. With this faith we will be able to hew out of the mountain of despair a stone of hope. With this faith we will be able to transform the jangling discords of our nation into a beautiful symphony of brotherhood. With this faith we will be able to work together, pray together, struggle together, go to jail together, stand up for freedom together, knowing that we will be free one day.

'This will be the day when all of God's children will be able to sing with new meaning "My country 'tis of thee, sweet land of liberty, of thee I sing. Land where my fathers died, land of the pilgrim's pride, from every mountainside let freedom ring". And if America is to be a great nation this must become true. So let freedom ring from the prodigious hilltops of New Hampshire. Let freedom ring from the mighty mountains of New York. Let freedom ring from the heightening Alleghenies of Pennsylvania . . . But not only that; let freedom ring from Stone Mountain of Georgia. Let freedom ring from Lookout Mountain of Tennessee. Let freedom ring from every hill and mole hill of Mississippi. From every mountaintop, let freedom ring.

'When we let freedom ring, when we let it ring from every village and every hamlet, from every state and every city, we will be able to speed up that day when all of God's children, black men and white men, Jews and Gentiles, Protestants and Catholics, will be able to join hands and sing in the words of the old Negro spiritual, "Free at last! Free at last! Thank God almighty, we are free at last!"'

Martin Luther King, 1963 [335]

*
**

We should do Proverbs a poor service if we contrived to vest it in a priestly ephod or a prophet's mantle, for it is a book which seldom takes you to church. Like its own figure of Wisdom, it calls across to you in the street about some everyday matter, or points things out at home. Its function in Scripture is to put godliness into working clothes; to name business and society as spheres in which we are to acquit ourselves with credit to our Lord, and in which we are to look for his training.

If we could analyse the influences that build up a godly character to maturity, we might well find that the agencies which we call natural vastly outweighed those that we call supernatural. The book of Proverbs reassures us that this, if it is true, is no reflection on the efficiency of God's grace; for the hard facts of life, which knock some of the nonsense out of us, are *God's* facts and his appointed school of character;

they are not alternatives to his grace, but means of it; for everything *is* of grace, from the power to know to the power to obey.

Derek Kidner, 1964 [336]

*
**

The Church, as 'the light of the world' and as 'the salt of the earth', should not have aligned itself with the militaristic purposes of the government. Rather, on the basis of our love for her and by the standard of our Christian conscience, we should have more correctly criticized the policies of our motherland. However, we made a statement at home and abroad in the name of the Kyodan that we approved of and supported the war and we prayed for victory.

Indeed, as our nation committed errors we, as a church, sinned with her. We neglected to perform our mission as a 'watchman.' Now, with deep pain in our heart, we confess this sin, seeking the forgiveness of our Lord, and from the churches and our brothers and sisters of the world, and in particular of Asian countries, and from the people of our own country.

United Church of Christ in Japan, 1967 [337]

*
**

Transcendence implies otherness and distinction, but not apartness or away-ness, and it is always *through* the world. It is through the natural that we encounter the supernatural, although the supernatural eludes the ability of the natural to exhaust its meaning. If it is the truth of the transcendent God, creator and redeemer, which secular Christianity so sadly misses, that truth will be presented with power and relevance by Christians who know that transcendence is always near to the world and through it.

Michael Ramsey, 1969 [338]

The kind of evangelicalism which concentrates exclusively on saving individual souls is not true evangelicalism. It is not evangelical because it is not biblical. It forgets that God did not create souls but body-souls called human beings, who are also social beings, and that he cares about their bodies and their society as well as about their relationship with himself and their eternal destiny. So true Christian love will care for people as people, and will seek to serve them, neglecting neither the soul for the body nor the body for the soul.

John Stott, 1970 [339]

**
*

We Christians are compelled to speak out and take accompanying actions on the following grounds:

> We are under God's command that we should be faithful to his Word in concrete historical situations. It is not a sense of triumphant victory that moves us today; rather it is a sense of confession of our sins before God; and yet we are commanded by God to speak the truth and act in the present situation in Korea. . . .

The firm foundation of our words and deeds is our faith in God the Lord of history, in Jesus the proclaimer of the Messianic Kingdom, and in the Spirit who moves vigorously among the people. We believe that God is the ultimate vindicator of the oppressed, the weak, and the poor; he judges the evil forces in history. We believe that Jesus the Messiah proclaimed the coming of the Messianic Kingdom, to be subversive to the evil powers, and that his Messianic Kingdom will be the haven of the dispossessed, the rejected, and the downtrodden. We also believe that the Spirit is working for the new creation of history and cosmos, as well as for the regeneration and sanctification of individual man.

Christian Ministers in South Korea, 1973 [340]

There is a mystery in the heart of the poor. Jesus says that everything we do for the hungry, the thirsty, the naked, the sick, the prisoner or the stranger, we do for him: 'All that you do for the least of my brothers, you do for me.' The poor, in their total insecurity, their anguish and their destitution, identify with Jesus. Hidden in their radical poverty, in their obvious wounds, is the mystery of the presence of God.

Of course people who have no security and are destitute need bread. But as well as the bread they need a presence, another human heart which says: 'Take heart: you are important in my eyes and I love you; you have a value; there is hope.' They need a presence which reveals God's mercy, the mercy of a God who is a father, who loves and gives life.

There is a covenant between Jesus and the poor. There is a great mystery there.

Jean Vanier, 1979 [341]

*
**

Conversion is no more than a trip to personal assurance, if we are encouraged to think it asks no questions about the company we keep. The call to follow Christ must always be in obedience to a vision of the Kingdom of God . . . that vision will lead us to be indignant at those features of life which contradict God's promise of the Kingdom.

David Sheppard, 1983 [342]

*
**

The Christological problem in the proclamation of the gospel is compounded by the way Christ has been manipulated, being treated as a private possession. Such treatment is often the fruit of an individualistic, pietist religiosity at the service of economic interests from local oligarchical and metropolitan powers. To be sure, lest I be misunderstood, pietism, as an expression of faith, or as an evangelical type of spirituality which stresses personal prayers, Bible reading and a high personal morality is a positive factor in the proclamation of the gospel. But a spirituality which isolates Christ from reality and interiorizes him in the individual domain of the private-self, is alienating and deadly for the Christian life and mission.

Orlando Costas, 1983 [343]

5
Progress

For at least three reasons Evangelicals have tended to be suspicious of the word 'progress'. To some, it smacks of evolutionist notions, as though the Christian life were a giant escalator, always going 'onwards and upwards'. Others suspect perfectionist ideas, which threaten to ignore basic fallibilities of sin and pride. Others, again, fear a re-birth of hierarchies and grades, with 'achievers' claiming superior status and (more importantly) threatening the essential equality of the 'priesthood of all believers'. All these fears have their justifications — and limitations.

St Paul chronicles his own experience in a typically balanced way in Philippians chapter 3. He concedes: 'Not that I have already obtained . . . or am already perfect . . . I do not consider that I have made it my own'. But he states: 'I press on . . . straining forward to what lies ahead, I press on toward the goal'. The movement forward 'to make it my own' is a simple response 'because Christ Jesus has made me his own'.

All progress is in Christ, and all progress is Christ. We can never go beyond him. We can never proceed beyond justification by faith; but we can allow justification and faith to proceed in us. The Christian life begins with a sacrifice; but that initial commitment will bring further consequences in its trail — more joyful, more painful, more liberating responses. Protestant theology has tended to resist very firmly occasional Catholic language of 'acquiring' gifts and graces from God; all is understood as gift — 'and every thought of holiness is his, and his alone'. Whatever we are considering, whether it be holiness, asurance or love, all is taken as deepening appreciation and reflection in human lives of the Christ at the Centre.

In different faces we see one or the other in fine clarity: an Isaac or a da Todi or a Studd consumed as a living sacrifice, an Anthony in our own day breathing the holiness of the God who is deeply intimate and breathtakingly Other, a Brooks or a Wesley secure in their assurance of God's commitment to them, a Lull or a David Watson freed to love without restraint. Even the plodding of a Carey or the intense self-dissatisfaction of a Martyn allow the miraculous patience of a dear God to breathe through. Common, right across the board, is a recklessness ('detachment', in Catholic language) which links the early martyrs with the modern missionaries and discovers 'holy folly' and 'madness for Christ' in Egyptian deserts, medieval Italy, nineteenth century Russia and twentieth century China — and England.

So progress is not just a deepening and rediscovery of what we already know (or thought we knew); it is also a movement into the future to discover what we have not yet fathomed and what we *know* we do not know; it is a journey into the trustworthy unknown of a personal God personally known. It is a way of admitting that we are permanently on the Way. It is a way of continually learning that discipleship means learning.

Growth

Accordingly, when he was a teacher he had the age of a teacher, not rejecting nor surpassing man, nor annulling his own law for the human race in himself, but sanctifying every age by its resemblance to himself. For he came to save all through himself – all, I say, who through him are regenerated into God, infants, children, boys, young men and elders. Therefore, he passed through every age, and became an infant for infants, sanctifying the infants; a child among children, sanctifying all of that age, at the same time being made an example for them of piety, righteousness and obedience. Among the young men he was a young man, becoming an example for young men, sanctifying them for the Lord. So also he became an elder among the elders so that he might become a perfect master in every particular, not only in the exposition of the truth, but also in the matter of age, thereby sanctifying the elders and becoming an example to them. Then he passed to his death, so that he might be 'the first-begotten from the dead'.

Irenaeus, 182–8 [344]

*
**

Every desire for the Beautiful which draws us on in this ascent is intensified by the soul's very progress towards it. And this is the real meaning of seeing God: never to have this desire satisfied. But fixing our eyes on those things which help us to see, we must ever keep alive in us the desire to see more and more. And so no limit can be set to our progress towards God: first of all, because no limitation can be put upon the beautiful, and secondly because the increase in our desire for the beautiful cannot be stopped by any sense of satisfaction.

Gregory of Nyssa, 390–5 [345]

*
**

My brother, may the Son of God who is already formed in you, grow in you so that for you he will become immeasurable, and that in you he will become laughter, exultation, the fulness of joy which no one will take from you.

Isaac of Stella, 1165–9 [346]

*
**

The beginning of right living is spiritual, where the inner feeling of the mind is unfeignedly dedicated to God for the cultivation of holiness and righteousness.

But no one in this earthly prison of the body has sufficient strength to press on with due eagerness; and weakness so weighs down the greater number that, with wavering and limping and even creeping along the ground, they move at a feeble rate. Let each one of us, then, proceed according to the measure of his puny capacity and set out upon the journey we have begun. No one shall set out so inauspiciously as not daily to make some headway, though it be slight. Therefore, let us not cease so to act that we may make some unceasing progress in the way of the Lord. And let us not despair at the slightness of our success; for even though attainment may not correspond to desire, when today outstrips yesterday the effort is not lost. Only let us look toward our mark with sincere simplicity and aspire to our goal; not fondly flattering ourselves, nor excluding our own evil deeds, but with continuous effort striving toward this end: that we may surpass ourselves in goodness until we attain to goodness itself. It is this, indeed, which through the whole course of life we seek and follow. But we shall attain it only when we have cast off the weakness of the body, and are received into full fellowship with him.

Jean Calvin, 1559 [347]

***

Songs of the soul in rapture at having arrived at the height of perfection, which is union with God by the road of spiritual negation

Upon a gloomy night,
With all my cares to loving ardours flushed,
(O venture of delight!)
With nobody in sight
I went abroad when all my house was hushed.

In safety, in disguise,
In darkness up the secret stair I crept,
(O happy enterprise!)
Concealed from other eyes
When all my house at length in silence slept.

Upon that lucky night
In secrecy, inscrutable to sight,
I went without discerning
And with no other light
Except for that which in my heart was burning.

It lit and led me through
More certain than the light of noonday clear
To where One waited near
Whose presence well I knew,
There where no other presence might appear.

Oh night that was my guide!
Oh darkness dearer than the morning's pride,
Oh night that joined the lover
To the beloved bride
Transfiguring them each into the other.

Within my flowering breast
Which only for himself entire I save
He sank into his rest
And all my gifts I gave
Lulled by the airs with which the cedars wave.

Over the ramparts fanned
While the fresh wind was fluttering his tresses,
With his serenest hand
My neck he wounded, and
Suspended every sense with its caresses.

Lost to myself I stayed
My face upon my lover having laid
From all endeavour ceasing:
And all my cares releasing
Threw them amongst the lilies there to fade.

John of the Cross, 1579–81 [348]

*
**

Though you destroy the flesh, and offer violence unto that, yet there is the inward man, that is growing up daily, though the outward man fail. It is true, violence must be offered to the flesh, you must be content to part with pleasures, and the outward man, in that sense, must suffer somewhat, but remember what you gain, there is the inward man that so much the more provides for itself, and if you will not deny yourself, you deny not your disease that will slay you.

John Preston, 1630 [349]

*
**

Grace is little at the first. There are several ages in Christians, some babes, some young men: grace is as 'a grain of mustard seed,' Matt. 17:20. Nothing so little as grace at first, and nothing more glorious afterward: things of

279

greatest perfection are longest in coming to their growth. Man, the perfectest creature, comes to perfection by little and little; worthless things, as mushrooms and the like, like Jonah's gourd, soon spring up, and soon vanish. A new creature is the most excellent frame in all the world, therefore it groweth up by degrees; we see in nature that a mighty oak riseth of an acorn . . . It is with a Christian as it was with Christ, who sprang out of the dead stock of Jesse, out of David's family, Isa. 53:2, when it was at the lowest, but he grew up higher than the heavens. It is not with the trees of righteousness as it was with the trees of paradise, which were created all perfect at the first . . . All these glorious fireworks of zeal and holiness in the saints had their beginning from a few sparks.

Let us not therefore be discouraged at the small beginnings of grace, but look on ourselves, as 'elected to be blameless and without spot,' Eph. 1:4. Let us only look on our imperfect beginning to enforce further strife to perfection, and to keep us in a low conceit. Otherwise, in case of discouragement, we must consider ourselves as Christ doth, who looks on us as such as he intendeth to fit for himself. Christ valueth us by what we shall be, and by that we are elected unto. We call a little plant a tree, because it is growing up to be so. 'Who is he that despiseth the day of little things?' Zech. 4:10. Christ would not have us despise little things.

Richard Sibbes, 1630 [350]

*
**

You say you are not as you once were. It is generally true that the time of espousals, the beginning of our profession, is attended with sensible sweetness and a liveliness of spirit which we afterwards look back upon with regret when we are led into a different dispensation. The young believer is like a tree in blossom. But I have a good hope that if you seem to have lost in point of sensible affections you have proportionally gained in knowledge, judgment, and an establishment in the faith. You see more of your own heart than you did or could in those early days; and you have a clearer view of the wisdom, glory, and faithfulness of God, as manifested in the person of Christ. Though the blossoms have gone off the fruit is found, and, I trust, ripening for glory. The Lord deals with us as children. Children, when they are young, have many little indulgences. As they grow up, they are subject to discipline and must learn obedience. So when faith and knowledge are in their infancy, the Lord helps this weakness by cordials and sensible comforts; but when they are advanced in growth he exercises and proves them by many changes and trials, and calls us to live more directly upon his power and promises in the face of all. discouragements, to hope even against hope, and at times seems to deprive us of every subsidiary support, that we may lean only and entirely upon our beloved.

John Newton, 1770 [351]

*
**

Eustace, if after my removal anyone should think it worth his while to write my life, I will give you a criterion by which you may judge of its correctness. If he give me credit for being a plodder he will describe me justly. Anything beyond this will be too much. I can plod. That is my only genius. I can persevere in any definite pursuit. To this I owe everything.

William Carey, early 19th cent. [352]

*
**

When we have nothing to call forth particular feelings, we go on in the common jog-trot way.

Charles Simeon, 1812 [353]

God does not, by the instant gift of his Spirit, make us always feel right, desire good, love purity, aspire after him and his will. Therefore either he will not, or he cannot. If he will not, it must because it would not be well to do so. If he cannot, then he would not if he could; else a better condition than God's is conceivable to the mind of God. . . . The truth is this: he wants to make us in his own image, *choosing* the good, *refusing* the evil. How should he effect this if he were *always* moving us from within, as he does at divine intervals, toward the beauty of holiness? . . . For God made our individuality as well as, and a greater marvel than, our dependence; made our *apartness* from himself, that freedom should bind us divinely dearer to himself, with a new and inscrutable marvel of love.

George MacDonald, 1867 [354]

***

If we could see beneath the surface of many a life, we would see that thousands of people within the Church are suffering spiritually from 'arrested development'; they never reach spiritual maturity; they never do all the good they were intended to do: and this is due to the fact that at some point in their lives they refused to go further; some act of self-sacrifice was required of them, and they felt they could not and would not make it; some habit had to be given up, some personal relation altered or renounced, and they would not change their ways; they refused to take the one step which would have opened up for them a new and vital development. They are 'stunted souls'.

Olive Wyon, 1943 [355]

***

It seems to me the most absurd thing in the world to be upset because I am weak and distracted and blind and constantly make mistakes! What else do I expect! Does God love me any less because I can't make myself a saint by my own power and in my own way? He loves me more because I am so clumsy and helpless without him – and underneath what I am he sees me as I will one day be by his pure gift and that pleases him – and therefore it pleases me and I attend to his great love which is my joy.

Thomas Merton, 1953 [356]

＊
＊＊

When is the Search ended? In one sense, it is finished when our hand, stretched out to God in the name of his appointed mediator Jesus Christ, feels the answering grasp and knows that he is there. But in another sense the searching never ends, for the first discovery is quickly followed by another, and that by another, and so it goes on.

To find *that he is*, is the mere starting point of our search. We are lured on to explore *what he is*, and that search is never finished, and it grows more thrilling the farther one proceeds.

Isobel Kuhn, 1957 [357]

＊
＊＊

Our Lord did not say 'I am come that ye may have safety, and have it more abundantly'. Some of us would indeed give anything to feel safe, about our life in this world as in the next, but we cannot have it both ways: safety or life, we must choose.

Gerald Vann, 1960 [358]

＊
＊＊

I have seen many people who will even go so far as to lie to themselves rather than admit that they are disappointed. They seemed to be looking forward to the future, but in reality their eyes were fixed on the past . . .

Take, for example, the case of a man who once was roused by the powerful inspiration of the Holy Spirit. Now he strives, by disciplining himself, to retain the old spontaneous ardour. But he fails. He reproaches himself for his lukewarmness, for the ineffectiveness, not only of his actions, but also of his prayers and resolutions. He reproaches himself for not having been able to preserve the 'heavenly gift', as the apostle urges. But in spiritual matters nothing is preserved, nothing can be saved up. This man is mistaking a psychological problem for a religious one. He refuses to recognize the law of adventure, which is that it dies as it achieves its object. The first requirement of religion is that we accept the laws of life. The spiritual life consists only in a series of new births. There must be new flowerings, new prophets, new adventures – always new adventures – if the heart of man, albeit in fits and starts, is to go on beating.

Paul Tournier, 1966 [359]

Sacrifice

When the soul grows tearful, weeps, and is filled with tenderness, and all this without having striven for it, then let us run, for the Lord has arrived uninvited and is holding out to us the sponge of loving sorrow, the cool waters of blessed sadness with which to wipe away the record of our sins. Guard these tears like the apple of your eye until they go away, for they have a power greater than anything that comes from our own efforts and our own meditation.

John Climacus, 7th cent. [360]

**

When you reach the place of tears, then know that your spirit has come out from the prison of this world and has set its foot upon the path that leads towards the new age. Your spirit begins at this moment to breathe the wonderful air which is there, and it starts to shed tears. The moment for the birth of the spiritual child is now at hand, and the travail of childbirth become intense. Grace, the common mother of us all, makes haste to give birth mystically to the soul, God's image, bringing it forth into the light of the age to come. And when the time for the birth has arrived, the intellect begins to sense something of the things of that other world – as a faint perfume, or as a breath of life which a newborn child receives into its bodily frame. But we are not accustomed to such an experience and, finding it hard to endure, our body is suddenly overcome by a weeping mingled with joy which excels the sweetness of honey. Together with the growing of the child within there will be an increase of tears . . . when the eyes become fountains of water for a period of nearly two years. This happens during a transition period . . . At the end of the period of tears you will reach peace in your deliberations . . . As soon as you have entered the place where deliberations are set at peace, then the violence of weeping is again taken from you and you reach the state of moderation.

Isaac of Nineveh, d. 700 [361]

*
**

'I was aforetime', he says, 'in the Court of the Emperor and I learned to be a fool, to the end that I might gather together money; and the Emperor has spoken to me so often of the Passion of Jesus Christ and of the nobility of God, that I desire to be a fool that I may give honour and glory to him, and I will have no art nor device in my words by reason of the greatness of my love.'

Ramon Lull, 1283-4 [362]

*
**

Sense and nobleness it seems to me to go mad for the
  beautiful Messiah.
It seems to me great wisdom in a man if he wishes to go
  mad for God;
in Paris there has never been seen such great philosophy
  as this.
Whoever goes mad for Christ seems afflicted and in
  tribulation;
but he is an exalted master of nature and theology.
Whoever goes mad for Christ certainly seems crazy to
  people;
it seems he is off the road to anyone without experience
  of the state.
Whoever wishes to enter this school will discover new
  learning,

he who has not experienced madness does not yet know
    what it is.
Whoever wishes to enter this dance will find unbounded
    love;
a hundred days' indulgence to whoever reviles him.
But whoever goes seeking honour is not worthy of his
    love,
for Jesus remained on the cross between two thieves.
But whoever seeks in humility will, I am sure, arrive
    quickly;
let him not go to Bologna to learn another doctrine.

Iacopone da Todi, 13th cent. [363]

* *

Take, Lord, and receive all my liberty, my memory, my
understanding, and my entire will, all that I have and
possess. Thou hast given it all to me. To thee, O Lord, I
return it. All is thine, dispose of it wholly according to thy
will. Give me thy love and thy grace, for this is sufficient for
me.

Ignatius of Loyola, ?1522-3 [364]

* *

The most material directions which have occurred to me,
relating to the progress of the day, are these:–

1. For seriousness in devotion, whether public or domestic;
let us take a few moments, before we enter upon such
solemnities, to pause, and reflect, on the perfections of the
God we are addressing, on the importance of the business
we are coming about, on the pleasure and advantage of a
regular and devote attendance, and on the guilt and folly of
an hypocritical formality. When engaged, let us maintain a
strict watchfulness over our own spirits and check the first
wanderings of thought. And when the duty is over, let us

immediately reflect on the manner on which it has been performed, and ask our own consciences whether we have reason to conclude, that we are accepted of God in it? For there is a certain manner of going through these offices which our own heart will immediately tell us, it is impossible for God to approve: and if we have inadvertently fallen into it, we ought to be deeply humbled before God for it, lest our prayer become sin.

2. As for the hours of worldly business; whether it be, as with you, that of the hands; or whether it be the labour of a learned life, not immediately relating to religious matters; let us set to the prosecution of it with a sense of God's authority, and with a regard to his glory. Let us avoid a dreaming, sluggish, indolent temper, which nods over its work, and does only the business of an hour in two or three. In opposition to this which runs through the life of some people, who yet think they are never idle, let us endeavour to dispatch as much as we well can in a little time; considering, that it is but a little we have in all. And let us be habitually sensible of the need we have of the divine blessing, to make our labours successful.

3. For seasons of diversion; let us take care, that our recreations be well chosen; that they be pursued with a good intention, to fit us for a renewed application to the labours of life; and thus that they be only used in subordination to the honour of God, the great end of all our actions. Let us take heed, that our hearts be not estranged from God by them; and that they do not take up too much of our time: always remembering that the faculties of the human nature, that the advantages of the christian revelation, were not given us in vain; but that we are always to be in pursuit of some great and honourable end, and to indulge ourselves in amusements and diversions no farther, than as they may make a part in a scheme of rational and manly, benevolent and pious conduct.

4. For the observation of providences: it will be useful to regard the divine interposition, in our comforts and in our afflictions. In our comforts, whether more common or extraordinary: that we find ourselves in continual health; that we are furnished with food for support and pleasure; that we have so many agreeable ways of employing our time; that we have so many friends, and those so good, and so happy; that our business goes on prosperously; that we go out and come in safely; and that we enjoy composure and cheerfulness of spirit, without which nothing else could be enjoyed: all these should be regarded as providential favours, and due acknowledgements should be made to God on these accounts, as we pass thro' such agreeable scenes. On the other hand, Providence is to be regarded in every disappointment, in every loss, in every pain, in every instance of unkindness from those who have professed friendship: and we should endeavour to argue ourselves into a patient submission, from this consideration that the hand of God is always mediately, if not immediately in each of them; and that if they are not properly the work of Providence, they are at least under its direction. It is a reflection, which we should particularly make with relation to those little cross accidents, (as we are ready to call them), and these infirmities and follies in the temper and conduct of our intimate friends, which else may be ready to discompose us. And it is the more necessary to guard our minds here, as wise and good men often lose the command of themselves on these comparatively little occasions; who calling up reason and religion to their assistance, stand the shock of great calamities with fortitude and resolution.

Philip Doddridge, 1745 [365]

*
**

I do not undervalue joy; but I suspect it, when it is not blended with the deepest humiliation and contrition . . .

I confess that this is the religion which I love; I would

have conscious unworthiness to pervade every act and habit of my soul; and whether the woof be more or less brilliant, I would have humility to be the warp.

Charles Simeon, early 19th cent. [366]

*
**

A day more unprofitable than the foregoing; the depravity of my heart, as it is in its natural frame, appeared to me today almost unconquerable. I could not, however long in prayer, keep the presence of God, or the power of the world to come, in my mind at all. It sunk down to its most lukewarm state, and continued in general so, in spite of my endeavours. Oh how I need a deep heart-rending work of the Spirit upon my self, before I shall save myself, or them that hear me. What I hear about my future destination has proved a trial to me today . . . I almost think that to be prevented going among the heathen as a missionary, would break my heart. Whether it be self-will or aught else, I cannot yet rightly ascertain . . .

I feel pressed in spirit to do something for God. Every body is diligent, but I am idle; all employed in their proper work, but I tossed in uncertainty; I want nothing but grace; I want to be perfectly holy, and to save myself and those that hear me. I have hitherto lived to little purpose, more like a clod than a servant of God; now let me burn out for God.

Henry Martyn, 1806 [367]

*
**

Yea let him take all!

Take my life, and let it be
Consecrated, Lord, to thee.

Take my moments and my days;
Let them flow in ceaseless praise.

Take my hands, and let them move
At the impulse of thy love.

Take my feet, and let them be
Swift and 'beautiful' for thee.

Take my voice, and let me sing
Always, only, for my King.

Take my lips, and let them be
Filled with messages from thee.

Take my silver and my gold;
Not a mite would I withhold.

Take my intellect, and use
Every power as thou shalt choose.

Take my will, and make it thine;
It shall be no longer mine.

Take my heart; it *is* thine own;
It shall be thy royal throne.

Take my love; my Lord, I pour
At thy feet its treasure-store.

Take myself, and I will be
Ever, *only*, ALL for thee.

Francis Ridley Havergal, 1874 [368]

*
**

How are we going to treat the Lord Jesus Christ with reference to this command? Shall we definitely drop the title Lord as applied to him, and take the ground that we are quite willing to recognize him as our Saviour, so far as the penalty of sin is concerned, but are not prepared to own ourselves 'bought with a price', or him as having any claim to our unquestioning obedience? Shall we say that we are our own masters, willing to yield something as his due, who bought us with his blood, provided he does not ask too much? Our lives, our loved ones, our possessions are our own, not his: we will give him what we think fit, and obey any of his requirements that do not demand too great a sacrifice? To be taken to heaven by Jesus Christ we are more than willing, but we will not have this Man to *reign* over us?

The heart of every Christian will undoubtedly reject the proposition, so formulated; but have not countless lives in each generation been lived as though it were proper ground to take? How few of the Lord's people have practically recognized the truth that Christ is either *Lord of all*, or is *not Lord at all!* If we can judge God's Word as much or as little as we like, then *we* are lords and he is the indebted one, to be grateful for our dole and obliged by our compliance with his wishes. If, on the other hand, he is Lord, let us treat him as such. 'Why call ye me, Lord, Lord, and do not the things which I say?'

Hudson Taylor, 1889 [369]

*
**

Prayer of Abandonment

Father,
I abandon myself into your hands;
do with me what you will.
Whatever you may do, I thank you:
I am ready for all, I accept all.
Let only your will be done in me,
and in all your creatures –
I wish no more than this, O Lord.

Into your hands I commend my soul;
I offer it to you with all the love of my heart.
For I love you, Lord,
and so need to give myself,
to surrender myself into your hands,

without reserve,
and with boundless confidence.

For you are my Father.

Brother Charles of Jesus, 1916 [370]

*
**

There are more than twice as many Christian uniformed
officers at home among peaceful Britain's 40 million
evangelized inhabitants, than the whole number of Christ's
forces fighting at the front among 1,200 million heathen!
And yet such call themselves soldiers of Christ! What do the
angels call them, I wonder? The 'Let's-save-Britain-first'
brigade are in the succession of the 'I-pray-thee-have-me-
excused' apostles.

Christ's call is to feed the hungry, not the full; to save the
lost, not the stiff-necked; not to call the scoffers, but sinners
to repentance; not to build and furnish comfortable chapels,
churches, and cathedrals at home in which to rock Christian
professors to sleep by means of clever essays, stereotyped
prayers and artistic musical performances, but to raise living
churches of souls among the destitute, to capture men from
the devil's clutches and snatch them from the very jaws of
hell, to enlist and train them for Jesus, and make them into
an Almighty Army of God. *But this can only be accomplished
by a red-hot, unconventional, unfettered Holy Ghost religion,*
where neither Church nor State, neither man nor traditions
are worshipped or preached, but only Christ and him
crucified. Not to confess Christ by fancy collars, clothes,
silver croziers or gold watch-chain crosses, church steeples
or richly embroidered altar-cloths, but by *reckless sacrifice
and heroism* in the foremost trenches.

When in hand-to-hand conflict with the world and the
devil, neat little biblical confectionery is like shooting lions
with a pea-shooter: one needs a man who will let himself go

and deliver blows right and left as hard as he can hit, trusting in the Holy Ghost. It's experience, not preaching, that hurts the devil and confounds the world, because unanswerable; the training is not that of the schools, but of the market; it's the hot, free heart and not the balanced head that knocks the devil out. Nothing but forked-lightning Christians will count. A lost reputation is the best degree for Christ's sake.

The difficulty is to believe that he can deign to use such scallywags as us, but of course he wants faith and fools rather than talents and culture. All God wants is a heart, any old turnip will do for a head; so long as we are empty, all is well, for then he fills with the Holy Ghost.

The fiery baptism of the Holy Ghost will change soft, sleek Christians into hot, lively heroes for Christ, who will advance and fight and die, but not mark time.

Fools would 'cut' the devil, pretending they do not see him; others erect a tablet over his supposed grave. Be wise; don't cut nor bury him; kill him with the bayonet of evangelism.

Hugh Latimer was an inextinguishable candle; the devil lit him, and ever since has been kicking himself for his folly. Won't someone else tempt the devil to make a fool of himself again?

Nail the colours to the mast! That is the right thing to do, and, therefore, that is what we must do, and do it now. What colours? The colours of Christ, the work he has given us to do – the evangelization of the unevangelized. *Christ wants not nibblers of the possible, but grabbers of the impossible*, by faith in the omnipotence, fidelity and wisdom of the Almighty Saviour who gave the command. Is there a wall in our path? By our God we will leap over it! Are there lions and scorpions in our way? We will trample them under our feet! Does a mountain bar our progress? Saying, 'Be thou removed and cast into the sea,' we will march on. Soldiers of Jesus! Never surrender! Nail the colours to the mast!

C. T. Studd, 1915 [371]

Revival has always come through persons for whom ador-
ing and realistic attention to God and total self-giving to
God's purpose have been the first interests of life. These
persons it is true have become fully effective only when
associated in groups: but the ultimate source of power has
been the dedication of the individual heart.

Evelyn Underhill, 1936 [372]

*
**

If the alabaster box is not broken, the pure spikenard will
not flow forth. Strange to say, many are still treasuring the
alabaster box, thinking that its value exceeds that of the
ointment. Many think that their outward man is more
precious than their inward man. This becomes the problem
in the Church. One will treasure his cleverness, thinking he
is quite important; another will treasure his own emotions,
esteeming himself as an important person; others highly
regard themselves, feeling they are better than others, their
eloquence surpasses that of others, their quickness of action
and exactness of judgment are superior, and so forth.
However, we are not antique collectors; we are not vase
admirers; we are those who desire to smell only the fragrance of the ointment. Without the breaking of the outward, the inward will not come forth. Thus individually we
have no flowing out, but even the Church does not have a
living way. Why then should we hold ourselves as so
previous, if our outward contains instead of releases the
fragrance? . . .

   . . . So the Treasure is in the earthen vessel, but if the
earthen vessel is not broken, who can see the Treasure
within? What is the final objective of the Lord's working in
our lives? It is to break this earthen vessel, to break our
alabaster box, to crack open our shell. The Lord longs to
find a way to bless the world through those who belong
to him. Brokenness is the way of blessing, the way of

fragrance, the way of fruitfulness, but it is also a path sprinkled with blood. Yes, there is blood from many wounds. When we offer ourselves to the Lord to be at his service, we cannot afford to be lenient, to spare ourselves. We must allow the Lord utterly to crack our outward man, so that he may find a way for his out working.

Watchman Nee, 1966 [373]

Holiness

O Most dreadful God, for the passion of your Son, I beseech you to accept of your poor Prodigal now prostrating himself at your door; I have fallen from you by my Iniquity, and am by nature a Son of Death, and a thousandfold more the Child of Hell by my wicked practice; but of your infinite grace you have promised mercy to me in Christ if I will but turn to you with all my heart: therefore upon the call of your Gospel, I am now come in, and throwing down my weapons, submit myself to your mercy.

And because you require, as the condition of my peace with you, that I should put away my Idols, and be at defiance with all your enemies, which I acknowledge I have wickedly sided with against you, I here from the bottom of my heart renounce them all; firmly covenanting with you, not to allow myself in any known sin, but conscientiously to use all the means that I know you have prescribed for the death and utter destruction of all my Corruptions. And whereas I have formerly, inordinately and idolatrously let out my Affections upon the World, I do here resign my Heart to you that made it; humbly protesting before your glorious Majesty that it is the firm resolution of my heart, and that I do unfeignedly desire grace from you, that when you shall call me hereunto, I may practice this my Resolution, to forsake all that is dear to me in this World, rather than turn from you, to the ways of Sin: and that I will watch against all Temptations, whether of prosperity or adversity, lest they withdraw my heart from you; beseeching you also to help me against the temptations of Satan, to whose wicked suggestions I resolve, by your grace, never to yield.

And forasmuch as you have, of your bottomless mercy, offered most graciously to me, wretched Sinner, to be again my God through Christ, if I would accept of you; I call heaven and earth to record this day that I do here solemnly avouch you for the Lord my God; and with all veneration bowing the neck of my soul under the feet of your most sacred Majesty, I do here take you the Lord Jehovah, Father, Son, and Holy Ghost, for my portion; and do give up myself, body and soul, for your Servant; promising and vowing to serve you in holiness and righteousness, all the days of my life. And since you have appointed the Lord Jesus Christ the only means of coming unto you I do here upon the bended knees of my soul accept of him as the only new and living way, by which Sinners may have access to you; and do solemnly join myself in a marriage-covenant to him.

O blessed Jesus, I come to you hungry, wretched, miserable, blind, and naked; a most loathsome, polluted wretch, a guilty, condemned malefactor, unworthy to wash the feet of the Servants of my Lord, much more to be solemnly married to the King of Glory; but since such is your unparalleled love, I do here with all my power accept you, and take you for my Head and Husband, for better, for worse, for richer, for poorer, for all times and conditions, to love, honour, and obey you before all others, and this to the death. I embrace you in all your offices: I renounce my own worthiness, and do here avow you for the Lord my Righteousness: I renounce my own wisdom, and do here take you for my only guide; I renounce my own will, and take your will for my law.

And now, glory be to you, O God the Father, whom I shall be bold from this day forward to look upon as my God and Father; that ever you should find out such a way for the recovery of undone Sinners. Glory be to you, O God the Son, who have loved me, and washed me from my sins in your own blood, and are now become my Saviour and Redeemer. Glory be to you, O God the Holy Ghost, who by the Finger of your almighty power have turned about my heart from Sin to God.

O dreadful Jehovah, the Lord God Omnipotent, Father, Son, and Holy Ghost, you are now become my Covenant-Friend, and I, through your infinite grace, am become your Covenant-Servant. Amen. So be it. And the Covenant which I have made on earth, let it be ratified in heaven.

John Wesley, 1780 [374]

*
**

I was not holy, and I recognised why not. I was not meaning to be. There were one or two pet little ways of my own I meant to keep; a pet prejudice or two I meant not to lay aside, and I could see that just here was the reason of my dropping holiness out of my scheme of life and teaching. The folly of this, the absolute inconsistency of it, appeared to me; and I changed my prayer for light on holiness into a prayer for holiness, dropping my hesitations and aversions and reserves entirely. The answer to my prayer came at once; I was like the woman in the gospel, I felt in myself that I was whole of that plague.

You will see it was a new experience I gained rather than new thought. But I will try to illustrate one of the new thoughts supplied me. You remember there is an ascription in a Psalm *'the name of the Lord is a strong tower; the righteous runneth into it and is safe.'* Now the truth which I experienced – *not my experience*, but the *truth* it presented to me – is like that. In wayward, sinful, petulant, wordly, base moods, it is possible for me to remind myself that these are of the flesh, and that I am – pardon my bold, blunt way of putting it, it may help you if you see that I do not shrink here – of the Spirit.

The holy life is just the divine life flowing through us, living in us and we in it; and this is not a figure of speech, but a reality.

Alexander Mackennal, 1887 [375]

All progress is progress in holiness.

W. E. Sangster, mid 20th cent. [376]

**

When learning looks down upon holiness the age of intellectual sterility is in sight, for again and again it is in the simple piety and holiness of one generation that we find the secret of great creative intellectual and artistic achievements in the next.

J. E. Fison, 1958 [377]

**

The prevalence of bad so-called sacred art everywhere constitutes a really grave spiritual problem, comparable, for example, to the analogous problem of polluted air in some of our big industrial centres. One breathes the bad air, aware only of a slight general discomfort, headache, stinging of the eyes; but in the long run the effect is grave. One looks at the bad art, in Church, in pious magazines, in some missals and liturgical books, on so called 'holy' pictures; one is aware of a vague spiritual uneasiness and distaste.

Or perhaps, worse still, one *likes* the cheap, emotional, immature and even sensual image that is presented. To *like* bad sacred art, and to feel that one is *helped* by it in prayer, can be a symptom of real spiritual disorders of which one may be entirely unconscious, and for which perhaps one may have no personal responsibility. The disease is there – and it is catching! . . .

Let us be aware of the dynamic and vitalizing spiritual effect of a purer and more traditional artistic sense. Let us realize that desire for a more living liturgy, a keener appreciation of theology and scripture, a greater awareness of the spiritual depth and of the contemplative possibilities of Christian life, cries out for the help that will be afforded by a sane and spiritual formation in sacred art.

All these things go together. Man is a living unity, an integrated whole. He is not sanctified just in his mind, or in his will. The whole man must be made holy, body and soul together, imagination and senses, intelligence, heart and spirit.

Thomas Merton, 1961 [378]

**
*

All holiness is God's holiness in us: it is a holiness that is participation and, in a certain way, more than participation, because as we participate in what we can receive from God, we become a revelation of that which transcends us. Being a limited light, we reveal the Light. But we should also remember that in this life in which we are striving towards holiness, our spirituality should be defined in very objective and precise terms. When we read books on spirituality or engage in studying the subject, we see that spirituality, explicitly or implicitly, is repeatedly defined as an attitude, a state of soul, an inner condition, a type of interiority, and so on. In reality, if you look for the ultimate definition and try to discover the inner core of spirituality, you find that spirituality does not consist of the states of soul that are familiar to us, but that it is the presence and action of the Holy Spirit in us, by us, and through us in the world.

Metropolitan Anthony, 1971 [379]

Assurance

It is one mercy for God to love the soul, and another mercy for God to assure the soul of his love. God writes many a man's name in the book of life, and yet will not let him know it till his hour of death, as the experience of many precious souls doth clearly evidence. Assurance is a flower of paradise that God sticks but in a few men's bosoms. It is one thing to be an heir of heaven, and another thing for a man to know or see himself an heir of heaven. The child in the arms may be heir to a crown, a kingdom, and yet not understand it; so many a saint may be heir to a crown, a kingdom of glory, and yet not know it.

Thomas Brooks, 1657 [380]

**
*

Some are fond of the expression [assurances]: I am not; I hardly ever use it. But I will simply declare (having neither leisure nor inclination to draw the saw of controversy concerning it) what are my present sentiments with regard to the thing which is usually meant thereby.

I believe a few, but very few, Christians have an assurance from God of everlasting salvation; and that is the thing which the Apostle terms the plerophory or full assurance of hope.

I believe more have such an assurance of being now in the favour of God as excludes all doubt and fear. And this, if I do not mistake, the Apostle means by the plerophory or full assurance of faith.

I believe a consciousness of being in the favour of God (which I do not term plerophory, or full assurance, since it is frequently weakened, nay, perhaps interrupted, by returns of doubt or fear) is the common privilege of Christians, fearing God and working righteousness.

Yet I do not affirm there are no exceptions to this general rule. Possibly some may be in the favour of God, and yet go mourning all the day long. But I believe this is usually owing either to disorder of body or ignorance of the gospel promises.

Therefore I have not for many years thought a consciousness of acceptance to be essential to justifying faith.

John Wesley, 1768 [381]

**
**
** **

Would you have assurance? The true solid assurance is to be obtained no other way. When young Christians are greatly comforted with the Lord's love and presence, their doubts and fears are for that season at an end. But this is not assurance; so soon as the Lord hides his face, they are troubled, and ready to question the very foundation of hope. Assurance grows by repeated conflict, by our repeated experimental proof of the Lord's power and goodness to save; when we have been brought very low and helped, sorely wounded and healed, cast down and raised again, have given up all hope, and been suddenly snatched from danger, and placed in safety; and when these things have been repeated to us and in us a thousand times over, we begin to learn to trust simply to the word and power of God, beyond and against appearances; and this trust, when habitual and strong, bears the name of assurance; for even assurance has degrees . . .

The best mark to judge by, and which he has given us for that purpose, is to inquire if his word and will have a prevailing, governing influence upon our lives and temper. If we love him, we do endeavour to keep his commandments; and it will hold the other way; if we have a desire to please him, we undoubtedly love him. Obedience is the best test; and when, amidst all our imperfections, we can humbly appeal concerning the sincerity of our view, this is a mercy for which we ought to be greatly thankful. He that has brought us to will, will likewise enable us to do according to his good pleasure.

John Newton, 1764 [382]

*
**

Assurance of Faith

A debtor to mercy alone,
    Of covenant mercy I sing;
Nor fear with thy righteousness on,
    My person and off'rings to bring:
The terrors of law, and of God,
    With me can have nothing to do;
My Saviour's obedience and blood,
    Hide all my transgressions from view.

The work which his goodness began,
    The arm of his strength will complete;
His promise is Yea, and Amen,
    And never was forfeited yet:
Things future, nor things that are now,
    Not all things below nor above,
Can make him his purpose forego,
    Or sever my soul from his love.

My name from the palms of his hands,
    Eternity will not erase;
Impress'd on his heart it remains,
    In marks of indelible grace;
Yes, I to the end shall endure,
    As sure as the earnest is giv'n;
More happy but not more secure,
    The glorified spirits in heav'n.

Augustus M. Toplady, 1771 [383]

I think it clear, even to demonstration, that *assurance* is not necessary to saving faith; a simple reliance on Christ for salvation is that faith which the word of God requires; assurance is a privilege, but not a duty. The true source of all the mistakes that are made in the religious world about assurance is, that men do not distinguish as they ought, between an assurance of *faith* and an assurance of *hope*. There are three kinds of full assurance spoken of in the Scriptures (as I have shown in one of my printed Skeletons); a full assurance of understanding (Col. 2:2), of faith (Heb. 10:22), and of hope (Heb. 6:11). The first relates to a clear view of revealed truth in all its parts; the second to the power and willingness of Christ to save to the uttermost all that come unto God by him; and the third (which is generally understood by the word *assurance*) to our own personal interest in Christ. This last may doubtless be enjoyed; but a person may possess saving faith without it, and even a full assurance of faith without it; he may be fully assured of Christ's power and willingness to save him, and yet not be assured that Christ has actually imparted salvation to him. The truth is, that these two kinds of assurance, namely, of faith and of hope, have respect to very different things; assurance of faith having respect only to the truth of God in his word, whilst assurance of hope is founded on the correspondence with that word: the one believes, that God will fulfil his promises to persons of a particular description; and the other, that we ourselves are of that very character to whom they are and shall be fulfilled. This latter, therefore, I say again, is not a duty, but a privilege; (an inestimable privilege no doubt); and it is certain that our Lord himself very highly commended the faith of the Canaanitish woman and others, who possessed the former assurance without one atom of the latter.

Charles Simeon, 1813 [384]

Love

The soul is led by a heavenly love and desire when once the beauty and glory of the Word of God has been perceived, he falls in love with his splendour and by this receives from him some dart and wound of love. For this Word is the image and brightness of the invisible God, the First Born of all creation, in whom all things were created, in heaven and on earth, visible and invisible (cf. Col. 1:15f.; Heb. 1:3). Therefore, if anyone has been able to hold in the breadth of his mind and to consider the glory and splendour of all those things created in him, he will be struck by their very beauty and transfixed by the magnificence of their brilliance or, as the prophet says, 'by the chosen arrow' (Is. 49:2). And he will receive from him the saving wound and will burn with the blessed fire of his love.

Origen, c. 240 [385]

*
**

If God is always being sought, when is he found? . . . Faith has already found him, but hope still seeks him. But love has found him through faith, and seeks to have him by sight, where he will then be found so as to satisfy us, and no longer to need our search . . . When we shall have seen him face to face as he is, will he still have to be sought, and to be sought without end, because to be loved without end? For we say to anyone present, 'I am not looking for you'; meaning, I do not like you. And thus he who is loved, is sought even when present, while there is constant love . . . Besides, he who loves anyone, even when he sees him, without ever being tired of him, wishes him ever to be present, that is, he always seeks his presence. And surely this is the sense of the words, *Seek his face evermore*; meaning that discovery should not terminate that seeking, by which love is testified, but with the increase of love the seeking of the discovered one should increase.

Augustine, 420 [386]

**

He, who is so great, loves us so much; he loves us freely, little and poor and worthless as we are. That is why I said in the beginning that measure of our love for God there should be none. For since love given to God is given to the infinite and measureless, what measure or what limit could it have?

He, the unmeasured and eternal God, he who is Love beyond all human ken, whose greatness knows no bounds, whose wisdom has no end, *loves*. Shall we, then, set a limit to our love for him? I will love thee, O Lord my strength, my stony rock and my defence, my Saviour, my one desire and love. My God, my helper, I will love thee with all the power thou hast given me; not worthily, for that can never be, but to the full of my capacity. Do what I will, I never can discharge my debt to thee, and I can love thee only according to the power that thou hast given me. But I will love thee more and more, as thou seest fit to give the further power; yet never, never, as thou shouldst be loved.

Bernard of Clairvaux, ?1130's [387]

**

The Lover said to his Beloved, 'You are all, and through all, and in all, and with all. I will have you wholly that I may have, and be, myself wholly.' The Beloved answered, 'You cannot have me wholly unless you are mine.' And the Lover said, 'Let me be yours wholly, and you be mine wholly.' The Beloved answered, 'So what will your son have, and your brother, and your father?' The Lover replied, 'You,

my Beloved, are so great a whole that you can abound and
be wholly of each one who gives himself wholly to you.'

Ramon Lull, 1283–4 [388]

**
*

I ask you, Lord Jesus,
   to develop in me, your lover,
   an immeasurable urge towards you,
   an affection that is unbounded,
   a longing that is unrestrained,
   a fervour that throws discretion to the winds!
The more worthwhile our love for you,
   all the more pressing does it become.
Reason cannot hold it in check,
   fear does not make it tremble,
   wise judgment does not temper it.

There is no one more blessed than he who dies because he
loves so much. No creature can love God too much.

Richard Rolle, 1343 [389]

**
*

The love of God the end of life

Since life in sorrow must be spent,
So be it – I am well content,
And meekly wait my last remove,
Seeking only growth in Love.

No bliss I seek, but to fulfil
In life, in death, thy lovely will;
No succours in my woes I want,
Save what thou art pleas'd to grant.

Our days are number'd, let us spare
Our anxious hearts a needless care:
'Tis thine, to number out our days;
Ours, to give them to thy praise.

Love is our only bus'ness here,
Love, simple, constant, and sincere;
O blessed days, thy servants see,
Spent, O Lord! in pleasing thee.

William Cowper, 1801 [390]

**

The Gospel offers a man life. Never offer men a thimbleful of Gospel. Do not offer them merely joy, or merely peace, or merely rest, or merely safety; tell them how Christ came to give men a more abundant life than they have, a life abundant in love, and therefore abundant in salvation for themselves, and large in enterprise for the alleviation and redemption of the world. Then only can the Gospel take hold of the whole of a man, body, soul, and spirit, and give to each part of his nature its exercise and reward. Many of the current Gospels are addressed only to a part of man's nature. They offer peace, not life; faith, not Love; justification, not regeneration. And men slip back again from such religion because it has never really held them. Their nature was not all in it. It offered no deeper and gladder life-current than the life that was lived before. Surely it stands to reason that only a fuller love can compete with the love of the world.

To love abundantly is to live abundantly, and to love for ever is to live for ever. Hence, eternal life is inextricably bound up with love.

Henry Drummond, 1890 [391]

**

Do not keep accounts with our Lord and say, 'I did him such an injury, therefore he owes me such a grudge. He cannot be on good terms with me because I have not paid him this or that; it would not be just otherwise'.

Go bankrupt! Let our Lord love you without justice! Say frankly, 'He loves me because I do not deserve it; that is the wonderful thing about him; and that is why I, in my turn, love him as well as I can without worrying whether I deserve to be allowed to love him. He loves me although I am not worthy; I love him without being worthy to love'.

I know no other way of loving God. Therefore burn your account books! You may say, 'I love him and yet I constantly offend him. How can these two things go together?' You actually ask me how these two things can go together in human nature, in this nature of ours which is continuously full of contradictions?

You will always offend God in some way; that is only one reason the more for making amends, both to yourself and to him, by loving him always and for evermore . . .

You want to compete with his affection before you have understood it; that is your mistake.

Come then! show a little deference to our Lord and allow him to go first. Let him love you a great deal, a very great deal, long before you have succeeded in loving him, even a little, as you would wish to love him.

Abbé Henri de Tourville, between 1881–1903 [392]

**

About one a.m. on Advent Sunday morning, I had a bad asthmatic attack. In my helplessness, I cried out to God to speak to me. I'm not very good at listening to God, but between one and three a.m. God spoke to me so powerfully and painfully that I have never felt so broken before him (and still do).

He showed me that all my preaching, writing and other ministry was absolutely *nothing* compared to my love-relationship with him. In fact, my sheer busyness had squeezed out the close intimacy I had know with him during the first few months of the year after my operation.

God also showed me that any 'love' for him meant *nothing* unless I was truly able to love from my heart my brother or sister in Christ. As the Lord put various names into my mind I began to write letters to about twelve people asking for forgiveness for hurting them, for still being inwardly angry against them — or whatever. It was the most painful pruning and purging I can remember in my entire Christian life. But fruitful! Already some replies to my letters have reduced me to tears.

David Watson, 1984 [393]

6
Crisis

'Can he have followed far/Who has no wound? No scar?'
wrote Amy Carmichael, and Christians who follow Christ
sooner or later recognise that they do so along the way of the
cross (Luke 8:23). Go back to the Old Testament, to Job, to
the Psalms in particular, and there is a whole literature of
crisis, a calling out to God from the depths. Where do these
crises come from, and what can we do about them?

One obvious source is our own disobedience or sinfulness
(and here the material overlaps with the holiness section of
'Progress' in particular). It may be that sensitivity to sin is
part of Christian growth; it may be that we need sharp
reminders of our total dependence on Christ's righteousness
to stop falling into a complacent reliance on a routine of
Christian observances in an increasingly unrepentant spirit.
But there is a danger that an echo of Paul's cry in Romans 7
– 'What a wretched man I am!' – is not followed by the
affirmation of Romans 8 – 'Those who are in Christ Jesus
are not condemned'. The resulting despair is a very different
kind of crisis, and its cure constant reflection on the loving,
forgiving nature of Christ. 'Up and out' of scrupulosity is
difficult, because solutions may seem to come from the
superficial, those who are strangers to much combat with
the Devil, as Bunyan put it. And there may be a more

difficult truth, that we are entering into a darkness which is God's. This transforming darkness, known to mystical writers as the cloud of unknowing, or the dark night of the soul, can be as painful as the result is glorious, as John of the Cross' image of the wood consumed by fire makes clear. Thomas Goodwin's title, *A Child of Light Walking in Darkness* (based on Isaiah 50:10) is appropriate here, as is his advice, an interesting mixture of be patient and be importunate – pray aggressively, remind God of the promises, and you may come out into the light again.

Suffering and healing can be similarly inscrutable; whether they transform, or, in some way, show the works of God (cf. John 9:3) isn't always clear to us before that moment foretold in Revelation when God will wipe away all tears. While all suffering seems to have some spiritual dimension the insights of medicine and psychiatry have their place, too. Some Christians have been called upon to endure persecution, even to martyrdom, and it is their witness which comes through most impressively in this section. What does come through from start to finish is that Christ has been there before, in his physical agony and his cry of spiritual dereliction on the cross. And where he has been, there is the promise of new birth.

Darkness and Struggle

Often enough when we approach the altar to pray our hearts are dry and lukewarm. But if we persevere, there comes an unexpected infusion of grace, our breast expands as it were, and our interior is filled with an overflowing love.

Bernard of Clairvaux, d. 1153 [394]

*
**

Sin is the sharpest scourge that any elect soul can be flogged with. It is the scourge which so reduces a man or woman and makes him loathsome in his own sight that it is not long before he thinks himself fit only to sink down to hell . . . until the touch of the Holy Spirit forces him to contrition, and turns his bitterness to the hope of God's mercy. Then he begins to heal his wounds, and to rouse his soul as it turns to the life of Holy Church. The Holy Spirit leads him on to confession, so that he deliberately reveals his sins in all their nakedness and reality, and admits with great sorrow and shame that he has befouled the fair image of God. . . .

Our courteous Lord does not want his servants to despair even if they fall frequently and grievously. Our falling does not stop his loving us. Peace and love are always at work in us, but we are not always in peace and love. But he wants us in this way to realize that he is the foundation of the whole of our life in love, and furthermore that he is our eternal protector, and mighty defender against our enemies who are so very fierce and wicked. And, alas, our need is all the greater since we give them every opportunity by our failures.

Julian of Norwich, 1393 [395]

A safe stronghold our God is still,
  A trusty shield and weapon;
He'll help us clear from all the ill
    That hath us now o'ertaken.
      The ancient prince of hell
      Hath risen with purpose fell;
      Strong mail of craft and power
      He weareth in his hour;
    On earth is not his fellow.

With force of arms we nothing can,
  Full soon were we down-ridden;
But for us fights the proper Man,
    Whom God himself hath bidden.
      Ask ye who is this same?
      Christ Jesus is his name,
      The Lord Sabaoth's Son;
      He, and no other one,
    Shall conquer in the battle.

And were this world all devils o'er,
  And watching to devour us,
We lay it not to heart so sore;
    Not they can overpower us.
      And let the prince of ill
      Look grim as e'er he will,
      He harms us not a whit;
      For why his doom is writ;
    A word shall quickly slay him.

God's Word, for all their craft and force,
  One moment will not linger,
But, spite of hell, shall have its course;
    'Tis written by his finger.
      And, though they take our life,
      Goods, honour, children, wife,
      Yet is their profit small;
      These things shall vanish all:
    The city of God remaineth.

Martin Luther, c. 1527 [396]

But let us, who are of the day, be sober, putting on the breastplate of faith and love, and for a helmet the hope of salvation. I Thess. 5:8.

Paul adds this in order that he may shake us the better out of our torpor. He calls us as it were to arms, to impress upon us that it is no time for sleep. He does not, indeed, mention war. But when he bids us to arm with a breastplate and a helmet, he is in fact calling us to warfare. It goes without saying that anyone who expects a surprise attack must rouse himself and keep watching. Having warned us to be watchful while we have the truth of the gospel for light, he now stirs us up with the argument that we have a battle to fight with the enemy, and that it is much too dangerous to be doing nothing. We know that soldiers, who may ordinarily be rather loose-living fellows, when they are near the enemy and in danger of being killed, avoid getting drunk or any other way of 'having fun' so that they may watch and be wary. So, since Satan is always breathing down our necks, and is ready and scheming to plunge us into a thousand perils, we ought to be no less watchful and on our guard.

Jean Calvin, 1540 [397]

**

O beloved reader, our weapons are not swords and spears, but patience, silence, and hope, and the Word of God. With these we must maintain our heavy warfare and fight our battle. Paul says, the weapons of our warfare are not carnal; but mighty through God. With these we intend and desire to storm the kingdom of the devil; and not with sword, spears, cannon, and coats of mail. For he esteemeth iron as straw, and brass as rotten wood. Thus may we with our Prince, Teacher, and Example Christ Jesus, raise the father against the son, and the son against the father, and may we cast down imagination and every high thing that exalteth itself against the knowledge of God, and bring into captivity every thought in obedience to Christ.

Menno Simons, 1552 [398]

Pardon me and pray for me, pray for me, I say. For I am sometimes so fearful, that I would creep into a mouse-hole; sometimes God doth visit me again with his comfort. So he cometh and goeth.

Hugh Latimer, 1556 [399]

*
**

For the sake of further clarity in this matter, we ought to note that this purgative and loving knowledge or divine light we are speaking of has the same effect on a soul that fire has on a log of wood. The soul is purged and prepared for union with the divine light just as the wood is prepared for transformation into the fire. Fire, when applied to wood, first dehumidifies it, dispelling all moisture and making it give off any water it contains. Then it gradually turns the wood black, makes it dark and ugly, and even causes it to emit a bad odour. By drying out the wood, the fire brings to light and expels all those ugly and dark accidents which are contrary to fire. Finally, by heating and enkindling it from without, the fire transforms the wood into itself and makes it as beautiful as it is itself. Once transformed, the wood no longer has any activity or passivity of its own, except for its weight and its quantity which is denser than the fire. For it possesses the properties and performs the actions of fire: it is dry and it dries; it is hot and it gives off heat; it is brilliant and it illumines; and it is also light, much lighter than before. It is the fire that produces all these properties in the wood.

Similarly, we should philosophize about this divine, loving fire of contemplation. Before transforming the soul, it purges it of all contrary qualities. It produces blackness and darkness and brings to the fore the soul's ugliness; thus the soul seems worse than before and unsightly and abominable. This divine purge stirs up all the foul and vicious humours of which the soul was never before aware; never did it realize there was so much evil in itself, since these humours were so deeply rooted. And now that they may be expelled and annihilated they are brought to light and seen clearly through the illumination of this dark light of divine contemplation. Although the soul is no worse than before, neither in itself nor in its relationship with God, it feels undoubtedly so bad as to be not only unworthy that God should see it but deserving of his abhorrence; in fact, it feels that God now does abhor it.

John of the Cross, 1583–4 [400]

*
**

Batter my heart, three personed God; for, you
As yet but knock, breathe, shine, and seek to mend;
That I may rise, and stand, o'erthrow me, and bend
Your force, to break, blow, burn and make me new.
I, like an usurped town, to another due,
Labour to admit you, but oh, to no end,
Reason your viceroy in me, me should defend,
But is captived, and proves weak or untrue.
Yet dearly'I love you, and would be loved fain,
But am betrothed unto your enemy,
Divorce me, untie, or break that knot again,
Take me to you, imprison me, for I
Except you enthral me, never shall be free,
Nor ever chaste, except you ravish me.

John Donne, c. 1609–11? [401]

*
**

All our life is a continual burden, yet we must not groan; a continual squeezing, yet we must not pant; and as in the tenderness of our childhood, we suffer, and yet are whipped if we cry, so we are complained of if we complain, and are made delinquents if we call the time ill. And that which adds weight to weight, and multiplies the sadness of this consideration, is this, that still the best men have had the most laid upon them. As soon as I hear God say, that he hath found *an upright man, that fears God, and eschews evil*, in the next lines I find a commission to Satan, to bring in Sabeans and Chaldeans upon his cattle, and servants, and fire and tempest upon his children and loathsome diseases upon himself. As soon as I hear God say, that he hath found *a man according to his own heart*, I see his sons ravish his daughters, and then murder one another, and then rebel against the father, and put him into straits for his life. As soon as I hear God testify of Christ at his baptism, *This is my beloved son in whom I am well pleased*, I find that son of his *led up by the Spirit, to be tempted of the Devil*. And after I hear God ratify the same testimony again, at his Transfiguration, (*This is my beloved Son, in whom I am well pleased*) I find that beloved son of his deserted, abandoned, and given over to Scribes, and Pharisees, and Publicans, and Herodians, and Priests, and soldiers, and people, and judges, and witnesses, and executioners, and he that was called the beloved Son of God, and made partaker of the glory of heaven, in this world, in his Transfiguration, is made now the sewer of all the corruption, of all the sins of this world, as no Son of God, but a mere man, as no man, but a contemptible worm. As though the greatest weakness in this world were man, and the greatest fault in man were to be good, man is more miserable than other creatures, and good men more miserable than any other men.

But then there is *Pondus Gloriae, an exceeding weight of eternal glory*, and that turns the scale; for as it makes all worldly prosperity as dung, so it makes all worldly adversity as feathers.

John Donne, 1625/6 [402]

**
**

No man can have his heart weaned from sin, divorced from sin which he hath been wedded to all his life, except he find another husband, in whom he may delight more . . . Now

319

if thou look on God as a judge, that will turn thee away from him, that makes thee continue still in sin; but when thou lookest upon one that loves thee, as one that favours thee, as one that is thy friend, that accepts thee, this will win thine heart, this will cause a man's heart to turn from sin.

John Preston, 1630 [403]

*
**

Some think, when they begin once to be troubled with the smoke of corruption more than they were before, therefore they are worse than they were. It is true, that corruptions appear now more than before, but they are less.

For, first, sin, the more it is seen the more it is hated, and thereupon is the less. Motes are in a room before the sun shines, but they then only appear.

Secondly, contraries, the nearer they are one to another, the sharper is the conflict betwixt them: now of all enemies the spirit and the flesh are nearest one to another, being both in the soul of a regenerate man, and in faculties of the soul, and in every action that springeth from those faculties, and therefore it is no marvel the soul, the seat of this battle, thus divided in itself, be as smoking flax.

Thirdly, the more grace, the more spiritual life, and the more spiritual life, the more antipathy to the contrary; whence none are so sensible of corruption, as those that have the most living souls.

Richard Sibbes, 1630 [404]

*
**

Christ's work, both in the church and in the hearts of Christians, often goeth backward that it may go the better forward. As seed roots in the ground in the winter time, but after comes better up, and the harder the winter the more flourishing the spring, so we learn to stand by falls, and get strength by weakness discovered – *virtutis custos infirmitas* – we take deeper root by shaking . . .

Let us assure ourselves that God's grace, even in this imperfect estate, is stronger than man's free will in the state of first perfection, being founded now in Christ, who, as he is the author, so will be 'the finisher, of our faith,' Heb. 12:2; we are under a more gracious covenant.

That which some say of faith rooted, *fides radicata*, that it continueth, but weak faith may come to nothing, seemeth to be crossed by this Scripture; for, as the strongest faith may be shaken, so the weakest where truth is, is so far rooted, that it will prevail. Weakness with watchfulness will stand out, when strength with too much confidence faileth. Weakness, with acknowledging of it, is the fittest seat and subject for God to perfect his strength in; for consciousness of our infirmities driveth us out of ourselves to him in whom our strength lieth.

Hereupon it followeth that weakness may stand with the assurance of salvation; the disciples, notwithstanding all their weaknesses, are bidden to rejoice, Luke 10:20, that their names are written in heaven. Failings, with conflict, in sanctification should not weaken the peace of our justification, and assurance of salvation. It mattereth not so much what ill is in us, as what good; not what corruptions, but how we stand affected to them; not what our particular failings be, so much as what is the thread and tenor of our lives; for Christ's mislike of that which is amiss in us, redounds not to the hatred of our persons, but to the victorious subduing of all our infirmities.

Some have, after conflict, wondered at the goodness of God, that so little and shaking faith should have upheld them in so great combats, when Satan had almost catched them. And, indeed, it is to be wondered how much a little grace will prevail with God for acceptance, and over our enemies for victory, if the heart be upright. Such is the goodness of our sweet Saviour, that he delighteth still to shew his strength in our weakness.

Richard Sibbes, 1630 [405]

*
**

One who truly fears God, and is obedient to him, may be in a condition of darkness, and have no light; and he may walk many days and years in that condition . . .

Wait upon God, thus trusting in his name, in the constant use of all ordinances and means of comfort. Waiting is indeed but an act of faith further stretched out. As an allegory is but a continued metaphor, so waiting is but a continuing to believe on God, and to look for help from him with submission, though he stays long ere he comes. Waiting is an act of faith resting on God; and an act of hope expecting help from him; an act of patience, the mind quietly contenting itself till God doth come; and of submission if he should not come.

And waiting thus, go on to use all the means of grace more diligently, more constantly, though thou findest a long while no good by them. Omit no ordinance God hath appointed for thy comfort and recovery. As in a long sickness, you still use means though many have failed; as the woman who had the bloody issue spent all upon physicians, in the use of means for her recovery. That trouble of mind doth only hurt you that drives you from the means. Therefore the devil endeavours nothing more than to keep such souls from the word, from good company, from the sacraments, from prayer, by objecting their unprofitableness unto them, and that all is in vain, and that you do but increase your condemnation.

But first, if thou learnest no other lesson in the use of the means but that thou art of thyself most unprofitable, and that unless God teacheth thee to profit no good is done, and so learnest to depend upon God in the ordinance; this is a great degree of profiting.

And, secondly, as when men are sick and eat, and cast up again, you use to say, yet take something down, for some strength is gotten, something remains in the stomach which keeps life and soul together: so I say here, though thou shouldest forget in a manner all thou hearest, seemest to reap no benefit by it, yet hear, for some secret strength is gotten by it. And as for increasing thy condemnation, know that utterly to neglect and despise the means is greater condemnation; and that to use the means would lessen thy condemnation. Therefore read, pray, meditate, hear, confer, receive the sacraments, forbear not these your appointed meals. Indeed when the body is sick ye use to forbear your appointed food, but when the soul is sick there is more need of them than ever. All these are both meat and medicine, food, physic, cordials, and all.

Thomas Goodwin, 1636 [406]

*
**

Afflictions are sweet preservatives to keep the saints from sin.

Thomas Brooks, 1652 [407]

*
**

It is impossible for that man to get the conquest of sin, that plays and sports with the occasions of sin. God will not remove the temptation, except you turn from the occasion. It is a just and righteous thing with God, that he should fall into the pit, that will adventure to dance upon the brink of the pit, and that he should be a slave to sin, that will not flee from the occasions of sin. As long as there is fuel in our hearts for a temptation, we cannot be secure. He that hath gunpowder about him had need keep far enough off from sparkles. To rush upon the occasions of sin, is both to tempt ourselves, and to tempt Satan to tempt our souls.

Thomas Brooks, 1652 [408]

***

Whatever ye are addicted to, the Tempter will come in that thing; and when he can trouble you, then he gets advantage over you, and then ye are gone. Stand still in that which is pure, after ye see yourselves; and then mercy comes in. After thou seest thy thoughts, and the temptation, do not think, but submit, and then power comes. Stand still in that which shows and discovers, and there doth strength immediately come. And stand still in the Light, and submit to it, and the other will be hushed and gone; and then content comes. And when temptations and troubles appear, sink down in that which is pure, and all will be hushed and fly away. And earthly reason will tell you what ye shall lose. Hearken not to that, but stand still in the Light, that shows them to you, and then strength comes from the Lord, and help, contrary to your expectation. When your thoughts are out abroad, then troubles move you; but come to stay your minds upon that Spirit, which was before the letter. Here ye learn to read the Scriptures aright. If ye do anything in your own wills, then ye tempt God; but stand still in the Power, which brings peace.

George Fox, 1652 [409]

***

Knowing God without knowing our own wretchedness makes for pride.

Knowing our own wretchedness without knowing God makes for despair.

Knowing Jesus Christ strikes the balance because he shows us both God and our own wretchedness.

324

Jesus is a God whom we can approach without pride and before whom we can humble ourselves without despair.

Blaise Pascal, 1658 [410]

*
**

As a father pities his child when it is sick, and in the rage and reveries of a fever, though it even utter reproachful words against himself, shall not our dearest Father both forgive and pity those thoughts in any child of his, that arise not from any wilful hatred of him, but are kindled in hell within them? . . .

In the meantime, when these assaults come thickest and violentest upon you, throw yourself down at his footstool and say O God, Father of mercies, save me from this hell within me. . . . Thus, or in whatever frame your soul shall be carried to vent itself into his bosom, be sure your words, yea your silent sighs and breathings shall not be lost, but shall have a most powerful voice and ascend into his ear and shall return to you with messages of peace and love in due time.

Robert Leighton, late 17th century [411]

*
**

I do not feel the wrath of God abiding on me, nor can I believe it does; and yet this is the mystery, I seem never to have loved God. I never did. Therefore I never believed in the Christian sense of the word. Therefore I am only an honest heathen, a proselyte of the temple. And yet to be so employed of God and so hedged in that I can neither go forward nor backward. Surely there was never such an instance before, from the beginning of the world. I have no direct witness. I cannot even say that I am a child of God.

John Wesley, c. 1720s [412]

Wrestling Jacob

Come, O thou Traveller unknown,
  Whom still I hold, but cannot see!
My company before is gone,
  And I am left alone with thee;
With thee all night I mean to stay,
And wrestle till the break of day.

I need not tell thee who I am,
  My misery or sin declare;
Thyself hast called me by my name,
  Look on thy hands, and read it there.
But who, I ask thee, who art thou?
Tell me thy name, and tell me now.

In vain thou strugglest to get free,
  I never will unloose my hold;
Art thou the Man that died for me?
  The secret of thy love unfold:
Wrestling, I will not let thee go
Till I thy name, thy nature know.

Wilt thou not yet to me reveal
  Thy new, unutterable name?
Tell me, I still beseech thee, tell;
  To know it now resolved I am:
Wrestling, I will not let thee go
Till I thy name, thy nature know.

What though my shrinking flesh complain
  And murmur to contend so long?
I rise superior to my pain:
  When I am weak, then I am strong;
And when my all of strength shall fail
I shall with the God-man prevail.

Yield to me now – for I am weak,
  But confident in self-despair!
Speak to my heart, in blessings speak,
  Be conquered by my instant prayer:
Speak, or thou never hence shalt move,
And tell me if thy name is *LOVE*.

'Tis Love! 'Tis Love! Thou diedst for me;
  I hear thy whisper in my heart.
The morning breaks, the shadows flee,
  Pure Universal Love thou art:
To me, to all, thy bowels move –
Thy nature, and thy name, is *LOVE*.

My prayer hath power with God; the grace
  Unspeakable I now receive;
Through faith I see thee face to face;
  I see thee face to face, and live!
In vain I have not wept and strove –
Thy nature, and thy name is *LOVE*.

I know thee, Saviour, who thou art –
  Jesus, the feeble sinner's friend;
Nor wilt thou with the night depart,
  But stay, and love me to the end:
Thy mercies never shall remove,
Thy nature, and thy name, is *LOVE*.

The Sun of Righteousness on me
  Hath rose with healing in his wings;
Withered my nature's strength; from thee
  My soul its life and succour brings;
My help is all laid up above:
Thy nature, and thy name, is *LOVE*.

Contented now upon my thigh
   I halt, till life's short journey end;
All helplessness, all weakness, I
   On thee alone for strength depend;
Nor have I power from thee to move:
Thy nature, and thy name, is *LOVE*.

Lame as I am, I take the prey,
   Hell, earth, and sin with ease o'ercome;
I leap for joy, pursue my way,
   And as a bounding heart fly home,
Through all eternity to prove,
Thy nature, and thy name, is *LOVE*.

Charles Wesley, 1742 [413]

*
**

April 25, 1752

O Lord, our heavenly Father, almighty and most merciful God, in whose hands are life and death, who givest and takest away, castest down and raisest up, look with mercy on the affliction of thy unworthy servant, turn away thine anger from me, and speak peace to my troubled soul. Grant me the assistance and comfort of thy Holy Spirit, that I may remember with thankfulness the blessings so long enjoyed by me in the society of my departed wife make me so to think on her precepts and example, that I may imitate whatever was in her life acceptable in thy sight, and avoid all by which she offended thee. Forgive me, O merciful Lord, all my sins, and enable me to begin and perfect that reformation which I promised her, and to persevere in that resolution, which she implored thee to continue, in the purposes which I recorded in thy sight, when she lay dead before me, in obedience to thy laws, and faith in thy word. And now, O Lord, release me from my sorrow, fill me with just hopes, true faith, and holy consolations, and enable me to do my duty in that state of life to which thou hast been pleased to call me, without disturbance from fruitless grief, or tumultuous imaginations; that in all my thoughts, words, and actions, I may glorify thy Holy Name, and finally obtain, what I hope thou hast granted to thy departed servant, everlasting joy and felicity, through our Lord Jesus Christ. Amen.

Easter Eve, 1761

Since the communion of last Easter, I have led a life so dissipated and useless, and my terrors and perplexities have so much increased, that I am under great depression and discouragement; yet I purpose to present myself before God tomorrow, with humble hope that he will not break the bruised reed.

Samuel Johnson [414]

**

The foulest stain and highest absurdity in our nature is pride. And yet this base hedgehog so rolls himself up in his bristly coat, we can seldom get a sight of his claws. It is the root of unbelief. Men cannot submit to the righteousness of Christ, and pride cleaves to them like a pitched shirt to the skin, or like leprosy to the wall. No sharp culture of ploughing and harrowing will clear the ground of it. The foul weed will be sure to spring up again with the next kindly rain. This diabolical sin has brought more scourges on my back than anything else; and it is of so insinuating a nature, that I know not how to part with it. I hate it, and love it; I quarrel with it, and embrace it; I dread it, and yet suffer it to lie in my bosom. It pleads a right, through the fall, to be a tenant for life; and has such a wonderful appetite, that it can feed kindly both on grace and garbage – will be as warm and snug in a cloister as a palace, and be as much delighted with a fine prayer as a foul oath.

John Berridge, 1771 [415]

I would not be the sport and prey of wild, vain, foolish, and worse imaginations; but this evil is present with me: my heart is like a highway, like a city without walls or gates. Nothing so false, so frivolous, so absurd, so impossible, or so horrid, but it can obtain access, and that at any time, or in any place: neither the study, the pulpit, or even the Lord's table, exempt me from their intrusion. I sometimes compare my words to the treble of an instrument, which my thoughts accompany with a kind of base, or rather anti-base, in which every rule of harmony is broken, every possible combination of discord and confusion is introduced, utterly inconsistent with, and contradictory to, the intended melody. Ah! what music would my praying and preaching often make in the ears of the Lord of Hosts, if he listened to them as they are mine only! By men, the upper part only (if I may so speak) is heard; and small cause there is for self-gratulation, if they should happen to commend, when conscience tells me they would be struck with astonishment and abhorrence could they hear the whole.

John Newton, 1772 [416]

***
****

By enduring temptation, you, as a living member of the body of Christ, have the honour of being conformed to your head. He suffered, being tempted; and because he loves you, he calls you to a participation of his sufferings, and to taste of his cup; not the cup of the wrath of God; this he drank alone, and he drank it all. But in affliction he allows his people to have fellowship with him; thus they fill up the measure of his sufferings, and can say, As he was, so are we in the world.

John Newton, 1774 [417]

When a man turns his back upon someone and walks away, it is so easy to see that he walks away, but when a man hits upon a method of turning his face towards the one he is walking away from, hits upon a method of walking backwards while with appearance and glance and salutations he greets the person, giving assurances again and again that he is coming immediately, or incessantly saying 'Here I am' – although he gets farther and farther away by walking backwards – then it is not so easy to become aware. And so it is with the one who, rich in good intentions and quick to promise, retreats backwards farther and farther from the good. With the help of intentions and promises he maintains an orientation towards the good, he is turned towards the good, and with this orientation towards the good he moves backwards farther and farther away from it. With every renewed intention and promise it seems as if he takes a step forward, and yet he not only remains standing still but really takes a step backward. The intention taken in vain, the unfulfilled promise leaves a residue of despondency, dejection, which perhaps soon again flares up in more passionate protestations of intention, which leave behind only greater languor. As a drunkard constantly requires stronger and stronger stimulation – in order to become intoxicated, likewise the one who has fallen into intentions and promises constantly requires more and more stimulation – in order to walk backward.

Søren Kierkegaard, 1847 [418]

*
**

In case one were to think of a house, consisting of cellar, ground-floor and *premier étage*, so tenanted, or rather so arranged, that it was planned for a distinction of rank between the dwellers on the several floors; and in case one were to make a comparison between such a house and what it is to be a man – then unfortunately this is the sorry and

331

ludicrous condition of the majority of men, that in their own house they prefer to live in the cellar. The soulish-bodily synthesis in every man is planned with a view to being spirit, such is the building; but the man prefers to dwell in the cellar, that is, in the determinants of sensuousness. And not only does he prefer to dwell in the cellar; no, he loves that to such a degree that he becomes furious if anyone would propose to him to occupy the *bel étage* which stands empty at his disposition – for in fact he is dwelling in his own house.

Søren Kierkegaard, 1849 [419]

***

All – Nothing

God creates everything out of nothing – and everything which God is to use he first reduces to nothing.

Søren Kierkegaard, 1854 [420]

***

No worst, there is none. Pitched past pitch of grief,
More pangs will, schooled at forepangs, wilder wring.
Comforter, where, where is your comforting?
Mary, mother of us, where is your relief?
My cries heave, herds-long; huddle in a main, a chief-
woe, world-sorrow; on an age-old anvil wince and sing –
Then lull, then leave off. Fury had shrieked 'No ling-
ering! Let me be fell: force I must be brief'.
O the mind, mind has mountains; cliffs of fall
Frightful, sheer, no-man-fathomed. Hold them cheap
May who ne'er hung there. Nor does long our small
Durance deal with that steep or deep. Here! creep,
Wretch, under a comfort serves in a whirlwind: all
Life death does end and each day dies with sleep.

Gerard Manley Hopkins, 1885 [421]

332

Those who come to the Lord with empty hands get them filled from his hand, and the hands of the Lord are marked with the nails of Calvary.

Bishop Taylor Smith, 1926 [422]

**

> Hast thou no scar?
> No hidden scar on foot, or side, or hand?
> I hear thee sung as mighty in the land,
> I hear them hail thy brightest ascendant star:
> Hast thou no scar?
>
> Hast thou no wound?
> Yet, I was wounded by the archers, spent,
> Leaned me against the tree to die, and rent
> By ravening beasts that compassed me, I swooned:
> Hast thou no wound?
>
> No wound? No scar?
> Yes, as the master shall the servant be.
> And pierced are the feet that follow me;
> But thine are whole. Can he have followed far
> Who has no wound? No scar?

Amy Carmichael, 1936 [423]

**

When we hit a nail with a hammer, the whole of the shock received by the large head of the nail passes into the point without any of it being lost, although it is only a point. If the hammer and the head of the nail were infinitely big it would be just the same. The point of the nail would transmit this infinite shock at the point to which it was applied.

Extreme affliction, which means physical pain, distress of soul and social degradation, all at the same time, constitutes the nail. The point is applied at the very centre of the soul. The head of the nail is all the necessity which spreads throughout the totality of space and time.

Affliction is a marvel of divine technique. It is a simple and ingenious device which introduces into the soul of a finite creature the immensity of force, blind, brutal and cold. The infinite distance which separates God from the creature is entirely concentrated into one point to pierce the soul in its centre.

The man to whom such a thing happens has no part in the operation. He struggles like a butterfly which is pinned alive into an album. But through all the horror he can continue to want to love. There is nothing impossible in that, no obstacle, one might almost say no difficulty. For the greatest suffering, so long as it does not cause fainting, does not touch the part of the soul which consents to a right direction.

It is only necessary to know that love is a direction and not a state of the soul. If one is unaware of this, one falls into despair at the first onslaught of affliction.

He whose soul remains ever turned in the direction of God while the nail pierces it, finds himself nailed on to the very centre of the universe. It is the true centre, it is not in the middle, it is beyond space and time, it is God. In a dimension which does not belong to space, which is not time, which is indeed quite a different dimension, this nail has pierced a hole through all creation, through the thickness of the screen which separates the soul from God.

Simone Weil, 1942 [424]

*
**

God marched on to victory in those dark days. How many were praying for me I little realised. He began to show me something of what he was doing. I recall with great clarity sitting down in the corner of my room and following Jacob over the brook Jabbok in my mind's eye. The struggle of the angel with Jacob as a man walking in the flesh portrayed my state so perfectly. He had touched me in the seat of my natural strength and now, broken and shattered through solitary confinement with everything gone, my work, my liberty, my Bible, and now it seemed life itself, I could only cling to him for his blessing. I would no doubt never be the same again. Then like a shaft of light in the mind, the relevance of Jacob's act of faith in Hebrews, where he is seen leaning on his staff in worship, to the conflict with the representative of the Camp of God, flashed into my mind. What does it matter if I come up from the waters limping? What does it matter if I am never the same again, provided my name is Israel? Then as a prince with God, having no confidence in the flesh, will I lean on my staff for my lameness and worship 'til the day dawn and the shadows flee away. Let that be my highest and final act of faith towards God my Strength and my Redeemer, and I remembered that God's Word said that, as Jacob passed over Penuel, the sun rose upon him. So after this I viewed everything as walking into the dawning, going on into the golden day-break and the morning without a cloud.

Geoffrey Bull, 1951 [425]

**
*

One difficult element in [the] disease of scrupulosity is that it confuses the mind, making it almost impossible to see things as they really are. Anxious introspection leads such people to believe that they have committed some sin, at least in thought, for which they suffer agonies of self-reproach. Very often these anxieties have no basis in fact; they are simply spectres of the mind, without reality. It is not until these spectres have been eliminated that such people can begin to see their real sins and imperfections, which they can then face quietly, and in true penitence, without being plunged into despair. For now they know that God is greater than all their sin; and they are able to turn away from themselves to God, in his love and mercy, and then to the needs of other people. The one thing to do is to turn away from useless introspection, up, and out, into the fresh air of God's loving and gracious Presence, till all our fears are blotted out in his embrace.

Olive Wyon, 1962 [426]

*
**

Dread, an unhallowed and horrible thing in itself, can become holy dread. The safe and proper way to encounter and overcome the dread within us is not to fit out an expedition to journey into the interior. Those who do enter their own 'darkest Africa' this way, are apt to lose themselves in its jungles. The Christian does not enter upon this, the hardest task of his life, at the place and time of his own choosing. He waits for God. To know that he has a journey to make which will threaten his peace, overcome his resistances and disturb his demons cannot be learnt too early in adult life. But the purpose of the Christian journey is not prompted by an introverted curiosity. It is not the cult of a fuller personality. It is obedience to God. The Christian has no particular interest in the symbolic fauna of the dark valley, of the wilderness, or of the deep sea of the unconscious. He encounters them as he encounters the Cross, in the course of a journey, the object of which is beyond all these things. He has to pass through them, or they through him, for they are now God's purgatives. The soul becomes cleaner and clearer for having passed through them. To follow Christ, the Lamb of God, wherever he goes, is to be attacked by the wolves. This is simply the nature of the case as it was for Jesus and as it will be for the Christian. To obey the living Truth when every fibre of one's nature protests is to enter a mental defile. All the more painful decisions of life involve our dying to at least one aspect of our mental defences.

Frank Lake, 1966 [427]

Paradoxes

O CHANGELESS GOD,
Under the conviction of thy Spirit I learn that
   the more I do, the worse I am,
   the more I know, the less I know,
   the more holiness I have, the more sinful I am,
   the more I love, the more there is to love.
     O wretched man that I am!

O Lord,
   I have a wild heart,
     and cannot stand before thee;
I am like a bird before a man.
How little I love thy truth and ways!
I neglect prayer,
   by thinking I have prayed enough and earnestly,
   by knowing thou hast saved my soul.
Of all hypocrites, grant that I may not be an evangelical
     hypocrite,
   who sins more safely because grace abounds,
   who tells his lusts that Christ's blood cleanseth them,
   who reasons that God cannot cast him into hell, for he
     is saved,
   who loves evangelical preaching, churches, Christians,
     but lives unholily.
My mind is a bucket without a bottom,
   with no spiritual understanding,
   no desire for the Lord's Day,
   ever learning but never reaching the truth,
   always at the gospel-well but never holding water.
My conscience is without conviction or contrition,
   with nothing to repent of.
My will is without power of decision or resolution.
   My heart is without affection, and full of leaks.
My memory has no retention,
   so I forget easily the lessons learned,

and thy truths seep away.
Give me a broken heart that yet carries home the water
   of grace.

Arthur Bennett, 1975 [428]

*
**

It was granted me to carry away from my prison years on
my bent back, which nearly broke beneath its load, this
essential experience: *how* a human being becomes evil and
how good. In the intoxication of youthful successes I had felt
myself to be infallible, and I was therefore cruel. In the
surfeit of power I was a murderer, and an oppressor. In my
most evil moments I was convinced that I was doing good,
and I was well supplied with systematic arguments. And it
was only when I lay there on rotting prison straw that I
sensed within myself the first stirrings of good. Gradually it
was disclosed to me that the line separating good and evil
passes not through states, nor between classes, nor between
political parties either – but right through every human
heart – and through all human hearts. This line shifts. Inside
us, it oscillates with the years. And even within hearts
overwhelmed by evil, one small bridgehead of good is
retained. And even in the best of all hearts there remains . . .
an unuprooted small corner of evil.

Since then I have come to understand the truth of all the
religions of the world: They struggle with the *evil inside a
human being* (inside every human being). It is impossible to
expel evil from the world in its entirety, but it is possible to
constrict it within each person.

And since that time I have come to understand the
falsehood of all the revolutions in history: They destroy
only *those carriers* of evil contemporary with them (and also
fail, out of haste, to discriminate the carriers of good as
well). And they then take to themselves as their heritage the

actual evil itself, magnified still more . . .

And that is why I turn back to the years of my imprisonment and say, sometimes to the astonishment of those about me: *'Bless you, prison!'* . . .

I nourished my soul there, and I say without hesitation: *'Bless you, prison,* for having been in my life!'

(And from beyond the grave come replies: It is very well for you to say that – when you came out of it alive!)

Alexander Solzhenitsyn, 1975 [429]

*
**

Like the vast army of the beast, the small army, which seems so ludicrous to Satan, also marches under a standard that is indicative of its weapons. On this standard a symbol can be seen bearing the opposite characteristics of the beast – the image of the Lamb! In contrast to the beast, whose appearance is terrible and frightening, the Lamb's appearance is heart-moving. He is wounded, and from his wounds blood is flowing. He lies there, surrendered to all the suffering and to all the malice that others vent on him, the innocent Lamb. He sheds his blood for others, whereas the beast sheds the blood of all his victims, whom he crushes with his teeth of iron. The Lamb of God, who suffers for the wickedness of man, gazes lovingly at his tormentors and lets himself be slain for their sakes. He loves the sons of men. This sacrificial love, exemplified by Jesus, is the banner of victory under which the army of the Lamb advances as it fights to gain the victory for him.

Basilea Schlink, 1976 [430]

I've Heard

I've heard
that Saint Thomas
recommended three ways
to combat melancholy
sleeping
bathing
and study of the sufferings of Christ

I've noticed
that my friends advise
in such cases
sleeping with someone
drinking
and study of one's own suffering

I imagine
other of my friends
if I could ask them
would recommend
watchfulness
work
and study of a world map
pinpointing illiteracy
and manufacturers of arms

But these friends
whose advice could help
set me right
live far away
behind walls

Dorothee Sölle, 1979 [431]

Suffering and Healing

Be comforted then, for God leads into hell and out again; he makes us sad and joyful again; he gives death and also life, and after great storms he makes the sun shine again. Therefore wait patiently for the redemption of your bodies, and do not grow faint or weary in the race. Do not look back either, but see to it that the love in your hearts does not grow cold and die. Do not be ashamed of the bonds and suffering of Christ; rejoice in them with your whole heart. You know that on this earth you are not promised anything but suffering and death, fear and need, and that the godless will persecute, torment, and dishonour you. This is the true sign of all God's faithful children; it is the sign of Christ, of the Son of Man and all his members. This sign will appear at the end-time too, according to the Word of the Lord; cross and tribulation are very fitting for all God's children. They are an honour in the sight of God the Most High and of all the believers, a glory and a garland of joy before him. Christ the Lord had to suffer, and so did all the patriarchs and prophets and disciples, indeed, all the chosen from the beginning of the world.

If such things befall us for the sake of truth, we should remember what this means; we are not enemies of God but rather his friends and children. For the Lord himself says, 'I discipline those whom I love.' Every son whom the Father receives he chastises; he will not spoil him. But those who will not accept this discipline are not children of God but of the Babylonian harlot. It is written, 'Happy are those who suffer the chastisement of the Lord.' Throughout Scripture, those who stand the test and remain steadfast are called blessed by the Holy Spirit and given high praise before God. 'Blessed are they who mourn, for they shall be comforted.'

This means those who for the Lord's sake bear sadness and grief and those who are persecuted for the sake of truth, for theirs is the Kingdom of Heaven. 'Blessed are you when men revile you on my account; rejoice and be glad, for great is your reward in Heaven, for in the same way men persecuted the holy prophets before you.' It is as if Christ were saying: 'By this you shall clearly recognize that you are made holy and are truly pleasing to God.'

Jakob Hutter, 1534 [432]

***

Ten meditations for the sick

1 That by afflictions, God may not only correct our sins past: but also work in us, a deeper loathing of our natural corruption; and so prevent us from falling into many other sins, which otherwise we would commit . . .

2 God sendeth affliction, to seal unto us our adoption: for every child whom God loveth he correcteth . . .

3 God sendeth affliction, to wean our hearts, from too much loving this world and worldly vanities: and to cause us the more earnestly to desire and long for eternal life . . .

4 By affliction and sickness, God exerciseth his children, and the graces which he bestoweth upon them. He refineth, and trieth their faith, as the goldsmith doth his gold, in the furnace, to make it shine more glistering, and bright . . .

5 God sendeth affliction, to demonstrate unto the world, the trueness of his children's love and service. Every hypocrite will serve God, whilst he prospereth and blesseth him . . . but who (save his loving child) will love and serve him in adversity, when God seemeth to be angry and displeased with him?

6 Sanctified affliction, is a singular help to further our true conversion: and to drive us home by repentance to our heavenly Father . . .

7 Afflictions work in us pity and compassion towards our fellow-brethren, that be in distress and misery: whereby we learn to have a fellow-feeling of their calamities; and to condole their estate, as if we suffered with them. And for this cause Christ himself would suffer . . .

8 God useth our sicknesses and afflictions, as means and examples, both to manifest unto others the faith and virtues which he hath bestowed upon us; as also to strengthen those who have not received so great a measure of faith as we . . .

9 By afflictions God makes us conformable to the Image of Christ his Son, who being the captain of our salvation, was made perfect through sufferings . . .

10 Lastly, that the godly may be humbled in respect of their own state and misery: and God glorified by delivering them out of their trials and afflictions, when we call upon him for his help and succour.

Lewis Bayly, 1613 [433]

*
**

Hymn to God my God, in my Sickness

Since I am coming to that holy room,
   Where, with thy choir of saints for evermore,
I shall be made thy music; as I come
    I tune the instrument here at the door,
    And what I must do then, think here before.

Whilst my physicians by their love are grown
   Cosmographers, and I their map, who lie
Flat on this bed, that by them may be shown
    That this is my south-west discovery
    Per fretum febris, by these straits to die,

I joy, that in these straits, I see my west;
   For, though their currents yield return to none,
What shall my west hurt me? As west and east
   In all flat maps (and I am one) are one,
   So death doth touch the resurrection.

Is the Pacific Sea my home? Or are
   The eastern riches? Is Jerusalem?
Anyan, and Magellan, and Gibraltar,
   All straits, and none but straits, are ways to them,
   Whether where Japhet dwelt, or Cham, or Shem.

We think that Paradise and Calvary,
   Christ's Cross, and Adam's tree, stood in one place;
Look Lord, and find both Adams met in me;
   As the first Adam's sweat surrounds my face,
   May the last Adam's blood my soul embrace.

So, in his purple wrapped receive me Lord,
   By these his thorns give me his other crown;
And as to others' souls I preached thy word,
   Be this my text, my sermon to mine own,
   Therefore that he may raise the Lord throws down.

John Donne, 1623? [434]

      *
     **

God will have low voices, as well as high; God will be
glorified *de profundis*, as well as *in excelsis*; God will have his
tribute of praise out of our adversity, as well as out of our
prosperity . . . even in the depth of any spiritual night, in
the shadow of death, in the midnight of afflictions and
tribulations, God brings light out of darkness, and gives his
saints occasions of glorifying him, not only in the dark
(though it be dark) but from the dark (because it is dark).
This is a way unconceivable by any, unexpressible to any,
but those who have felt that manner of God's proceeding in
themselves, that be the night what night it will, be the

oppression of what extension, or of what duration it can, all this retards not their zeal to God's service; nay, they see God better in the dark, than they did in the light; their tribulation hath brought them to a nearer distance to God, and God to a clearer manifestation to them.

John Donne, 1627 [435]

*
**

Oh, what owe I to the file, to the hammer, to the furnace of my Lord Jesus! who hath now let me see how good the wheat of Christ is, that goeth through his mill, and his oven, to be made bread for his own table. Grace tried is better than grace, and it is more than grace; it is glory in its infancy. I now see that godliness is more than the outside, and this world's passments and their buskings. Who knoweth the truth of grace without a trial? Oh, how little getteth Christ of us, but that which he winneth (to speak so) with much toil and pains! And how soon would faith freeze without a cross! How many dumb crosses have been laid upon my back, that had never a tongue to speak the sweetness of Christ, as this hath! When Christ blesseth his own crosses with a tongue, they breathe out Christ's love, wisdom, kindness, and care of us. Why should I start at the plough of my Lord, that maketh deep furrows on my soul? I know that he is no idle husbandman, he purposeth a crop. O that this white, withered lea-ground were made fertile to bear a crop for him, by whom it is so painfully dressed; and that this fallow-ground were broken up! Why was I (a fool!) grieved that he put his garland and his rose upon my head – the glory and honour of his faithful witnesses? I desire now to make no more pleas with Christ. Verily he hath not put me to a loss by what I suffer; he oweth me nothing; for in my bonds how sweet and comfortable have the thoughts of him been to me, wherein I find a sufficient recompense of reward!

Samuel Rutherford, 1637 [436]

Leave God to order all thy ways,
    And hope in him what'er betide,
Thou'lt find him in the evil days
    Thy all-sufficient strength and guide;
Who trusts in God's unchanging love,
Builds on the rock that nought can move.

What can these anxious cares avail,
    These never-ceasing moans and sighs?
What can it help us to bewail
    Each painful moment as it flies?
Our cross and trials do but press
The heavier for our bitterness.

Only thy restless heart keep still,
    And wait in cheerful hope; content
To take whate'er his gracious will,
    His all-discerning love hath sent.
Doubt not our inmost wants are known
To him who chose us for his own.

He knows when joyful hours are best,
    He sends them as he sees it meet;
When thou hast borne the fiery test,
    And art made free from all deceit,
He comes to thee all unaware,
And makes thee own his loving care.

Nor, in the heat of pain and strife,
    Think God hath cast thee off unheard,
And that the man, whose prosperous life
    Thou enviest, is of him preferr'd.
Time passes and much change doth bring,
And sets a bound to everything.

All are alike before his face;
    'Tis easy to our God most high
To make the rich man poor and base,
    To give the poor man wealth and joy.

True wonders still by him are wrought,
Who setteth up, and brings to nought.

Sing, pray, and swerve not from his ways,
   But do thine own part faithfully,
Trust his rich promises of grace,
   So shall they be fulfill'd in thee;
God never yet forsook at need
The soul that trusted him indeed.

Georg Neumarck, 1657, tr. C. Winkworth 1855 [437]

**

Imagine hidden in a simpler exterior a secret receptacle wherein the most precious treasure is deposited – there is a spring which has to be pressed, but the spring is hidden, and the pressure must have a certain strength, so that an accidental pressure would not be sufficient – so likewise is the hope of eternity hidden in man's inmost parts, and affliction is the pressure. When it presses the hidden spring, and strongly enough, then the contents appear in all their glory.

Søren Kierkegaard, 1848 [438]

**

Such is the mercy of God that he will hold his children in the consuming fire of his distance until they pay the uttermost farthing, until they drop the purse of selfishness with all the dross that is in it, and rush home to the Father and the Son and the many brethren – rush inside the centre of the life-giving fire whose outer circles burn.

George MacDonald, 1889 [439]

God has created the heavens and the earth,
None is mightier than he.
God will end the conflict of these days.
Come quickly, let us pray.
We are following thee.
Someone wants to inflict evil on us.
Our God, Jesus, our Brother,
Jesus, snatch us from misery.
Come, Jesus, help us here on earth.
We are listening to thee.
For our enemies we are performing all the labour
They demand of us.
But they do not see the truth about our cause [*a reference
    to Kimbanguism*].
Our Father and Mother, we are obedient.
If conflict arises
Then we shall resist with our prayers.
Jesus was a prisoner,
Jesus was smitten.
They are smiting us, too,
We, the blacks, are prisoners.
The whites are free.
The enemy has snatched from us the staff [*the sign of
    prophetic power, the prophet himself*].
All kinds of suffering befall us.
We are afflicted, our tears flow.
Come, help us, Holy Spirit,
Come, come, come, help us!
We are all following thee.
Blacks and whites are praying,
And we do not know the day of thy Return.

Kimbanguist Hymn, 1922-5 [440]

It is infinitely easier to suffer in obedience to a human command than to accept suffering as free, responsible men. It is infinitely easier to suffer with others than to suffer alone. It is infinitely easier to suffer as public heroes than to suffer apart and in ignominy. It is infinitely easier to suffer physical death than to endure spiritual suffering. Christ suffered as a free man alone, apart and in ignominy, in body and spirit, and since that day many Christians have suffered with him.

Dietrich Bonhoeffer, 1942 [441]

**

O Lord,
remember not only the men and women of goodwill,
but also those of ill will.
But do not only remember the suffering they have
    inflicted on us,
remember the fruits we bought thanks to this suffering,
our comradeship, our loyalty, our humility,
the courage, the generosity,
the greatness of heart which has grown out of all this.
And when they come to judgement
let all the fruits that we have borne
be their forgiveness.   AMEN   AMEN   AMEN

Written on a piece of wrapping paper near the body of a dead child in Ravensbrück where 92,000 women and children died, 1945 [442]

**

Consolation in trouble

I made a record of my experience. I have copied it for you:
    As I beheld him in his silent majesty hanging upon his Cross with the eyes of my soul, I saw in his gaze upon this

world from his place of pain that there was no smallest trace of reproach, complaint, or blame, but only unutterable overwhelming love.

I saw that his love was our judgement; that as the eye must quail before the light of the sun because of the exceeding brightness of that light, so the soul must quail before his love because of the exceeding splendour of that love; and that that love was the greatest of all forces, the perfection of all power.

Then there came to me three distinct messages. The first *to all the world*: his love went forth from him in silent power but his silence said, with greater clearness than any spoken words, 'Your sin has never lessened my love; here on the Cross I love you with an everlasting love.'

The second was *to all sufferers*: 'I am God,' he said, 'Suffering is not natural to me; as God I cannot suffer, but when I gave to certain of my creatures free wills and they admitted selfishness and sin into my universe, then of necessity there followed suffering, and suffering can only leave my universe when sin has departed from it. But when I saw my creatures suffering, I took upon me a human nature that I might make their suffering my suffering. All the suffering of the world is my suffering; I have made it mine in love; they that love me may make my suffering theirs.'

The third was *to all the disillusioned, disappointed, bereaved, and out of heart*: 'Behold me,' he said, 'Here am I dying in the dark, and I came to bring light to the world. I am dying at the hands of hate, and I came to bring love to the world. Death is closing in upon me, and I came to bring life to the world. But I remain true to my faith; dying in the dark I believe in the Light; killed by hate I trust Love; with death closing in upon me I believe in Life; on the third day I shall rise again. Do you then cling to your ideals; in any darkness still trust the Light, in any hatred still trust Love, and be sure that, though all consciousness be slipping from you and you yourself seem to be sinking into a void, eternal Life is yours.'

So the message was given, and the silence was full of peace.

Father Andrew, 1945 [443]

*
**

Jesus did not come to explain suffering nor to take it away: he came to fill it with his presence.

Paul Claudel, d. 1955 [444]

*
**

The Holy Spirit, who is the giver of the gift of healing, simply cannot be circumscribed within the walls of a church. He cannot abide it and he will not, but will dim his power in any church that dares to claim him as the exclusive tool of the clergy. For indeed the healing Spirit of God is in the wind and the sun and in the little creeping things upon the earth and is most certainly available to the one who prays with faith, be he minister or layman, man, woman or child.

Agnes Sanford, 1966 [445]

*
**

The paradox of evil is this, however, that the providence of God uses the intense suffering it permits to perfect the Son himself and to perfect all those who, by holy baptism, have been made sons. The fiery baptism of pain becomes, by Christ's bearing of it and deliberately going under it on the Cross, a resource which God uses when, by the Holy Spirit, he draws alongside all those who are undergoing the same affliction. The Holy Spirit, the hovering Dove over the still waters in the baptism of Jordan and at every font, becomes the groaning

Spirit of Christ crucified and afflicted. All God's breakers
and billows crash over his head. He is drowning under the
curse of sin and vicarious suffering. The metaphors gather
at the Cross, the Lamb of God is dipped in the deep waters
of redemptive suffering.

Frank Lake, 1966 [446]

*
**

I have summarized in my own heart the specific lessons of
my months in captivity to help me not to lose anything of
their wonder and their worth.

   1. *Participation in his suffering is necessary* to each one if we
are to fulfil his will in this world;

   2. *The pre-eminence of his Son is essential* that we may know
in very truth his all-sufficiency at all times;

   3. *Praise through his sacrifice is possible* even in the midst of
danger and horror, as we rejoice in his working out his
purposes.

   Above all, I have learnt a little of the tremendous privilege
of walking with him, of being identified with him. Christ
not only bore my sin; he was made sin for me. He identified
himself utterly with us sinners that he might redeem us.
Now if he should seek a body, a vessel, in whom to live, that
he might identify himself with the deepest needs and hungers of Congolese hearts, was I willing to be this vessel?
More than willing! I entered into the great privilege of
bearing about the One who had paid the supreme cost.

Helen Roseveare, 1966 [447]

*
**

I have seen Christians in communist prisons with 50 lbs. of
chains on their feet, tortured with red-hot iron pokers, in
whose throats spoonfuls of salt had been forced, being kept
afterwards without water, starving, whipped, suffering

from cold, and praying with fervour for the communists. This is humanly inexplicable! It is the love of Christ which was shed into our hearts.

Richard Wurmbrand, 1967 [448]

***

We are to share in Christ's sorrow, and the realm in which we do this is not the realm of a special kind of mystical experience, but the realm of everyday ministry. It does not mean that we are to be ashamed of our own little griefs or worries. We do not cease to be hurt and sensitive, and Christ understands our hurts and disappointments. But in and through them we are drawn near to Christ's sorrow. It makes all the difference. The setbacks, the plans that misfire, the unfairness of other people, the sickness, or whatever the trial may be – let these be the door into Christ's sorrow. And as he wept over the city of Jerusalem which did not know the things which belonged to its peace, so may he wish us to weep with him over the cities and villages and populations where his love is rejected or unknown and his people suffer. He draws us to watch with him, and to watch will mean to bear and to grieve.

But the door into his sorrow is also the door into his joy. As the cloud of the presence in the tabernacle was pierced from within by a burning light, so the sorrow of Jesus is the place of reconciling love pouring itself into the world, and his joy there is radiant.

Michael Ramsey, 1972 [449]

***

The idea behind inner healing is simply that we can ask Jesus Christ to walk back to the time we were hurt and to free us from the effects of that wound in the present. This involves two things then:

1) *Bringing to light* the things that have hurt us. Usually this is best done with another person; even the talking out of the problem is in itself a healing process.

2) *Praying* the Lord to heal the binding effects of the hurtful incidents of the past . . .

Jesus, as Lord of time, is able to do what we cannot: he can heal those wounds of the past that still cause us suffering. The most I was ever able to do as a counsellor was to help the person bring to the foreground of consciousness the things that were buried in the past, so that he could consciously cope with them in the present. Now I am discovering that the Lord can heal these wounds – sometimes immediately – and can bring the counselling process to its completion in a deep healing.

At times, these hurts may seem slight to an adult mind, but we must be sensitive to see things as a child would. I remember once praying for a woman whose complaint was that her inner life was always bleak and boring, even though her professional life was in itself full and exciting. When we finally found what had caused her to shut off the flow of life it was an incident that happened when she was ten years old.

Francis MacNutt, 1974 [450]

**

Why hast thou forsaken me?

My God, my God, oh why hast thou forsaken me?
I am but the travesty of a man
   despised of the people,
laughed unto scorn in every daily paper.
Their armoured cars encompass me,
their machine-gunners have set their sights on me,
barbed wire besets me round.
From morning until evening
I must answer to my name;
they have tattooed me with a number.

They have photographed me
  hedged about by an electric fence.
My bones may all be told as on an X-ray screen.
They have taken my identity away from me.
They have led me naked to the gas-chamber;
and they have parted my garments among them –
  yea even down to my shoes.
I call out for morphia but no one hears;
I call out in the strait-jacket,
call out all night long in lunatic asylums –
in the ward for terminal cases,
in the isolation wing,
in the home for the aged.
Drenched in sweat, I suffer
in the psychiatric clinic, stifle
in the oxygen-tent, and weep
in the police station,
    in the prison yard,
      in the torture chamber,
        in the orphanage;
I am contaminated by radioactivity
  and all men shun me lest it might smite them.

But my words shall be of thee before my brethren,
and I shall exalt thee before the congregation of our
  people;
my hymns shall rise up in the midst of a multitude.
There will be a banquet set before those that are poor.
And there shall be a great feast among our people:
the new people, that is to be born.

Ernesto Cardenal, 1975 [451]

**

There is both a faith that rebels and a faith that accepts, and
they belong together. Jesus consistently attacked the power
of evil. In no recorded case did he ever advise the handi-

355

capped and the sick to accept their lot; his unfailing response to their presence was to put forth his power to heal. He sent out his disciples with a commission to do the same. And yet he also told them that they must of necessity suffer, just as he would have to suffer. This paradox is at the very heart of the gospel. 'He saved others; himself he cannot save.' It belongs to the mission of the church to the end. The power given to the church to meet the power of evil is just the power to follow Jesus on the road that leads through suffering, through total surrender to the Father, to the gift of new life and a new world.

Lesslie Newbigin, 1978 [452]

*
**

Jesus was there at Hiroshima and Nagasaki. He was beside the woman who left only a shadow on a wall. Jesus was with the victims. He felt their terror and their pain because he was among them in the inferno. What was done to them was done to him. 'As you did it to one of the least of these my brethren, you did it to me.'

On the cross, Jesus took upon himself every sin, every hate, every fear, every violence, and every death, including those of Hiroshima and Nagasaki. He took our place. He represented us. Jesus bore in his own body the wrath that we deserved. The death of the Japanese thousands, and the spirit of violence that killed them, fell on Jesus at Calvary. The crucified God bore the pain of the victims of Hiroshima and Nagasaki. He was there with them. By remembering the weight of the sin he bore at Calvary, we have an intimation of his agony at Hiroshima and Nagasaki. By seeing him there, we begin to understand the sufferings of those places.

Perhaps we can better comprehend the deaths of millions in a nuclear war if we realize that Jesus would be the central victim. He would know each victim. Each hair on every

head he would have numbered. Each passion, fear, and love
would be familiar to him. Jesus would be there with every
father, mother, and terrified child in thousands of infernos.
He would feel every death.

Jim Wallis, 1981 [453]

7
Endings

While Jesus' disciples were fascinated by the question of the end of the age (Matthew 24), Jesus himself was committed to loving them to another 'end' (John 13): the glory of God through the 'end' of his life on the Cross. Here is based the central vision that Christ himself is the End to which all things are being led by the Spirit.

Unfortunately, the church's stance has more often seemed to coincide with that of the disciples than that of Jesus. The false security of the time-tabling mentality, coupled with a belligerent literalism and an over-eager readiness to dispatch people to hell has produced mountains of macabre, morbid and bizarre writing. It is true that, at root, apocalyptic hopes are born out of the very conditions of persecution and oppression which the church itself has often experienced; but it is also true that Roman and pagan ideas of judgment have constantly threatened to replace Old Testament and Hebrew hopes for justice. Fortunately, the creeds leave all these matters open, and hold firmly to the essentials. Hendrikus Berkhof is right to remind us that there is much that we simply do not know, and must not pretend to know.

In an age which is, perhaps, not surprisingly short on hope, it is vital to hold to basic New Testament texts: Jesus

Christ is the same yesterday, today and for ever. He is, he was, and he is to come. The One who is to come is the One who has been revealed to us above all in Cross and Resurrection. The One who brings judgment brings justice. 'The Crucified God' is the basis of any 'Theology of Hope'. We must hold all together, just as many Holy Tables of Evangelical churches in the past proclaimed the Lord's death 'till he come'. Here is the source and goal of our longing – that our individual histories, and the world's history, which, in faith, are already pregnant with Christ, may gloriously give birth to what is now so painfully hidden.

Longing and Expectation

Strike that thick cloud of unknowing with the sharp dart of longing love, and on no account whatever think of giving up.

Cloud of Unknowing, c. 1370 [454]

*
**

For so commonly it fareth with the most sort of men, that if any scourge of God's hand do fall upon us, we weep and wail, as though there were none other hell. And if we flourish a while in any wealth, we laugh and sing as though there were no other heaven, yea and almost care for no other life. But we that be Christians are taught by the Scriptures another lesson, whether we be in wealth or woe, to turn our minds from the consideration of things here present, and to cheer up our hearts with the expectation of higher things, of better things, of eternal things, of things to come, and therein to occupy our studies, and exercise our senses, not passing for the old, and dead things of this world, which, as St Paul saith, *are past already.* And what should men pass then for things that be past? What should we care for things that be conquered? *Care ye not,* saith Christ: *be bold, I have overcome the world.* Or what should we regard things that be none of ours? For what have we to do with the world, which are redeemed out of the world? . . . This world is none of ours, let them have it to whom it belongeth. Our kingdom is there where our king is: our country where our head is: our city where our freedom standeth. Seeing therefore we be here but strangers, let us pass forward as strangers, through the desert of this desolate world. What should we travellers take long rest in our inns? And though it should chance upon us, as it happened to the Israelites, to lay our bones here, as they did in the desert, yet let us hold the hope fast of the promised land in the generation to come, which I trust in Christ, well beloved, doth approach apace. And though as yet we have not bodily entered into it, yet with the eyes of our faith let us look about us, and see upward where they are lifted, and behold the glory of them, at least afar off. So shall we lightly shake off the love and lust of this transitory, and conquered desert.

John Foxe, 1570 [455]

*
**

No man ever saw God and lived; and yet, I shall not live until I see God; and when I have seen him I shall never die . . .

As he that fears God, fears nothing else, so he that sees God sees everything else; when we shall see God, *sicuti est*, as he is, we shall see all things *sicuti sunt*, as they are; for that's their essence, as they conduce to his glory. We shall be no more deluded with outward appearances; for, when this sight which we intend here comes, there will be no delusory thing to be seen. All that we have made as though we saw, in this world, will be vanished, and I shall see nothing but God, and what is in him.

John Donne, 1620 [456]

*
**

A little of God would make my soul bankfull. Oh that I had but Christ's odd off-fallings; that he would let but the meanest of his love-rays and love-beams fall from him, so as I might gather and carry them with me! I would not be ill to please with Christ, and vailed visions of Christ; neither would I be dainty in seeing and enjoying of him: a kiss of Christ blown over his shoulder, the parings and crumbs of glory that fall under his table in heaven, a shower like a thin

361

May-mist of his love, would make me green, and sappy, and joyful, till the summer-sun of an eternal glory break up (Song 2:17). Oh that I had anything of Christ! Oh that I had a sip, or half a drop, out of the hollow of Christ's hand, of the sweetness and excellency of that lovely One! Oh that my Lord Jesus would rue upon me, and give me but the meanest alms of felt and believed salvation! Oh, how little were it for that infinite sea, that infinite fountain of love and joy, to fill as many thousand thousand little vessels (the like of me) as there are minutes of hours since the creation of God! I find it true that a poor soul, finding half a smell of the Godhead of Christ, hath desires (paining and wounding the poor hearts so with longings to be up at him) that makes it sometimes think, 'Were it not better never to have felt anything of Christ, than thus to lie dying twenty deaths, under these felt wounds, for the want of him?' Oh, where is he? O Fairest, where dwellest thou? O never-enough admired Godhead, how can clay win up to thee? How can creatures of yesterday be able to enjoy thee? Oh, what pain is it, that time and sin should be so many thousand miles betwixt a loved and longed-for Lord and a dwining and love-sick soul, who would rather than all the world have lodging with Christ! Oh, let this bit of love of ours, this inch and half-span length of heavenly longing, meet with thy infinite love! Oh, if the little I have were swallowed up with the infiniteness of that excellency which is in Christ! Oh that we little ones were in at the greatest Lord Jesus! Our wants should soon be swallowed up with his fulness.

Samuel Rutherford, 1637 [457]

**

My God, I am thine; What a comfort divine,
What a blessing to know that my Jesus is mine!
In the heavenly Lamb Thrice happy I am,
And my heart it doth dance at the sound of his name.

True pleasures abound In the rapturous sound;
And whoever hath found it hath paradise found.
My Jesus to know, And feel his blood flow,
'Tis life everlasting, 'tis heaven below!

Yet onward I haste To the heavenly feast;
That, that is the fullness, but this is the taste;
And this I shall prove, Till with joy I remove
To the heaven of heavens in Jesus's love.

Charles Wesley, 1749 [458]

**

Where is heaven? Is it some millions of leagues from us, far
beyond the sun and the fixed stars? What have immortal
spirits to do with space and place? Who knows, but a
heaven-born soul, who is freed from the clog of this vile
body, and filled with all the fulness of God, may pass as
easily and quickly from one verge of the creation to the
other, as our thoughts can change and fly from east to west,
from the past to the future? Perhaps, even now, we live in
the midst of this glorious assembly; heaven is there where
our God and Saviour displays himself; and do not you feel
him near you, nearer than any of his visible works? Perhaps
there is nothing but this thin partition of flesh and blood
between us and those blessed spirits that are before the
throne. If our eyes were open, we should see the mountains
around us covered with chariots and horses of fire; if our
ears were unstopped we should hear the praises of our great
Immanuel resounding in the air, as once the shepherds
heard. What a comfortable meditation is this to strengthen
our weak faith in such a dark declining day as this, when
sense would almost persuade us that we are left to serve God
alone!

John Newton, 1762 [459]

I shall walk slowly all the days of my life, under the shadow of the merit of the blood of the Cross, and I shall run the course in the same way, and as I run I shall stand still and see the full salvation that I shall find when I come to rest in the grave.

Ann Griffiths, 1796–1805 [460]

*

When shall these longings be sufficed
That stir my spirit night and day?
When shall I see my country lay
Her homage at the feet of Christ?

Of all I have, O Saviour sweet,
All gifts, all skill, all thoughts of mine,
A living garland I entwine,
And offer at thy lotus feet.

Narayam Vaman Tilak, d. 1919 [461]

*

It is not finished

It is not finished, Lord.
There is not one thing done,
There is no battle of my life,
That I have really won.
And now I come to tell thee
How I fought to fail,
My human, all too human, tale
Of weakness and futility.
And yet there is a faith in me,
That thou wilt find in it
One word that thou canst take
And make
The centre of a sentence

In thy book of poetry.
I cannot read this writing of the years,
My eyes are full of tears,
It gets all blurred, and won't make sense
It's full of contradictions
Like the scribblings of a child,
Such wild, wild
Hopes, and longing as intense
As pain, which trivial deeds
Make folly of – or worse:
I can but hand it in, and hope
That thy great mind, which reads
The writings of so many lives,
Will understand this scrawl
And what it strives
To say – but leaves unsaid.
I cannot write it over,
The stars are coming out,
My body needs its bed.
I have no strength for more,
So it must stand or fall – Dear Lord –
   That's all.

G. A. Studdert Kennedy, 1927 [462]

*
**

I believe, I believe, I believe
with a perfect faith
in the coming of the Messiah;
in the coming of the Messiah I believe.
And even though he tarry
I nevertheless believe.
Even though he tarry,
Yet, I believe in him,
I believe, I believe, I believe.

Unknown Jew, Warsaw Ghetto, 1943? [463]

We cannot arrive at the perfect possession of God in this life, and that is why we are travelling and in darkness. But we already possess him by grace, and therefore in that sense we have arrived and are dwelling in the light.

But oh! How far have I to go to find you in whom I have already arrived!

For now, oh my God, it is to you alone that I can talk, because nobody else will understand. I cannot bring any other man on this earth into the cloud where I dwell in your light, that is, your darkness, where I am lost and abashed. I cannot explain to any other man the anguish which is your joy nor the loss which is the possession of you, nor the distance from all things which is the arrival in you, nor the death which is the birth in you because I do not know anything about it myself and all I know is that I wish it were over – I wish it were begun.

Thomas Merton, 1948 [464]

*
**

To him we come –
Jesus Christ our Lord,
God's own living Word,
his dear Son:
in him there is no east and west,
in him all nations shall be blessed;
to all he offers peace and rest –
   loving Lord!

In him we live –
Christ our strength and stay,
life and truth and way,
friend divine:
his power can break the chains of sin,
still all life's storms without, within,
help us the daily fight to win –
   living Lord!

For him we go –
soldiers of the cross,
counting all things loss
him to know;
going to every land and race,
preaching to all redeeming grace,
building his church in every place –
   conquering Lord!

With him we serve –
his the work we share
with saints everywhere,
near and far;
one in the task which faith requires,
one in the zeal which never tires,
one in the hope his love inspires –
   coming Lord!

Onward we go –
faithful, bold, and true,
called his will to do
day by day;
till, at the last, with joy we'll see
Jesus, in glorious majesty;
live with him through eternity –
   reigning Lord!

James Seddon, c. 1964 [465]

*
**

Island hill-tops
Pierce the broads of mist
That roof the matutinal trees,
And smooth-flanked boulders
Nestle in the shock of green,
Like conus-emblems
In a chieftain's plaited hair.
Your Spirit,

Early-stirring in the morning atmosphere,
Accompanies the bell-birds'
Momently duet,
Reiterates
The red-breast cuckoo's monody.
Your herds glide silently
Among arboreal spears,
Obedient
To the beckoning Master of the wild;
And, with the honey-guide,
You chatter overhead
To plot
The complex flight-plan of the homing bees.
Within the palisaded clearing breathes
The rustling maize.
A dog is barking,
And the monitory cock
Awakes the sleeping village
From his makeshift minaret.
The blue-grey smoke-wisps curl
From every mushroom-thatch;
And soon the wattle doors
Are set aside,
And blanket-swaddled denizens emerge
To prod the dying embers
And to down
The early-morning can of gruel.
While in the compound
Watchful ancestors sleep on,
Their earthen coverlets
Pegged down with corner-sticks.
Yours is the thread of life that binds
The living and the dead,
And yours
The quick of our relatedness.
Among the millet-threshers

And the men that build
A neigbour's homestead,
Or the forest slash
To let the sun's rays sweeten
A new farm
Among the shouting fisher-folk
That splash
And scare the mudfish
From the shallow river bottoms,
For huntsmen, yes,
And honey-gatherers,
You are the bond.
You are the cloth that binds
The bobbing babies to the backs
Of mothers
In their rhythmic pounding
Of the grain,
The single calico that hides
The sponsor and the tearful bride
At village nuptials,
You, the milk-white paste
With which the earnest wedding-guests
Anoint the unassuming pair.

These, the faces
Of the Universal Brother,
Earthbound kindred's loving
Lineage-head,
Defender
Of diminished humankind.
You spark in us
The glint of recognition and
The present hope
Of sharing in divine community.
God's programme for
World-villagization.

Aylward Shorter, 1977 [466]

What point, then, can it still have for me, with reference to the end of the world, to speak not only – scientifically – of an end bang or of a disintegration of the universe but also, with a perfect right – theologically – of a *God who will bring to perfection the world and man*, as men have acknowledged again and again from time immemorial? I ask this in the midst of a great and sublime but also infinitely cruel history of the cosmos, with its disasters, disasters that have so often struck also human beings. I ask this in the midst of a history of humanity that is so often a history of blood, sweat and tears, a slaughter block of the nations, as Hegel says, a history of saints and gangsters, of exploiters and exploited. The more I reflect on the history of the world and humanity, must I not, again and again, in astonishment and horror, also ask: What is the meaning of the whole? Where is it all going? Into nothingness? Does this explain anything? Is reason satisfied with this? All that I treasure and love to end in nothingness, people around me, with all their thoughts and great desires, ideas, plans, all their work, life and love, all music, art and learning, all faith and final hope – all for nothing? Is nothingness to be the end also of the world of animals, of plants, of mountains and seas; is nothing the end of the stars, solar systems, galaxies, the whole cosmos? Is all this to come to nothing, to count for nothing? Can anyone blame me for thinking that almost any other alternative seems better, more human, more reasonable, than this single great unreason? What can the alternative be?

The only serious *alternative* – which pure reason, of course, cannot prove to me, because it transcends reason's horizon of experience – is that *the whole is oriented to that last end of ends, which we call God, in fact God the Finisher*. And if I cannot prove him any more than I could prove the Creator God, I can still with good reason affirm him: in that trust which for me is so reasonable, tested, enlightened, in which I have already affirmed his existence. For if the God who exists is truly God, he is God not only for me here and now, not only at the present time, but God also at the end, God for all eternity.

Is all this, however, perhaps merely an empty consolation? Am I perhaps hoping for a final consummation only to compensate for my frequently cruel lot on earth? Am I – as Marx thought – merely adorning my chains with flowers instead of doing what I could as an inhabitant of the world to change what ought to be changed, for the sake of the humanity of man and of society? No. Precisely because we look for the consummation, it is essential to remain faithful to the earth. It is in view of the future consummation that I can make my contribution to the fight for justice, freedom and peace: against the powers of evil, of injustice, of servitude, of desolation, of unkindness and death.

Hans Küng, 1978 [467]

Death and Resurrection

When the proconsul insisted and said: 'Take the oath and I will set you free; revile Christ,' Polycarp replied: 'For six and eighty years I have been serving him, and he has done no wrong to me; how, then, dare I blaspheme my King who has saved me!' . . .

Again he said to him: 'If you make little of the beasts, I shall have you consumed by fire unless you change your mind.'

'The fire which you threaten,' replied Polycarp, 'is one that burns for a little while, and after a short time goes out. You evidently do not know the fire of the judgment to come and the eternal punishment, which awaits the wicked. But why do you delay? Go ahead; do what you want.'

Martyrdom of Polycarp, 155 [468]

*
**

For as when a tyrant is conquered by a legitimate king and is bound hand and foot, all passers-by mock him and strike and deride him, no longer afraid of his fury or brutality because of the king who has overcome him; even so has death been conquered and branded by the Saviour on the cross and bound hand and foot, and all Christian passers-by trample on it, bearing witness to Christ but mocking at death, charging it and saying what has been written above against it: *'Where is your victory, death, where your sting, hell?'*

Athanasius, 318 or 335–6 [469]

*
**

When you come to welcome us, may you find us ready, schooled by the fear of you, untroubled, unhesitant on the last day. May you wrench us away from the things of earth in so far as our love of the world and the flesh is excessive, and make us turn with a will towards the life of eternal bliss, the life that is in Christ Jesus, our Lord. Glory to him throughout the unending succession of ages. Amen.

Gregory of Nazianzus, c. 369 [470]

**
*

'Alleluia' indicates praise of God; hence, to us who are labouring it signifies the attainment of our rest. For, when we come to that rest after this period of labour, our sole occupation will be the praise of God, our action there will be 'Alleluia'. What does 'Alleluia' mean? Praise God. Who would faultlessly praise God except the angels? They do not experience hunger or thirst or sickness or death. But we also have sung 'Alleluia'. It was sung here early in the morning, and when we were present, we sang 'Alleluia' a little while ago. A certain suggestion of the divine praise and of that peace reaches us, but, for the greater part, our mortality presses us down. We grow weary from speaking, and we wish to rest our limbs. If we were to say 'Alleluia' for a long period of time, the praise of God would become a burden for us because of the weight of our body. But, after the labours of this world, there will be an unceasing repetition of 'Alleluia'. What are we to do, then, my brethren? Let us say it as often as we can so that we may merit to say it eternally. There 'Alleluia' will be our food; 'Alleluia' will be our drink; 'Alleluia' will be our peaceful action; 'Alleluia' will be our whole joy, that is, the praise of God.

Augustine, 393–403 [471]

**
*

This shall be our whole duty, an unceasing Hallelujah . . . Brethren, we shall never be satiated with the praise of God, with the love of God. If love could fail, praise could fail. But if love be eternal, as there will there be beauty inexhaustible, fear not lest thou be not able to praise for ever him whom thou shalt be able to love for ever.

Augustine, 420 [472]

**

When we die, we will not be criticised for having failed to work miracles. We will not be accused of having failed to be theologians or contemplatives. But we will certainly have some explanation to offer to God for not having mourned unceasingly.

John Climacus, 7th cent. [473]

**

Christ rose again that he might have us as companions in the life to come. He was raised by the Father, inasmuch as he was Head of the church, from which the Father in no way allows him to be severed. He was raised by the power of the Holy Spirit, the Quickener of us in common with him.

Jean Calvin, 1559 [474]

**

The child of God may pass to heaven by the very gulfs of hell. The love of God is like a sea, into which when a man is cast, he neither feels bottom nor sees bank. I conclude therefore, that despair, whether it arise out of weakness of nature, or of conscience of sin, though it fall out about the time of death, cannot prejudice the salvation of them that are effectually called. As for other strange events which fall out in death, they are the effects of diseases . . . we ought not so much to stand upon the strangeness of any man's end, when we know the goodness of his life; for we must judge a man not by his death, but by his life.

William Perkins, 1595 [475]

We must not judge of our graves as they appear to the bodily eye, but we must look upon them by the eye of faith, and consider them as they are altered and changed by the death and burial of Christ, who having vanquished death on the cross, pursued him afterward to his own den, and foiled him there, and deprived him of his power. And by this means Christ in his own death has buried our death, and by the virtue of his burial, as sweet incense hath sweetened and perfumed our graves.

William Perkins, 1595 [476]

*
**

The Final Joy

Wake, awake, for night is flying,
The watchmen on the heights are crying;
   Awake, Jerusalem, at last!
Midnight hears the welcome voices,
And at the thrilling cry rejoices:
   Come forth, ye virgins, night is past!
     The Bridegroom comes, awake,
     Your lamps with gladness take;
      Hallelujah!
And for his marriage-feast prepare,
For ye must go to meet him there.

Zion hears the watchmen singing,
And all her heart with joy is springing,
   She wakes, she rises from her gloom;
For her Lord comes down all-glorious,
The strong in grace, in truth victorious,
   Her Star is risen, her Light is come!
     Ah come, thou blessed Lord,
     O Jesus, Son of God,
      Hallelujah!
We follow till the halls we see
Where thou hast bid us sup with thee.

Now let all the heavens adore thee,
And men and angels sing before thee
  With harp and cymbal's clearest tone;
Of one pearl each shining portal,
Where we are with the choir immortal
  Of angels round thy dazzling throne;
    Nor eye hath seen, nor ear
    Hath yet attain'd to hear
      What there is ours,
    But we rejoice, and sing to thee
    Our hymn of joy eternally.

Philipp Nicolai, 1598, tr. Catherine Winkworth, 1858 [477]

*
**

I would always raise your hearts, and dilate your hearts, to a holy joy, a joy in the Holy Ghost . . . for under the shadow of his wings, you may, you should, rejoice.

If you look upon this world in a map, you find two hemispheres, two half worlds. If you crush heaven into a map, you may find two hemispheres too, two half heavens; half will be joy, and half will be glory; for in these two, the joy of heaven, and the glory of heaven, is all heaven often represented unto us. And as of those two hemispheres of the world, the first hath been known long before, but the other, (that of America, which is the richer in treasure) God reserved for later discoveries; so though he reserve that hemisphere of heaven, which is the glory thereof, to the resurrection, yet the other hemisphere, the joy of heaven, God opens to our discovery, and delivers for our habitation even whilst we dwell in this world . . .

The true joy of a good soul in this world is the very joy of heaven; and we go thither, not that being without joy, we might have joy infused into us, but that as Christ says, our joy might be full, perfected, sealed with an everlastingness;

for, as he promises, that no man shall take away our joy from us, so neither shall death itself take it away, nor so much as interrupt it, or discontinue it, but as in the face of death, when he lays hold upon me, and in the face of the devil, when he attempts me, I shall see the face of God (for everything shall be a glass, to reflect God upon me) so in the agonies of death, in the anguish of that dissolution, in the sorrows of that valediction, in the irreversibleness of that transmigration, I shall have a joy, which shall no more evaporate, than my soul shall evaporate, a joy that shall pass up, and put on a more glorious garment above, and be joy super-invested in glory.

John Donne, 1625/6 [478]

*
**

But for them that have slept in Christ . . . they shall awake as Jacob did, and say as Jacob did, 'Surely the Lord is in this place', and 'this is no other but the house of God, and the gate of heaven', and into that gate they shall enter, and in that house they shall dwell, where there shall be no cloud nor sun, no darkness nor dazzling, but one equal light, no noise nor silence, but one equal music, no fears nor hopes, but one equal possession, no foes nor friends, but one equal communion and identity, no ends nor beginnings, but one equal eternity.

John Donne, 1627/8 [479]

*
**

Consider:
That thou must presently pass to an impartial, strict, the highest and last tribunal, which can never be appealed from, or repealed: there to give an exact account of all things done in the flesh: for every thought of thine heart, every word of

thy mouth, every glance of thine eye, every movement of thy time, every omission of any holy duty or good deed, every action thou hast undertaken, with all the circumstances thereof, every office thou has born, and the discharge of it in every point and particular: every company thou hast come into, and all thy behaviour there: every sermon thou hast heard, every Sabbath thou hast spent, every motion of the Spirit which hath been made unto thy soul, etc. Let us then, while it is called *today*, call ourselves to account, examine, search and try thoroughly our hearts, lives and callings, our thoughts, words and deeds: let us arraign, accuse, judge, cast and condemn ourselves: and prostrated before God's mercy seat, with broken and bleeding affections, lowliness of spirit, and humblest adoration of his free grace . . . Let us therefore give our merciful God no rest, until we have sued out our pardon by the intercession of the Lord Jesus. And then we shall find the reckoning made up to our hand, and all matters fully answered beforehand. And (which is a point of unconceivable comfort) he that was our advocate upon earth, and purchased the pardon with his own heart's blood, shall then be our Judge.

Robert Bolton, 1635 [480]

*
**

When it comes to the trial, the question will not be, who hath preached most, or heard most, or talked most, but who hath loved most?

Richard Baxter, 1649 [481]

*
**

The Bridegroom's departure was not upon divorce; he did not leave us with a purpose to return no more; he hath left pledges enough to assure us; we have his word in pawn, his many promises, his sacraments, which show forth his death until he comes; and his Spirit, to direct, sanctify, and comfort, till he return . . . He that would come to suffer, will surely come to triumph: and he that would come to purchase, will surely come to possess. Alas, where else were all our hopes? What were become of our faith, our prayers, our tears and our waiting? What were all the patience of the saints worth to them? Were we not left of all men most miserable? . . . I have thought on it many a time, as a small emblem of that day, when I have seen a prevailing army drawing towards the towns and castles of their enemy. Oh with what glad hearts do all the poor prisoners within hear the news, and behold their approach? How do they run to their prison windows, and thence behold us with joy? How glad are they at the roaring report of the cannon, which is the enemy's terror? How do they clap each other on the back, and cry, *Deliverance, Deliverance?*

Richard Baxter, 1649 [482]

***

How weak the thoughts and vain
    Of self-deluding men!
Men, who fixed to earth alone
    Think their houses shall endure,
Fondly call their lands their own,
    To their distant heirs secure!

How happy then are we,
    Who build, O Lord, on thee!
What can our foundation shock?
    Though the shattered earth remove,
Stands our city on a rock,
    On the rock of heavenly love.

A house we call our own,
    Which cannot be o'erthrown:
In the general ruin sure,
    Storms and earthquakes it defies,
Built immovably secure,
    Built eternal in the skies.

379

High on Immanuel's land
  We see the fabric stand,
From a tottering world remove
  To our steadfast mansion there;
Our inheritance above
  Cannot pass from heir to heir.

Those amaranthine bowers,
  Unalienably ours,
Bloom, our infinite reward,
  Rise, our permanent abode,
From the founded world prepared,
  Purchased by the blood of God!

O might we quickly find
  The place for us designed;
See the long-expected day
  Of our full redemption here!
Let the shadows flee away!
  Let the new-made world appear!

High on thy great white throne,
  O king of saints, come down!
In the New Jerusalem
  Now triumphantly descend;
Let the final trump proclaim
  Joys begun which ne'er shall end!

Charles Wesley, 1750 [483]

* * *

Believers should not have a slavish dread of death. Where is
the infant that is afraid to go to sleep in its nurse's arms?

Augustus M. Toplady, d. 1778 [484]

* * *

Concerning my poor dear babe . . . truly I grieved, and felt
more than ever I felt before of that grief, which springs from

being bereaved of one much beloved: and my heart bleeds, if I may thus speak, at every remembrance of her. But I do not grieve *as one without hope*: hope of meeting her in glory, and spending a joyful eternity together – I do not grieve so as to *indulge* grief or complaining, or think (with Jonah) *I do well to be angry*, because my darling gourd is withered. God hath done well, and wisely, and graciously; and, whilst my heart is pained, my judgement is satisfied.

Thomas Scott, 1780 [485]

**
*

When my wife died, the world seemed to die with her, (I hope to revive no more.) I see little now, but my ministry and my christian profession, to make a continuance in life, for a single day, desirable; though I am willing to wait my appointed time. If the world cannot restore her to me, (not that I have the remotest wish that her return was possible,) it can do nothing for me. The Bank of England is too poor to compensate for such a loss as mine. But the Lord, the all-sufficient God, speaks, and it is done. Let those who know him, and trust him, be of good courage. He can give them strength according to their day; he can increase their strength as their trials are increased, to any assignable degree. And what he can do, he has promised he will do. The power and faithfulness on which the successive changes of day and night, and of the seasons of the year, depend, and which uphold the stars in their orbits, is equally engaged to support his people, and to lead them safely and unhurt (if their path be so appointed) through floods and flames. Though I believe she has never yet been (and probably never will be) out of my waking thoughts for five minutes at a time; though I sleep in the bed in which she suffered and languished so long; I have not had one uncomfortable day, nor one restless night, since she left me. I have lost a right hand, which I cannot but miss continually; but the Lord enables me to go on cheerfully without it.

John Newton, 1794[486]

*
**

Christians should watch. Ah! if Christ is at hand, take heed lest you be found unforgiven. Many Christians seem to live without a realizing view of Christ. The eye should be fixed on Christ. Your eye is shut. Oh! if you would abide in Christ, then let him come to-night – at even, or at midnight, or at cockcrow, or in the morning – he is welcome, thrice welcome! Even so, come, Lord Jesus. Take heed lest you be found in any course of sin. Many Christians seem to walk, if I mistake not, in courses of sin. It is hard to account for it; but so it seems to be. Some Christians seem to be sleeping – in luxury – in covetousness – in evil company. Ah! think how would you like to be overtaken thus by the coming Saviour. Try your daily occupations – your daily state of feeling – your daily enjoyments – try them by this test: Am I doing as I would wish to do on the day of his coming?

Robert Murray M'Cheyne, d. 1843 [487]

*
**

My dearest Maria,
You referred in your letter to those two angel boys. I cannot say how often I think of them. That beautiful Maurice with his bright black eyes has indeed a place in my inmost memories. I have often felt what the family loss is and the personal one to Walter, but all is ordered and they are safe and more than that 'present with the Lord'.

Let us all cultivate the spirit of thankful trust and seek unto God and unto God commit our cause – that is our life with all its *cares*, and *blanks*, and *needs* as well as its blessings to be accepted aright.

Catherine, Lady Buxton, 1889 [488]

There are only two kinds of people in the end: those who say to God 'Thy will be done,' and those to whom God says, in the end, 'Thy will be done.'

C. S. Lewis, 1946 [489]

***

Jesus Christ's coming again for judgment, his ultimate and universal manifestation is often described in the New Testament as *the* revelation. He will be revealed, not only to the Church but to everyone, as the Person he is. He will not only then be the judge, he is that already; but then for the first time it will become visible, that it is not a question of our Yes and No, our faith or lack of faith. In full clarity and publicity the 'it is finished' will come to light. For that the Church is waiting; and without knowing it the world is waiting too. . . . What is the future bringing? Not, once more, a turning-point in history, but the revelation of that which is. It is the future, but the future of that which the Church remembers, of that which has already taken place once and for all. The Alpha and the Omega are the same thing . . .

In the biblical world of thought the judge is not primarily the one who rewards some and punishes the others; he is the man who creates order and restores what has been destroyed. We may go to meet this judge, this restoration or, better, the revelation of this restoration with unconditioned confidence, because *he* is the judge. With unconditioned confidence, because we come from his revelation.

Karl Barth, 1949 [490]

***

When it comes time to die, make sure that all you have to do is die.

Jim Elliot, d. 1956 [491]

It is hard to have patience with people who say 'There is no death' or 'Death doesn't matter'. There is death. And whatever is matters. And whatever happens has consequences, and it and they are irrevocable and irreversible. You might as well say that birth doesn't matter. I look up at the night sky. Is anything more certain than that in all those vast times and spaces, if I were allowed to search them, I should nowhere find her face, her voice, her touch? She died. She is dead. Is the word so difficult to learn?

C. S. Lewis, 1961 [492]

**

Death is the physic;
There is no remedy less radical.
We cannot patch the threadbare goodness
with a small square of glory.
We have come to where the fragments must be fused
painfully into a unity
By resurrection out of a three-days tomb.

First, death of self-concern
Which stands outside the event
To keep the score of good or bad –
'How am I making out?' – 'That's better now'.
For we must be born into that action which is all ourself,
Total commitment when the cost's been weighed;
Authentic choice to be, without reserves in case it doesn't
    work.

Then, death to judgement of our brother;
The secret pleasure in his faults;
The double mind condemning while love wrestles to
    control.

Then last of all, the death to set us free
From testing God, setting the scene where he must play a
    part,

dance to our piping,
    ratify our schemes because we made him patron;
    doing our own will behind the Three-fold Name.
Dead, and alive in Christ
We find new trust.
Not flabby relaxation but poised rest;
the knife-edge of discernment's still to tread,
But always with the knowledge that he reigns
Both in the choosing and whatever comes
Out of that choice.

The grave clothes hold us,
They're all we know.
Give us the courage to be loosed and live.

Michael Hare Duke, 1970 [493]

*
* *

The structural redemption of mankind needs as its reverse
the redemption of innumerable people. When God abol-
ishes the oppressive structures, this means salvation for the
oppressed. Millions of people – the outlawed, the victims of
discrimination, the persecuted, the trampled upon, and the
martyred – were in this life never able to answer to God's
purpose, not because of their own sin, but due to the sins of
others. If God has in mind to banish sin and to resist sinners,
the judgment upon the oppressors must imply the deliverance of their victims. Else it would be meaningless. The
Bible is full of that expectation. Most of the time we have
overlooked that in our reading of the Bible. Yet how could
we stand in a world which offers such unequal opportuni-
ties, a world which is drenched in injustice, if we could not
also expect this from God?

Hendrikus Berkhof, 1973 [494]

We know that the covenant means that God's faithfulness ever and again does battle with man's unfaithfulness. What ultimately will be forced to yield: divine faithfulness or human unfaithfulness? Paul raised that question with respect to Israel, as the trial grounds of God's relationship to man; and he ends with the confession: 'God has consigned all men to disobedience, that he may have mercy upon all' (Romans 11:32). These considerations compel us, not to detract from the gravity of the human 'no' against God and its consequences, but to think just a little more of the divine 'yes' to recalcitrant humans. God is serious about the responsibility of our decision, but he is even more serious about the responsibility of his love. The darkness of rejection and God–forsakenness cannot and may not be urged away, but no more can and may it be eternalized. For God's sake we hope that hell will be a form of purification.

Hendrikus Berkhof, 1973 [495]

*\
**

Prayer for Marilyn Monroe

Lord accept this girl
called Marilyn Monroe throughout the world
though that was not her name
(but you know her real name, that of the orphan raped at
   nine
the shopgirl who tried to kill herself when aged sixteen)
who now goes into your presence without make-up
without her Press Agent
without her photographs or signing autographs
lonely as an astronaut facing the darkness of outer space.

When a girl, she dreamed she was naked in a church
     (according to *Time*)
standing in front of a prostrate multitude, heads to the
   ground,

and had to walk on tiptoe to avoid the heads.
You know our dreams better than all psychiatrists.
Church, house or cave all represent the safety of the womb
but also something more . . .
The heads are admirers, so much is clear (that
mass of heads in the darkness below the beam to the screen)
but the temple isn't the studios of 20th-Century Fox.
The temple, of marble and gold, is the temple of her body
in which the Son of Man stands whip in hand
driving out the money-changers of a 20th-Century Fox
who made your house of prayer a den of thieves.

Lord, in this world
contaminated equally by radioactivity and sin,
surely you will not blame a shopgirl
who (like any other shopgirl) dreamed of being a star.
And her dream became 'reality' (Technicolour reality).
All she did was follow the script we gave her,
that of our own lives, but it was meaningless.
Forgive her, Lord, and likewise all of us
for this our 20th Century
and the Mammoth Super-Production in whose making we
    all shared.

She was hungry for love and we offered her tranquillizers.
For the sadness of our not being saints
        they recommended psychoanalysis.
Remember, Lord, her increasing terror of the camera
and hatred of make-up (yet insistence on being newly
    made-up
for every scene) and how the terror grew
and how her unpunctuality at the studios grew.

Like any other shopgirl she dreamed
of being a star.
And her life was as unreal as a dream an analyst reads and
    files.

The Lord of the Journey

Her romances were kisses with closed eyes
which when the eyes are opened
are seen to have been played out beneath the spotlights
    but the spotlights have gone out,
and the two walls of the room (it was a set) are taken down
while the Director moves away notebook in hand,
    the scene being safely canned.
Or like a cruise on a yacht, a kiss in Singapore, a dance in
    Rio;
a reception in the mansion of the Duke and Duchess of
    Windsor
    viewed in the sad tawdriness of a cheap apartment.

The film ended without the final kiss.
They found her dead in bed, hand on the phone
And the detectives knew not whom she was about to call.
It was as
though somone had dialled the only friendly voice
and heard a pre-recorded tape just saying 'WRONG NUMBER'
or like someone wounded by gangsters, who
reaches out towards a disconnected phone.

Lord, whomsoever
it may have been that she was going to call
but did not (and perhaps it was no one at all
or Someone not named in the Los Angeles directory),
    Lord, answer that phone.

Ernesto Cardenal, 1975 [496]

*
**

The present theological and spiritual tendency consists in minimizing [judgment], and even rejecting it. We return to the terrestrial reality of the vocation of man, to his full historic dimension, to his condition as creator with God, as demiurge; we drop all this phantasmagoria of celestial combats (so inspired, are they not, by Near Eastern cultures) of damnations (Ashur and her demons are not far).

These ideas of judgment appear completely outmoded; modern man has come of age. For some it is complexes and fantasies that have produced this idea of damnation, while for others it is the state of famine and of the vital animal condition on the plane of subsistence, and for still others it is a mischievous invention of exploiters and the powerful in order to compel the poor and the oppressed to remain quiet. All these explanations are very fine and have no other foundation than the opinion of their authors. If we continue to consider that Jesus Christ is truly the Messiah and that he attests what Scripture tells us, which is to say if we remain Christians, it is impossible to reject this judgment of the creation by God. The whole is strictly coherent. The conception of judgment that we find as much in the prophets as in the psalms, as much in the Gospels as in the Epistles is not a cultural phenomenon: it rests upon that evident conviction that if God is God, both perfect and just, how can the encounter between this God and the world as we know it take place without some sparks being produced and without, at least, revealing in the absolute light what we have been *in truth*? The judgment being never juridical but revelatory, it is not the expression of the servile terror of men, but of their comprehension of the divine reality.

Jacques Ellul, 1975 [497]

**
*

Our eyes fell on the empty grave, a gaping hole in the earth. The words of the angel to the two women seeking Jesus's body flashed into our minds. 'Why do you seek the living among the dead?' Namirembe Hill resounded with the song that the *balokole* have taken as their own, *Tukutendereza Yesu:*

> Glory, glory, hallelujah!
> Glory, glory to the Lamb!
> Oh, the cleansing blood has reached me!
> Glory, glory to the Lamb!

We came away from the service praising, healed by the revelation of the empty grave. We greeted each other, using the words of the old Easter greeting: 'Christ is risen' – 'He is risen indeed!' Archbishop Sabiti spoke to me briefly as I was leaving: 'Why are we bothering about the body? Janani went straight to heaven.'

At our Sunday evening fellowship meeting there were many testimonies. 'When I heard the Archbishop was dead, I wanted to slaughter the men who had killed him. Now the Lord is convicting me to pray for his murderers that they will repent and be saved by the cleansing blood of Christ.' And from someone else: 'I know Christ has risen. He healed me today through the power of the resurrection.'

The resurrection is the heart of the gospel we proclaim and because I have tasted the reality of the resurrection, I know I must continue telling others, 'Christ lives.'

Margaret Ford, 1978 [498]

*
**

Christian faith is essentially faith in the resurrection. Faith in the resurrection means being born again to hope . . .

Faith in the resurrection does not look past death to eternity. Nor does it come to melancholy terms with this vale of tears. It sees the raising of the tortured and crucified Son of Man as *God's great protest* against death and against everyone who plays into death's hands and threatens life. For faith senses that the event of Christ's self-giving and his resurrection reflect God's infinite passion for life, and for the salvation and liberty of his creation. Faith shares this passion . . .

But it lives from measureless astonishment over the future, in the infinite joy of looking towards the new heaven and the new earth, in which righteousness will dwell, and towards eternal blessedness. 'How much more', says the apostle Paul, when he has ceased to talk about *liberation from* sin, law and death, and is talking about *freedom for* eternal life. 'How much more' is the 'added value' of hope, the surplus of promise beyond this life. The 'notwithstanding' with which we resist death and inertia is only the dark side of the shield whose reverse is the 'how much more' of the hope by which we are quickened.

If God's protest against death is to be experienced in the struggle against the forces of death, how and where are we to experience this 'added value', this surplus of hope? It is experienced in 'the feast'. Easter is a feast and is celebrated as the feast of freedom. For Easter is the beginning of the laughter of the redeemed and the dance of the liberated and the creative game of fantasy. Since earliest times Easter hymns have celebrated the victory of life by laughing at death, by mocking at hell, and by making the lords of this world absurd. Easter is God's protest against death. Easter is the feast of freedom from death. We must keep the two things together. Resistance is the protest of those who hope and hope is the festival of those who resist.

Jürgen Moltmann, 1980[499]

*
**

A Father's Prayer
upon the Murder of his Son

O God,
We remember not only Bahram but also his murderers;
Not because they killed him in the prime of his youth
    and made our hearts bleed and our tears flow,
Not because with this savage act they have brought
    further disgrace on the name of our country among
    the civilized nations of the world;
But because through their crime we now follow thy foot-
    steps more closely in the way of sacrifice.

The terrible fire of this calamity burns up all selfishness
   and possessiveness in us;
Its flame reveals the depth of depravity and meanness
   and suspicion, the dimension of hatred and the
   measure of sinfulness in human nature;
It makes obvious as never before our need to trust in
   God's love as shown in the cross of Jesus and his
   resurrection;
Love which makes us free from hate towards our
   persecutors;
Love which brings patience, forbearance, courage,
   loyalty, humility, generosity, greatness of heart;
Love which more than ever deepens our trust in God's
   final victory and his eternal designs for the Church
   and for the world;
Love which teaches us how to prepare ourselves to face
   our own day of death.

O God,
Bahram's blood has multiplied the fruit of the Spirit in
   the soil of our souls;
So when his murderers stand before thee on the day of
   judgement
Remember the fruit of the Spirit by which they have
   enriched our lives,
And forgive.

Hassan B. Dehqani-Tafti, 1981 [500]

*
**

In the sky
The song of the skylark
Greets the dawn.
In the fields wet with dew
The scent of the violets
Fills the air.

On such a lovely morning as this
Surely on such a lovely morning as this

Lord Jesus
Came forth
From the tomb.

Misuno Genzo, 1984 [501]

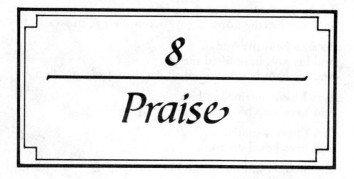

8
Praise

We close with a short, largely rhapsodic burst of praise, spanning the centuries even more swiftly than the previous sections. Praise has its functions in many areas of Christian understanding and experience, and it is generally important for praise to have content. It follows naturally from the last section, as heaven is a world of praise, and we join with the songs of the angels each time we lift our hearts in praise. And many of the greatest hymns of praise have been summaries, taking in the history of salvation from start to finish; so this section is not so much an appendix as an overview.

In our own times the note of praise has been found difficult; although in recent years the music of praise has been reborn, the words that go with it are strangely limp when unsupported on the page. Instead, we conclude with praise out of the furnace: of doubt in Dostoevsky's case, in the case of Genzo of a crippling cerebral palsy, from which he wrote poems through a system of eyelid signals understood by his mother. Out of such weakness God perfects praise.

As the sun is the joy to them who seek its daybreak,
So is my joy the Lord;

Because he is my Sun,
And his rays have lifted me up;
And his light has dismissed all darkness from my face.

Eyes I have obtained in him,
And have seen his holy day.

Ears I have acquired,
And have heard his truth.

The thought of knowledge I have acquired,
And have lived fully through him.

I repudiated the way of error,
And went towards him and received salvation from him
   abundantly.

And according to his generosity he gave to me,
And according to his excellent beauty he made me.

I put on incorruption through his name,
And took off corruption by his grace.

Death has been destroyed before my face,
And Sheol has been vanquished by my word.

And eternal life has arisen in the Lord's land,
And it has become known to his faithful ones,
And been given without limit to all that trust in him.

   Hallelujah.

Odes of Solomon, early 2nd cent. [502]

*
**

The Word of God
has left the lyre and the cithara,
instruments without a soul,

to tune the whole world, gathered into man,
in to himself through the Holy Spirit.
He makes use of him
as an instrument with many voices
and accompanying his song,
he plays to God
on that instrument that is man.

Clement of Alexandria (died c. 211–16) [503]

*
**

My whole heart I lay upon the altar of thy praise, an whole
burnt-offering of praise I offer to thee . . . Let the flame of
thy love . . . set on fire my whole heart, let nought in me be
left to myself, nought wherein I may look to myself, but
may I wholly burn towards thee, wholly be on fire towards
thee, wholly love thee, as though set on fire by thee.

Augustine, 420 [504]

*
**

You, oh Christ, are the Kingdom of Heaven; you, the land
  promised to the gentle;
You, the grazing lands of paradise; you, the hall of the
  celestial banquet;
You, the ineffable marriage chamber; you, the table set for
  all,
You, the bread of life; you, the unheard of drink;
You, both the urn for the water and the life-giving water;
You, moreover, the inextinguishable lamp for each one of
  the saints;
You, the garment and the crown and the one who distri-
  butes the crowns;
You, the joy and rest; you, the delight and glory;
You the gaiety; you, the mirth;

And your grace, my God, grace of the Spirit of all sanctity,
Will shine like the sun in all the saints;
And you, inaccessible sun, will shine in their midst
And all will shine brightly, to the degree
Of their faith, their asceticism, their hope and their love,
Their purification and their illumination by your Spirit.

Symeon the New Theologian, 980–1005 [505]

*
**

When all thy Mercies, O my God,
  My rising Soul surveys;
Transported with the View, I'm lost
  In Wonder, Love, and Praise:

O how shall Words with equal Warmth
  The Gratitude declare
That glows within my Ravish'd Heart!
  But Thou canst read it there.

Thy Providence my Life sustain'd
  And all my Wants redrest,
When in the silent Womb I lay,
  And hung upon the Breast.

To all my weak Complaints and Cries
  Thy Mercy lent an Ear,
Ere yet my feeble Thoughts had learnt
  To form themselves in Pray'r.

Unnumber'd Comforts to my Soul
  Thy tender Care bestow'd,
Before my Infant Heart conceiv'd
  From whom those Comforts flow'd.

When in the slipp'ry Paths of Youth
  With heedless Steps I ran,
Thine Arm unseen convey'd me safe
  And led me up to Man;

Through hidden Dangers, Toils, and Deaths,
  It gently clear'd my Way,
And through the pleasing Snares of Vice,
  More to be fear'd than they.

When worn with Sickness oft hast Thou
  With Health renew'd my Face,
And when in Sins and Sorrows sunk
  Revived my Soul with Grace.

Thy bounteous Hand with worldly Bliss
  Has made my Cup run o'er,
And in a kind and faithful Friend
  Has doubled all my Store.

Ten thousand thousand precious Gifts
  My Daily Thanks employ,
Nor is the least a chearful Heart,
  That tastes those Gifts with Joy.

Through ev'ry Period of my Life
  Thy Goodness I'll pursue,
And after Death in distant Worlds
  The glorious Theme renew.

When Nature fails, and Day and Night
  Divide thy Works no more,
My Ever-grateful Heart, O Lord,
  Thy Mercy shall adore.

Through all Eternity, to thee
  A grateful Song I'll raise;
But O Eternity's too short
  To utter all thy Praise!

Joseph Addison, 1712 [506]

Wonderful, wonderful in the sight of angels, a great wonder in the eyes of faith, to see the giver of being, the generous sustainer and ruler of everything that is, in the manger in swaddling clothes and with nowhere to lay his head, and yet the bright host of glory worshipping him now.

When Sinai is altogether on smoke, and the sound of the trumpet at its loudest, in Christ the Word I can go to feast across the boundary without being slain; in him all fullness dwells, enough to fill the gulf of man's perdition; in the breach, between the parties, he made reconciliation through his self-offering.

He is the satisfaction that was between the thieves, he suffered the pains of death, it was he who gave to the arms of his executioners the power to nail him there to the cross; when he pays the debt of brands plucked out of the burning and honours his Father's law, Righteousness shines with fiery blaze as it pardons within the terms of the free reconciliation.

O my soul, behold the place where lay the chief of kings, the author of peace, all creation moving in him, and he lying dead in the tomb; song and life of the lost, greatest wonder of the angels of heaven, the choir of them sees God in flesh and worships him together, crying out 'Unto him'.

Thanks for ever, and a hundred thousand thanks, thanks while there is breath in me, that there is an object to worship and a theme for a song to last for ever, in my nature, tempted like the lowest of mankind, a babe, weak, powerless, the infinite true and living God.

Instead of carrying a body of corruption, to penetrate ardently with the choir above into the endless wonders of the salvation wrought on Calvary, to live to see the Invisible who was dead and now is alive – eternal inseparable union and communion with my God!

There I shall exalt the Name which God has set forth to be a propitiation, without imagination, curtain or covering and with my soul fully in his likeness; in the fellowship of the mystery revealed in his wounds, I shall kiss the Son to all eternity, and never turn from him any more.

Ann Griffiths, 1796–1805 [507]

*
**

Praise to the Holiest in the height,
  And in the depth be praise:
In all his words most wonderful,
  Most sure in all his ways!

O loving wisdom of our God!
  When all was sin and shame,
A second Adam to the fight
  And to the rescue came.

O wisest love! that flesh and blood,
  Which did in Adam fail,
Should strive afresh against their foe,
  Should strive and should prevail.

And that a higher gift than grace
  Should flesh and blood refine,
God's Presence and his very Self,
  And Essence all-divine.

O generous love! that he who smote
  In man for man the foe,
The double agony in man
  For man should undergo;

And in the garden secretly,
  And on the Cross on high,
Should teach his brethren, and inspire
  To suffer and to die.

Praise to the Holiest in the height,
  And in the depth be praise,
In all his words most wonderful,
  Most sure in all his ways!

John Henry Newman, 1865 [508]

It is not as a boy that I believe in Christ and confess him, but my hosanna has passed through a great furnace of doubts.

Fyodor Dostoevsky, c. 1879 [509]

*
**

Just Give Thanks

I
can do nothing
for my family
for people
for the Lord.
For the abundant love
of the Lord
of people
of my family
I just give thanks
just give thanks.

Misuno Genzo, 1984 [510]

Further Reading

A SHORT-LIST OF RECENT BOOKS
NOT REFERRED TO IN THE NOTES

Louis Bouyer *A History of Christian Spirituality* (3 Vols Burns and Oates 1968)

George Every, Richard Harries, Kallistos Ware (eds) *Seasons of the Spirit* (SPCK 1984)

Anne Freemantle (ed) *The Protestant Mystics* (Weidenfeld and Nicholson 1964)

Grove Spirituality Series (Grove Books, Nottingham 1982–)

Michael Hennell *John Venn and the Clapham Sect* (Lutterworth, 1958); *Sons of the Prophets: Evangelical Leaders of the Victorian Church* (SPCK 1979)

Urban T. Holmes *A History of Christian Spirituality: An Analytical Introduction* (Seabury 1981)

Morton T. Kelsey *Encounter with God: A Theology of Christian Experience* (Hodder and Stoughton 1974)

Kenneth Leech *True God: An Exploration in Spiritual Theology* (Sheldon 1985)

Richard Lovelace *Dynamics of Spiritual Life: An Evangelical Theology of Renewal* (Paternoster 1979)

Ranald Macaulay and Jerram Barrs *Christianity with a human face* (IVP 1979)

Randle Manwaring *From Controversy to Co-Existence: Evangelicalism in the Church of England from 1914–1980* (CUP 1985)

Geoffrey Nuttall *The Holy Spirit in Puritan Faith and Experience* (Blackwell 1946)

Wolfhart Pannenberg *Christian Spirituality and Sacramental Community* (DLT 1984)

Simon Tugwell *Ways of Imperfection: An Exploration of Christian Spirituality* (DLT 1984)

Gordon S. Wakefield *Puritan Devotion* (Epworth 1957); (ed) *A Dictionary of Christian Spirituality* (SCM 1983)

Owen C. Watkins *The Puritan Experience* (Routledge and Kegan Paul, 1972)

Rowan Williams *The Wound of Knowledge: Christian Spirituality from the New Testament to St John of the Cross* (DLT 1979)

Sherwood Eliot Wirt (ed) *Exploring the Spiritual Life: Classics of Seventeenth-Century Devotion* (Lion 1983)

Veronica Zundel (ed) *The Lion Book of Christian Classics* (Lion 1985)

Notes on Sources

(Place of publication is London unless otherwise stated.)

ABBREVIATIONS

ACW	*Ancient Christian Writers* ed. J. Quasten & J.C. Plumpe (Longmans, Green 1946–)
ANF	*Ante-Nicene Fathers* (=American edition of Ante-Nicene Christian Library ed. A. Roberts & J. Donaldson 1867–; reprinted Grand Rapids: Eerdmans 1951–)
BOT	Banner of Truth Trust
Bull	Josiah Bull *Letters by the Rev. John Newton* (1869)
Carus	*Memoirs of the Life of the Rev. Charles Simeon . . .* ed. William Carus (1848)
CIM/OMF	China Inland Mission/Overseas Missionary Fellowship
CWSp	*Classics of Western Spirituality* (SPCK 1978–)
FC	*The Fathers of the Church* (NY: Fathers of the Church Inc. & Washington DC: Catholic University of America 1946–)
Inst.	Jean Calvin *Institutes of the Christian Religion* ed. John T. McNeill, tr. Ford Lewis Battles (Philadelphia: Westminster Press 1960; Library of Christian Classics XX–XXI)
LCC	*Library of Christian Classics* (SCM 1953–)
LF	*A Library of Fathers* ed. E.B. Pusey (Oxford 1837–)
LW	*Luther's Works* (American edition: Ed. Jaroslav Pelikan & Helmut T. Lehmann: Philadelphia: Muhlenberg & Fortress Press, & St Louis: Concordia Publishing House 1955–)
NPNF	*Nicene and Post-Nicene Fathers* ed. P. Schaff (NY: 1886–; repr. Eerdmans 1969–)
P&S	*The Sermons of John Donne* ed. George R. Potter & Evelyn M. Simpson (Berkeley: University of California Press 1953–62) 10 vols.
SC	*Sources Chrétiennes* (Paris: du Cerf 1942–)
STL	Send the Light (Bromley)

[1] 'Epistle of the Apostles' 21 in *New Testament Apocrypha* ed. E. Hennecke, W. Schneemelcher, R. McL. Wilson (SCM 1973) I,206.
[2] Basil the Great *On the Holy Spirit* (New York: St Vladimir's Seminary Press 1980) para. 44.
[3] Augustine *Confessions* tr. R.S. Pine-Coffin (Harmondsworth: Penguin 1961) VII, 10.
[4] Augustine *Confessions* X, 6.

[5] *The Works of St Patrick* tr. L. Bieler (Longmans, Green 1953; ACW) pp.69–72.

[6] Isaac of Nineveh *Directions on Spiritual Training* no.130 in *Early Fathers from the Philokalia* ed. E. Kadloubovsky and G.E.H. Palmer (Faber & Faber 1954). The *Philokalia* is a collection of texts on the spiritual life written during the 4th–15th centuries and collected by two Greek Orthodox monks in the 18th century.

[7] Anselm 'Prayer to St Paul' in *Prayers and Meditations of St Anselm* tr. Sister B. Ward (Harmondsworth: Penguin, 1973) pp.153–6.

[8] Isaac of Stella Sermon 5,122–7 from Isaac de l'Etoile *Sermons* I ed. A. Hoste & G. Salet (SC 1967), tr. Sr. Mary Magdalen CSMV.

[9] Francis of Assisi 'The Parchment given to Brother Leo' in *Francis and Clare: the Complete Works* ed. R.J. Armstrong and I.C. Brady (SPCK 1982: CWSp) pp.99–100.

[10] Julian of Norwich *Revelations of Divine Love* tr. Clifton Wolters (Harmondsworth: Penguin 1966) p.100.

[11] Verses 8–15 of Luther's 'Vom Himmel hoch' in *Lyra Germanica: Hymns for the Sundays and Chief Festivals of the Christian Year* ed. & tr. Catherine Winkworth (Longman 1855) pp.13–14.

[12] Martin Luther 'Lectures on Galatians' (1535) in *LW* 26, pp.28–30.

[13] Robert Southwell 'New Heaven. New Warre' in *The Poems of Robert Southwell SJ* ed. James H. McDonald & Nancy Pollard Brown (Oxford: Clarendon Press 1967) pp.14–15.

[14] Westminster Assembly *Shorter Catechism* (1648 edn.)

[15] Pascal *Pensées* tr. A.J. Krailsheimer (Harmondsworth: Penguin 1966) no.446, p.167.

[16] Thomas Brooks *An Ark for all God's Noahs* (1666).

[17] Free version of Joachim Neander's 'Meine Hoffnung' (1679) in *Hymns by Robert Bridges* (Oxford: Henry Daniel 1899) no.XXV.

[18] Charles Wesley *Nativity Hymns* (1746).

[19] From *George Macdonald: an Anthology* ed. C.S. Lewis (1946; Fontana 1983 edn.) pp.1 & 63.

[20] P.T. Forsyth *The Cruciality of the Cross* (Hodder 1909) pp.38–9.

[21] Karl Barth *Church Dogmatics* II/1 (Edinburgh: T. & T. Clark 1957) p.74.

[22] Karl Barth *Church Dogmatics* II/1 p.363.

[23] Karl Barth *Church Dogmatics* II/1 p.342.

[24] Vladimir Lossky *The Mystical Theology of the Eastern Church* (Cambridge: James Clarke 1957) pp.65–6.

[25] Kazoh Kitamori *Theology of the Pain of God* (SCM 1966) pp.19–20 & 167.

[26] Dorothy Sayers *The Zeal of thy House* (Gollancz 1952) pp.110–111.

[27] Klaus Klostermaier *Hindu and Christian in Vrindaban* (SCM 1969) [USA edition *In the Paradise of Krishna: Hindu and Christian Seekers (Westminster)*] pp.49–50.

[28] Metropolitan Anthony *God and Man* (Hodder 1971) pp.76–7.

[29] Fynn *Mr God This is Anna* (Collins 1974) p.118.

[30] Hans Küng *Does God Exist?* (Collins 1980) pp.632–4.

[31] Simon Barrington-Ward *CMS News-letter* no.463 (Nov. 1984).

[32] Augustine Sermon 241,2 in *St Augustine: Sermons on The Liturgical Seasons* (FC 38).

[33] Augustine *Expositions on the Book of Psalms* (LF II, 140) on Ps.XL.8.

[34] *St Francis of Assisi: Omnibus of Sources* ed. M.A. Habig (SPCK 2nd edn. 1979) pp.130–1.

[35] Julian of Norwich *Revelations of Divine Love* tr. Clifton Wolters (Harmondsworth: Penguin 1966) p.68.

[36] John Donne 'Preached at S. Pauls, in the Evening, upon Easter Day. 1625' *P&S* VI, 265.

[37] John Donne 'Sermon Preached at St Pauls for Easter Day 1628' *P&S* VIII, 224.

[38] Walter Charleton *The Darkness of Atheism Dispelled* (1652).

[39] Thomas Traherne *Poems, Centuries, and Three Thanksgivings* ed. A. Ridler (OUP 1966) pp.169–70.

[40] Thomas Traherne *Poems, Centuries and Three Thanksgivings* p.177.

[41] Thomas Traherne *Poems, Centuries and Three Thanksgivings* pp.377–8.

[42] Charles Simeon, during his last illness, in Carus p.806.

[43] Dr & Mrs Hudson Taylor *Hudson Taylor in Early Years* (CIM 1911) p.285.

[44] Francis Ridley Havergal in Janet Grierson *Francis Ridley Havergal: Worcestershire Hymnwriter* (The Havergal Society, 1979) pp.151–2.

[45] Gerard Manley Hopkins *Poems and Prose* (Harmondsworth: Penguin 1953) p.27.

[46] Gerard Manley Hopkins *Poems and Prose* p.51.

[47] Eric Gill, Introduction to *Twenty-Five Nudes* (Dent 1938) p.3.

[48] Simone Weil 'Forms of the Implicit Love of God' in *Waiting on God* (Fontana 1959) pp.126–7.

[49] D. Bonhoeffer *Letters & Papers from Prison* enlarged edn. ed. E. Bethge (SCM 1971) pp.168–9.

[50] Jack Clemo *The Invading Gospel* (Lakeland 1972) pp.70–1.

[51] Gerald Vann *To Heaven with Diana!: a study of Jordan of Saxony and Diana d'Andalò* (Collins 1960) pp.56–7.

[52] Helmut Thielicke *How the World Began* (Cambridge: James Clarke 1964) p.60.

[53] R.S. Thomas *Later Poems 1972–1982* (Macmillan 1983) p.201.

[54] Introductory Lecture, 16 in *Catechetical Lectures of S. Cyril* (LF).

[55] Augustine *The Trinity* VIII.7 from *Augustine: Later Works* ed. John Burnaby (SCM 1955, LCC VIII).

[56] Augustine *The Trinity* XV.2 from *Augustine: Later Works*.

Notes on Sources

[57] John Climacus *The Ladder of Divine Ascent* tr. Colm Luibhead and Norman Russell (SPCK 1982, CWSp) p.121.

[58] Martin Luther 'Holy Sacrament of Baptism' in *LW* 35, pp.30–1.

[59] Martin Luther 'The Greater Catechism' in *Luther's Primary Works* ed. H. Wace and C.A. Buchheim (Hodder 1896) pp.140 & 142.

[60] John Donne 'Sermon preached at Pauls upon Christmas Day, in the evening, 1624' in *P&S* VI, 172.

[61] John Preston *The Breast-plate of Faith and Love* (1630).

[62] Westminster Assembly *Shorter Catechism* (1648 edn.).

[63] Jonathan Edwards *Religious Affections* ed. J.E. Smith (New Haven: Yale UP 1959) pp.161–2.

[64] Jim Wallis *The Call to Conversion* (Tring: Lion 1982) pp.6–7, 123.

[65] Cyprian Treatise I (to Donatus), 3ff. in *The Treatises of S. Cyprian* (LF).

[66] Augustine *Confessions* tr. R.S. Pine-Coffin (Harmondsworth: Penguin 1967) VIII, 12, pp.177–8.

[67] Augustine *Confessions* X, 27.

[68] Martin Luther 'Preface to the Complete Edition of Luther's Latin Writings' (1545) in *LW* 34, 336–7.

[69] John Donne sermon preached at Lincolns Inn, 1618, in *P&S* II, 155.

[70] 'The Life of Dr Thomas Goodwin' (edited by his son) in Goodwin *Works* (1704) I, vii–ix.

[71] Blaise Pascal *Pensées* tr. A.J. Krailsheimer (Harmondsworth: Penguin 1966) no.913.

[72] John Bunyan *Grace Abounding to the Chief of Sinners* (1666) §203–7.

[73] Richard Baxter *The Autobiography* ed. J.M.Ll. Thompson (Dent, 1931) p.7.

[74] Jonathan Edwards *Memoirs of the Rev David Brainerd, Missionary to the Indians, chiefly taken from his own diary* (New Haven 1822 edn.; also available in vol II of Edwards' *Works*, published BOT).

[75] Charles Simeon in Carus pp.8–9.

[76] Charles Simeon to a missionary, Aug. 16, 1822 in Carus pp.570–1.

[77] *The Journals of Søren Kierkegaard 1835–1854* ed. A. Dru (Fontana 1958) p.142.

[78] W. Haslam *From Death into Life* (1880: repr. St Austell: Good News Crusade 1969) pp.69–70.

[79] Sadhu Sundar Singh 'With and without Christ' in A.J. Appasamy *Sundar Singh: A Biography* (Lutterworth 1958) p.21.

[80] C.S. Lewis *Surprised by Joy* (Fontana 1959 edn.) pp.182–3.

[81] Edwin Muir *An Autobiography* (Hogarth Press 1954) p.246.

[82] Basilea Schlink *When God Calls* (Lakeland 1970) pp.139–40.

[83] Geoffrey T. Bull *When Iron Gates Yield* (1955; Hodder & Stoughton 1976) p.140.

[84] Dag Hammarskjöld *Markings* tr. Leif Sjöberg & W.H. Auden (Faber & Faber 1964) p.169.

[85] John Berryman 'Eleven Addresses to the Lord, 7' *Love and Fame* (Faber & Faber 1971) p.90.

[86] Bilquis Sheikh *I Dared to Call Him Father* (Kingsway 1979) pp.51–3.

[87] Patrick Carpmael, Hilbre, Oakway, Reigate, previously unpublished.

[88] Melito of Sardis *On Pascha* tr. S.G. Hall (Oxford: Clarendon Press 1979) pp.100–3.

[89] Irenaeus *Against Heresies* 4.20.7, our tr.

[90] Interpolation in Guigo II *Scala Claustralium*, quoted in Simon Tugwell *Prayer* (Dublin: Veritas, 1974), I, 28–9.

[91] From George Herbert 'The Temple' in *Works* ed. F.E. Hutchinson (Oxford: Clarendon Press 1941).

[92] E.F. (=? Edward Fisher) *The Marrow of Modern Divinity*. Modern edition by C.G. McCrie (Glasgow: David Bryce 1902).

[93] Odes of Solomon no.3 from *The Odes of Solomon: the Syriac Texts* ed. and tr. J.H. Charlesworth (Missoula, Montana: Scholars Press 1977) p.19.

[94] Athanasius *De Incarnatione*, 14 in *Contra Gentes & De Incarnatione*, ed. and tr. R.W. Thomson (Oxford: Clarendon Press 1971).

[95] From *Intoxicated with God: the Fifty Spiritual Homilies of Macarius* tr. George A. Maloney SJ (Denville, NJ: Dimension Books 1978) Homily 30.4.

[96] From Eleanor Hull *Poem Book of the Gael* (Chatto, 1912) pp.119–20, adapted from a version by Mary Byrne in *Eriú* Vol.II (1905) pp.89–91, which also contains the original Gaelic.

[97] Symeon the New Theologian *Hymns of Divine Love* tr. George A. Maloney SJ (Denville, NJ: Dimension Books 1978) pp.168–9.

[98] Symeon the New Theologian *Ethics* X lines 879–885 & XI 167–172, tr. PS from *Traités Théologiques et Ethiques* ed. J. Darrouzès (SC 1967) II 322, 340.

[99] Desiderius Erasmus *Enchiridion* ed. R. Himelick (Indiana University Press, 1963) pp.130, 136.

[100] Martin Luther Fragment 45.20 from E. Vogelsang (ed.) *Unbekannte Fragmente aus Luthers zweite Psalmenvorlesung 1518* (Berlin 1940), quoted in Gordon Rupp *The Righteousness of God* (Hodder & Stoughton, 1953) p.225.

[101] Martin Luther 'Lectures on Galatians' (1535) in *LW* 26, pp.232–3.

[102] Martin Luther 'The Private Mass and the Consecration of Priests' (1533) in *LW* 38, 158.

[103] *Inst.* 3.2.24.

[104] John Bunyan *The Pilgrim's Progress* ed. J.B. Wharey, rev. Roger Sharrock (Oxford: Clarendon Press 1960) pp.32–3.

[105] Johann Andreas Rothe 1727, tr. John Wesley in *Hymns and Sacred Poems* (1740).

[106] John Newton to D. West esq., August 13, 1773 in Bull pp.136–7.

[107] *Journals & Letters of the Rev. Henry Martyn, B.D.* ed. S. Wilberforce (1837) I, 416–7, with *Life & Letters of the Rev. Henry Martyn, B.D.* ed. John Sargent (1819; new edn. 1885) p.140 interpolated.

[108] G.M. Hopkins *Poems and Prose* (Harmondsworth: Penguin 1953) p.51.

[109] Athene Seyler in J.H. Oldham *Florence Allshorn and the Story of St Julians* (St Julians, 1983) pp.xi–xii.

[110] Metropolitan Anthony *Living Prayer* (Darton, Longman & Todd 1966) p.115.

[111] Anselm 'Proslogion' in *Prayers and Meditations of St Anselm* tr. Sr Benedicta Ward (Harmondsworth: Penguin 1973) pp.243–4.

[112] Martin Luther, 'Preface to the Epistle of St Paul to the Romans' (1546) in *LW* 35, 370–1.

[113] *Inst.* 3.16.1.

[114] John Donne 'A Sermon preached to the Household at Whitehall. April 30.1626.' in *P&S* VII, 152–3.

[115] Pascal *Pensées* tr. A.J. Krailsheimer (Harmondsworth: Penguin 1966) no.424.

[116] Thomas Shepard *The Parable of the Ten Virgins* (1660).

[117] William Cowper 'Love Constraining to obedience' *Olney Hymns* (1779) no.54.

[118] Charles Simeon to Miss Mary Elliott, November 21, 1834 in Carus pp.738–40.

[119] Robert Murray M'Cheyne to Rev. Dan Edwards, 2 October 1840; in Andrew A. Bonar *Memoir and Remains of the Revd. R. Murray M'Cheyne* (Dundee, 1845); there is a modern reprint by BOT.

[120] Søren Kierkegaard, from *For Self-Examination* in *The Parables of Kierkegaard* ed. Thomas C. Oden (Princeton UP 1978) p.59.

[121] William Jay of Bath preaching, quoted by Spurgeon in *C.H. Spurgeon: the Early Years 1834–1859* (1897–1900; BOT edn., 1962) p.190.

[122] From *Spiritual Letters of Edward King D.D.* ed. B.W. Randolph (Mowbrays, 1910) p.15.

[123] George Mueller *Autobiography*, compiled by G.F. Bergin (1905) p.353.

[124] Edith Cherry, quoted in Elizabeth Elliott *Through Gates of Splendour* (Hodder & Stoughton 1957) p.156.

[125] J.H. Oldham *Florence Allshorn and the Story of St Julians* (St Julians, 1983 edn.) p.21.

[126] Helmut Thielicke 'The Festival of Light' in *Christ and the Meaning of Life* ed. and tr. John W. Doberstein (James Clarke 1965) p.28.

[127] Helder Camara *The Desert is Fertile* tr. Dinah Livingstone (Sheed & Ward 1974) p.38.

[128] V. Donovan *Christianity Rediscovered: An Epistle from the Masai* (SCM 1982) pp.62–3.

[129] Tertullian *On the Flesh of Christ*, V (ANF III, 525).

[130] The Epistle to Diognetus, 9, in *Early Christian Writings: the Apostolic Fathers* tr. Maxwell Staniforth (Penguin 1968) pp.180–1.

[131] Ephraem, in *Early Christian Prayers* ed. A. Hamman tr. W. Mitchell (Longmans 1967) p.180.

[132] In Erich Przywara *An Augustine Synthesis* (Sheed & Ward 1936) p.288.

[133] Anselm 'Meditation on Human Redemption' in *Prayers and Meditations of St Anselm* tr. Benedicta Ward (Penguin 1973) p.231.

[134] From Bonaventure 'The Tree of Life' in *Bonaventure: The Soul's Journey to God* ed. E. Cousins (SPCK 1978; CWSp) pp.148–9.

[135] Thomas à Kempis *The Imitation of Christ* tr. B.I. Knott (Fount 1978) 2.11.1.

[136] Martin Luther *Operationes in Psalmos* (1519–21) Weimar edn. V, 608; in Gordon Rupp *The Righteousness of God* (Hodder 1953) pp.240–1.

[137] Martin Luther *Operationes in Psalmos* (1519–21) Weimar edn. V, 602–3, our tr.

[138] John Bunyan *The Pilgrim's Progress* ed. J.B. Wharey, rev. Roger Sharrock (Oxford: Clarendon Press 1960) p.38.

[139] Isaac Watts *Hymns and Spiritual Songs* (1707).

[140] Isaac Watts *Hymns and Spiritual Songs* (1720 ed.).

[141] Charles Wesley *Hymns and Sacred Poems* (1739).

[142] Charles Simeon 'Christ Crucified, or Evangelical Religion Described' in *Let Wisdom Judge: University Addresses and Sermon Outlines by Charles Simeon* ed. A. Pollard (IVP, 1959) p.109.

[143] Charles Simeon 'On Justification by Faith', preached before Cambridge University in November 1815, in *Let Wisdom Judge: University Addresses and Sermon Outlines by Charles Simeon*, pp.74–5.

[144] Evan H. Hopkins *The Law of Liberty in the Spiritual Life* (1884) pp.132–3.

[145] J. Denney *The Second Epistle to the Corinthians* (Expositor's Bible, Hodder 1894) pp.221-2.

[146] P.T. Forsyth *The Cruciality of the Cross* (Hodder 1909) pp.52–3.

[147] G.A. Studdert Kennedy *The Word and the Work* (Longmans 1925) pp.57–8.

[148] Emil Brunner *The Mediator* tr. Olive Wyon (Lutterworth 1934) p.473.

[149] Dietrich Bonhoeffer *The Cost of Discipleship* (SCM 1959) p.79.

[150] Amy Carmichael *If* (SPCK 1963) pp.32, 40, 54, 58, 68.

[151] T.F. Torrance *Theology in Reconstruction* (SCM 1965) pp.162–3.

[152] Anon., quoted by Frank Lake *Clinical Theology* (Darton, Longman & Todd 1966) pp.820–1.

[153] Frank Lake *Clinical Theology* (Darton, Longman & Todd 1966) pp.794–5.

[154] Richard Wurmbrand *Sermons in Solitary Confinement* (Hodder & Stoughton 1969) p.96.

[155] D. Martyn Lloyd-Jones *Romans: Exposition of Chapter 5* (BOT 1971) pp.21–2.

[156] John Carden *Empty Shoes: A Way in to Pakistan* (Highway Press 1971) pp.34–6.

[157] Jürgen Moltmann *The Crucified God* tr. R.A. Wilson & John Bowden (SCM 1974) pp.242–3.

[158] Chandran Devanesen in G. & M. Harcourt *Short Prayers for the Long Day* (Collins 1978) p.103.

[159] Thomas Merton *The Wisdom of the Desert* (Sheldon Press 1974) p.50.

[160] *Catechetical Lectures of S. Cyril* (LF) XVI, 12.

[161] *Intoxicated with God: the Fifty Spiritual Homilies of Marcarius* ed. George A. Maloney SJ (Denville, N.J.: Dimension Books 1978) Homily 18.7,8.

[162] Edward Caswall *Lyra Catholica* (1849); revised by the compilers of *Hymns Ancient & Modern* (1861) as 'Come, Thou Holy Spirit, Come'.

[163] *Bar Hebraeus' Book of the Dove* tr. A.J. Wensinck (Leyden: E.J. Brill 1919) p.4.

[164] *Inst.* 1.9.3.

[165] *Inst.* 3.2.36 & 37.

[166] Lancelot Andrewes 'A Sermon preached before the King's majesty at Greenwich on the eighth of June, A.D. MDCVI, being Whitsunday; A Sermon of the Sending of the Holy Ghost' in *Ninety-Six Sermons* (Oxford 1841: Anglo-Catholic Library) III, 108–9.

[167] Thomas Brooks *Precious Remedies against Satan's Devices* (1652).

[168] Thomas Goodwin 'An Exposition of the Epistle to the Ephesians' *Works* (Edinburgh 1861–66) I,251.

[169] John Owen 'Pneumatologia: or, a discourse concerning the Holy Spirit' from *Works* (repr. BOT 1965) III, 194.

[170] John Wesley *The Witness of the Spirit* (1788) pp.15–6.

[171] Nicholas Motovilov (1809–1832) in Valentine Zander *St Seraphim of Sarov* tr. Sr. Gabriel Anne (SPCK 1975) pp.90–92.

[172] Robert Murray M'Cheyne 'Thanksgiving obtains the Spirit', sermon preached Nov. 24, 1839, in *Sermons* (BOT 1960).

[173] Roland Allen *Pentecost and the World* (OUP 1917); in *The Ministry of the Spirit* ed. D.M. Paton (World Dominion Press 1960) pp.45–7.

[174] Samuel Chadwick *The Way to Pentecost* (Hodder & Stoughton 1933) p.30.

[175] William Temple *Readings in St John's Gospel* (Macmillan 1945) pp.288–9.

[176] D.M. Lloyd-Jones *Christ our Sanctification* (IVF 1948) pp.20–21.

[177] Paul Claudel *I Believe in God* ed. Agnès du Sarment, tr. Helen Weaver (Harvill Press 1965) p.209.

[178] A.W. Tozer *The Divine Conquest* (STL 1984) p.98.

[179] H.U. von Balthasar *The Glory of the Lord: a Theological Aesthetics*, vol. I, 'Seeing the Form', ed. Joseph Fessio & John Riches, tr. Erasmo Leivà-Merikakis (Edinburgh: T.&T. Clark 1982) pp.493–4.

[180] Francis Schaeffer *True Spirituality* (STL 1979) pp.87–8.

[181] J.V. Taylor *The Go-Between God* (SCM 1972) pp.16ff.

[182] J.C. Haughey *The Conspiracy of God* (Image Books 1973) p.75.

[183] Cardinal L.J. Suenens *A New Pentecost?* (DLT 1975) p.161.

[184] C.S. Song *Third Eye Theology* (Lutterworth 1980) p.3.

[185] S. Barrington-Ward, *CMS Newsletter* no.448, July 1982.

[186] Steve Turner *Up to Date: Poems 1968–1982* (Hodder & Stoughton 1983) p.166.

[187] Tertullian *Apology* 39 (ANF III, 46ff.).

[188] Epistle to Diognetus, 5 in *Early Christian Writings: the Apostolic Fathers* tr. Maxwell Staniforth (Penguin 1968) pp.176–7.

[189] Gregory Thaumaturgus *Oration & Panegyric addressed to Origen*, VI (ANF VI, 28).

[190] Augustine 'Homilies on 1 John' (VII.8) in *Augustine: Later Works* ed. J. Burnaby (SCM 1955; LCC VIII).

[191] Christopher Ostorodt 'Treatise on the Chief Points of the Christian Religion' from *Every Need Supplied* ed. Donald F. Durnbaugh (Philadelphia: Temple UP 1974) p.139.

[192] Richard Sibbes 'The Bruised Reed and Smoking Flax' in *Works* (BOT reprint, 1973) I, 53.

[193] Jonathan Mitchel 'A letter' in *A Discourse of the Glory to which God hath called Believers* (2nd ed., Boston 1721).

[194] From the Diary of David Brainerd in Jonathan Edwards *Works* (BOT) II.

[195] John Wesley *Letters* ed. John Telford (Epworth Press 1931) III, 12–14.

[196] John Newton to the Rev. Mr Whitfield in Bull 42–3.

[197] John Wesley *Works* (3rd edn. 1819–21) V, 296.

[198] Charles Simeon to the Duchess of Beaufort in Carus, p.582.

[199] Charles Simeon to Miss Mary Elliott in Carus, pp.769–772.

[200] C.H. Spurgeon 'On Religious Grumblers' *John Ploughman's Talk* (1868) pp.19–21.

[201] Dietrich Bonhoeffer *Life Together* (SCM 1954) p.70.

202 Dietrich Bonhoeffer to his parents 14 June 1943, in *Letters and Papers from Prison* (SCM 1971) p.53.

203 A.W. Tozer *The Divine Conquest* (STL 1984) pp.13–4.

204 J.V. Taylor *The Primal Vision* (SCM 1963) pp.8–9.

205 Hans Küng *The Church* tr. R.&R. Ockenden (Search Press 1968) pp.238–9.

206 Francis Schaeffer *True Spirituality* (STL 1979) pp.176–7.

207 Henri Nouwen *Reaching Out* (Fount 1980) p.45.

208 C.M. Mwoleka 'Trinity and Community' in A. Shorter WF, *African Christian Spirituality* (Geoffrey Chapman 1978) p.124.

209 C. Lyimo 'An Ujamaa Theology' in A. Shorter WF, *African Christian Spirituality* p.128.

210 V. Donovan *Christianity Rediscovered: An Epistle from the Masai* (SCM 1982) pp.91–3.

211 Jean Vanier *The Challenge of L'Arche* (Darton, Longman & Todd 1982) p.268.

212 Source untraced.

213 Martin Luther 'Preface to the Old Testament' (1545) in *LW* 35, 236.

214 William Tyndale 'A Pathway into the Holy Scripture' in *The Work of William Tyndale* ed. G.E. Duffield (Appleford: Sutton Courtenay Press 1964) pp.4–5.

215 Thomas Cranmer, 'A Fruitful Exhortation to the Reading and Knowledge of Holy Scripture' in *The Book of Homilies* (1547).

216 Hugh Latimer 'Sermon of the Plough' in *Sermons by Hugh Latimer* (Cambridge: Parker Society 1844) p.62.

217 *Inst.* 1.7.5.

218 'Memoir of Rev. John Robinson' in *The Works of John Robinson, Pastor of the Pilgrim Fathers* ed. Robert Ashton (1851) I, xliv.

219 Westminster Assembly *Confession of Faith* (1648 edn.).

220 Robert Boyle *Some Considerations touching the Style of the Holy Scripture* (1661) pp.25–6.

221 Isaac Watts *The Psalms of David Imitated in the Language of the New Testament* (1719).

222 Augustus M. Toplady notebook entry, *Works* (1825) IV, 289.

223 John Newton *Letters* (BOT 1960) pp.79 & 81-2.

224 Thomas Scott Preface to *The Holy Bible . . . with explanatory notes, practical observations and copious marginal references* (6th ed., 1823).

225 Charles Simeon, Preface to *Horae Homileticae* (1819–28) I, xxiii–iv.

226 Charles Simeon in Carus p.811.

227 R. Payne Smith *Prophecy a Preparation for Christ* (Bampton Lectures 1869) pp.38–9.

228 C.H. Spurgeon *Metropolitan Tabernacle Pulpit XXIX* (1883), p.215.

229 William Booth in *The War Cry* May 30, 1885, from *The Founder Speaks Again* ed. Cyril J. Barnes (Salvationist Publishing 1960) p.198.

[230] Dietrich Bonhoeffer *Life Together* (SCM 1954) pp.38–9.

[231] Austin Farrer *The Glass of Vision* (Dacre Press 1948) pp.35–6.

[232] A.W. Tozer *The Pursuit of God* (STL 1984) p.69.

[233] T.F. Torrance *Theology in Reconstruction* (SCM 1965) pp.139–40.

[234] Hans Urs von Balthasar *The Glory of the Lord: A Theological Aesthetics*. Vol. I: 'Seeing the Form' (Edinburgh: T & T Clark 1982) p.31.

[235] 'The Didache', in *Early Christian Writings* tr. M. Staniforth (Harmondsworth: Penguin 1968) pp.231–2.

[236] Augustine *Homilies on the Gospel of John* (NPNF VII, 174–8) XXVII,1,6,11.

[237] H. Zwingli 'Of the Virtue of the Sacraments' [from *An Exposition of the Faith*] in *Zwingli and Bullinger* ed. G.W. Bromiley (SCM 1953; LCC XXIV) pp.263–4.

[238] M. Bucer 'The Censura' in *Martin Bucer and the Book of Common Prayer* ed. E.C. Whitaker (Mayhew-McCrimmon 1974; Alcuin Club) p.64, tr. slightly altered.

[239] *Inst.* 4.17.46.

[240] John Jewel 'An Apologie of the Church of England' in *English Reformers* ed. T.H.L. Parker (SCM 1966; LCC XXVI) pp.28–9.

[241] Lewis Bayly *Practice of Piety* (1613, 3rd edn.).

[242] John Preston *Three Sermons upon the Sacrament of the Lord's Supper* (Oxford 1613).

[243] C. Winkworth *Lyra Germanica: Second Series: The Christian Life* (1858) pp.96–8.

[244] Edward Taylor 'Preparatory Meditations' before the Lord's Supper, modernised from *Poems* ed. Donald E. Stanford (New Haven: Yale UP 1960) pp.18–9.

[245] *Edward Taylor's Treatise Concerning the Lord's Supper* ed. Norman S. Grabo (East Lansing: Michigan State UP 1966) pp.179–80.

[246] Charles Wesley *Hymns on the Lord's Supper* (1745) no.16.

[247] Charles Welsey *Hymns on the Lord's Supper* (1745) no.164.

[248] Philip Doddridge *Hymns founded on Various Texts in the Holy Scriptures* (1755), Hymn CLXXI.

[249] P.T. Forsyth *The Church and the Sacraments* (Independent Press 1947) p.141.

[250] G.C. Berkouwer *The Sacraments* (Eerdmans 1969) pp.240–1.

[251] J.V. Taylor *The Primal Vision* (SCM 1963) p.200.

[252] J. Neville Ward *The Use of Praying* (Epworth Press 1963) p.83.

[253] E. Schillebeeckx OP *The Eucharist* tr. N.D. Smith (Sheed & Ward 1968) p.137.

[254] Marie-Louise Martin *Kimbangu: An African Prophet and his Church* (Blackwell 1975) pp.179–81.

[255] T.F. Torrance *Theology in Reconciliation* (Geoffrey Chapman 1975) pp.119–20.

256 V. Donovan *Christianity Rediscovered* (SCM 1982) pp.60–1.

257 Evagrius 'On Prayer' 60, quoted in Kenneth Leech *Soul Friend* (Sheldon 1977) p.35.

258 Augustine *Expositions on the Book of Psalms* (NPNF VIII, 107) on Ps. XXXVIII, 13.

259 Isaac of Nineveh 'Directions on Spiritual Training' no.117, in *Early Fathers from the Philokalia* ed. & tr. E. Kadloubovsky & G.E.H. Palmer (Faber & Faber 1954).

260 From *The Art of Prayer* compiled by Igumen Chariton of Valamo, tr. E. Kadloubovsky & E.M. Palmer (Faber & Faber 1966) p.87.

261 *The Cloud of Unknowing* tr. William Johnston (Image Books 1973) p.48.

262 Martin Luther 'A Simple Way to Pray for a good friend. How one should pray; for Peter, the Master Barber' in *LW* 43. pp.198–200.

263 John Donne 'A Sermon preached at the funeral of Sir William Cockayne, 1626' in *P&S* VII, 264.

264 Richard Sibbes 'The Bruised Reed and Smoking Flax' in *Works* ed. Alexander Grosart (Edinburgh 1862–4), 1, 65.

265 John Preston *Three Sermons upon the Sacrament of the Lord's Supper* (Oxford 1631).

266 Richard Baxter *The Saints Everlasting Rest* (1650) ch.8.

267 Thomas Brooks *Precious Remedies against Satan's Devices* (1652).

268 Brother Lawrence *The Practice of the Presence of God* tr. E.M. Blaiklock (Hodder & Stoughton 1981) pp.44–5.

269 Charles Wesley *Hymns and Sacred Poems* (1742).

270 C.H. Spurgeon in H.E. Fosdick *The Meaning of Prayer* (1915; Fontana 1960) p.121.

271 From *The Art of Prayer* compiled by Igumen Chariton of Valamo, tr. E. Kadloubovsky & E.M. Palmer (Faber & Faber 1966) p.51.

272 From *The Art of Prayer* p.89.

273 *The Way of a Pilgrim* anon. Russian, 19th c., tr. R.M. French (SPCK 1972 edn.) pp.40–1.

274 *George Macdonald: An Anthology* ed. C.S. Lewis (Fount 1983 edn.) p.137.

275 J.O. Fraser in Mrs Howard Taylor *Behind the Ranges, a Biography of J.O. Fraser of Lisuland* (1944; OMF 1970) pp.111–3.

276 Jewish prisoner quoted in Monica Furlong *Contemplating Now* (Hodder 1971) p.68.

277 A.W. Tozer *The Pursuit of God* (Bromley: Send the Light 1981) pp.42–3.

278 Quoted in Michael Bourdeaux *Risen Indeed!* (DLT 1983) p.59.

279 Maurice Giuliani SJ 'Finding God in All Things' in *Finding God in All Things: Essays in Ignatian Spirituality* tr. W.J. Young SJ (Chicago: Henry Regnery 1958) p.13.

[280] John V. Taylor *The Go-Between God* (SCM 1972) pp.242–3.

[281] Metropolitan Anthony *God and Man* (Hodder & Stoughton 1971) pp.135–8.

[282] Simon Tugwell *Prayer Vol.2: Prayer in Practice* (Dublin: Veritas Publications 1974) pp.62–3, 65.

[283] Carlo Carretto *In Search of the Beyond* (Darton, Longman & Todd 1975) p.81.

[284] Lord Hailsham *The Door Wherein I Went* (Collins 1975) p.8.

[285] Jürgen Moltmann *The Open Church* (SCM 1978) p.44.

[286] Robert Faricy *Praying for Inner Healing* (SCM 1979) p.75.

[287] Origen *Contra Celsum* tr. H. Chadwick (Cambridge UP 1953) Preface, 1 & 2.

[288] In Samuel M. Zwemer *Raymond Lull: First Missionary to the Moslems* (NY: Funk & Wagnalls 1902) p.53.

[289] Erasmus *Treatise on Preaching* quoted in Eugene Stock *The History of the Church Missionary Society* (CMS 1899) I, 18–9.

[290] Henry James Coleridge SJ *The Life and Letters of St Francis Xavier* (Burns Oates 1881) I, 156–7.

[291] Richard Baxter *Poetical Fragments* (1681).

[292] 'An attempt at a memoir of brother Carey' in Eustace Carey *Memoir of William Carey D.D.* (1836) p.75.

[293] John Venn, address at the second Valedictory Meeting of the Church Missionary Society, January 13, 1806, quoted in Eugene Stock *The History of the Church Missionary Society* (CMS 1899) I, 85–6.

[294] Henry Venn, address to the Islington clerical meeting, January 10, 1865 in Max Warren *To Apply the Gospel: selections from the writings of Henry Venn* (Grand Rapids: Eerdmans 1971) p.119.

[295] Dr & Mrs Hudson Taylor *Biography of James Hudson Taylor* (OMF 1965) p.167.

[296] William Booth *In Darkest England and the Way Out* (1890) p.45.

[297] Roland Allen *Missionary Methods: St Paul's or ours?* (World Dominion Press 1930) pp.185–6.

[298] Roland Allen *Pentecost and the World* (OUP 1917) in *The Ministry of the Spirit: selected writings of Roland Allen* ed. D.M. Paton (World Dominion Press 1965) p.21.

[299] W.H.T. Gairdner *The Rebuke of Islam* (United Council for Missionary Education 1920) pp.136–7 (a revised edition of *The Reproach of Islam* 1909).

[300] From Mrs Howard Taylor *Behind the Ranges: Fraser of Lisuland* (1944: OMF 1970 edn.) p.229.

[301] Quoted in Stephen Neill *The Unfinished Task* (Edinburgh House and Lutterworth 1957) p.152.

[302] Kenneth Cragg *The Call of the Minaret* (NY: OUP 1956) p.256ff.

[303] Kenneth Cragg *The Call of the Minaret* p.334ff.

[304] Stephen Neill *The Unfinished Task* (Edinburgh House and Lutterworth 1957) p.162.

[305] Isobel Kuhn *By Searching* (OMF 1957) p.106.

[306] Max Warren, introduction to A.K. Cragg *Sandals at the Mosque* (SCM 1959) p.9.

[307] A.W. Tozer *The Knowledge of the Holy* (STL/Kingsway 1976) p.41.

[308] Klaus Klostermaier *Hindu and Christian in Vrindaban* (SCM 1969) [USA edition *In the Paradise of Krishna: Hindu and Christian Seekers* (Westminster)] p.102.

[309] Ayako Miura *The Wind is Howling* tr. Valerie Griffiths (Hodder 1978) pp.41–2.

[310] Lesslie Newbigin *The Open Secret* (SPCK 1978) pp.196–7.

[311] Kwame Bediako 'Christologies amid African Traditional Religions' in *Sharing Jesus in the Two-Thirds World* ed. Vinay Samuel and Chris Sugden (Partnership in Mission – Asia, 1983) p.148.

[312] Martin Luther *The Freedom of a Christian* (1520) in *LW* 21, 344.

[313] Martin Luther *The Freedom of a Christian* (1520) in *LW* 21, 366–8.

[314] Peter Riedemann *Account of our Religion, Doctrine & Faith* (ie of the Hutterian Brethren, 1540) from *Every Need Supplied: Mutual Aid and Christian Community in the Free Churches 1525–1675* ed. Donald F. Durnbaugh (Philadelphia: Temple UP 1974) p.109.

[315] From the fifth sermon on the Lord's Prayer, *Sermons by Hugh Latimer* (Cambridge: Parker Society 1844) p.399.

[316] William Perkins *A Treatise of Callings* (Cambridge 1602).

[317] William Bridge *A Lifting Up for the Downcast* (1648: BOT 1961) pp.213–4.

[318] George Fox 'To all the Magistrates in London . . .' (1657) in *Works* (1694) III.

[319] Richard Baxter 'A Christian Directory' Part IV, Christian Politics, in *Works* (1830) VI, 351.

[320] John Newton 'Thoughts upon the African Slave Trade' (1788) in *Works* ed. R. Cecil (2nd ed. 1816) pp.519–20, 523–4.

[321] Carus, p.80.

[322] John Wesley to William Wilberforce, *Letters* ed. John Telford (Epworth Press 1931) VIII, 265.

[323] William Carey *An Enquiry into the obligations of Christians to use Means for the conversion of the Heathen* (1792; facsimile intro. E.A. Payne, Carey Kingsgate Press 1961) p.86.

[324] William Wilberforce to the House of Commons June 22, 1813 *Parliamentary Debates* XXVI col.853.

[325] David Bogue *On Universal Peace* (Society for the Promotion of Permanent & Universal Peace, 1819).

[326] George Mueller *Autobiography*, compiled by G.F. Bergin (1905) p.81.

[327] John Caird 'A sermon preached at Crathie Church, October 14, 1855 before Her Majesty the Queen & Prince Albert'.

[328] F.D Maurice 'The Law of Christ the Law of Humanity', preached at Lincoln's Inn, 14 March, 1858, in *Sermons and Society* ed. Paul Welsby (Penguin 1970) pp.242–5.

[329] Andrew Murray *Abide in Christ* (Lakeland 1968 edn.) p.118.

[330] William Booth *In Darkest England and the Way Out* (1890) p.16.

[331] The Declaration of the National Free Synod [part of the movement known as the 'Confessing Church'] at Barmen, May 29–31, 1934; in E.H. Robertson *Christians against Hitler* (SCM 1962) pp.48–52.

[332] C.S. Lewis 'The Weight of Glory', a sermon preached at St Mary the Virgin Oxford, first pr. in *Theology* (November 1941); repr. in *Screwtape Proposes a Toast* (Fontana 1965) pp.109–10.

[333] Dietrich Bonhoeffer *Letters and Papers from Prison* (enlarged ed., SCM 1971) pp.369–70.

[334] Martin Luther King 'Loving your Enemies' in *Strength to Love* (Fontana 1969) pp.48–9.

[335] Martin Luther King quoted in Stephen B. Oates *Let the Trumpet Sound: the Life of Martin Luther King Jr.* (Search Press 1982) pp.260–2.

[336] Derek Kidner *Proverbs* (Tyndale Old Testament Commentary; Tyndale Press 1964) p.35.

[337] 'Confession on the Responsibility of the United Church of Christ in Japan during World War II' in *Asian Voices in Christian Theology* ed. Gerald H. Anderson (Maryknoll NY: Orbis 1976) pp.254–5.

[338] A.M. Ramsey *God, Christ and the World* (SCM 1969) pp.26–7.

[339] J.R.W. Stott *Christ the Controversialist* (Tyndale Press 1970) p.188.

[340] 'Theological Declaration by Christian Ministers in the Republic of Korea, 1973' in *Asian Voices in Christian Theology* ed. Gerald H. Anderson (Maryknoll NY: Orbis 1976) p.242.

[341] Jean Vanier *Community & Growth* (Darton Longman & Todd 1979) p.43.

[342] David Sheppard *Bias to the Poor* (Hodder & Stoughton 1983) p.89.

[343] Orlando E. Costas 'Proclaiming Christ in the Two-Thirds World' in *Sharing Jesus in the Two-Thirds World* ed. Vinay Samuel and Chris Sugden (Bangalore: Partnership in Mission – Asia, 1983) p.9.

[344] *The Treatise of Iranaeus of Lugdunum Against the Heresies* tr. F.R.M. Hitchcock (SPCK 1916) 2.22.4.

[345] Gregory of Nyssa 'The Life of Moses' in *From Glory to Glory: Texts from Gregory of Nyssa's Mystical Writings* sel. J. Danielou SJ tr. H. Musurillo SJ (John Murray 1962) p.147ff.

[346] Isaac of Stella Sermon 7 from the *Sermons* (SC), quoted in A.M. Allchin *The Dynamic of Tradition* (Darton, Longman & Todd 1981) p.100.

[347] *Inst.* 3.6.5.

[348] *Poems of St John of the Cross* tr. Roy Campbell (Harvill 1951) pp.11–13.

[349] John Preston *The Breast-plate of Faith and Love* (1630).

[350] Richard Sibbes 'The Bruised Reed and Smoking Flax', *Works* (BOT 1973) I, 49.

[351] John Newton to Mrs Wilberforce, January 18, 1770, in Bull pp.80–1.

[352] William Carey to his son, in F. Deaville Walker *William Carey: Missionary Pioneer and Statesman* (SCM 1926) p.47.

[353] Charles Simeon to Rev. Thomas Thomason, August 19, 1812, in Carus p.357.

[354] *George Macdonald: An Anthology* ed. C.S. Lewis (Fount 1983) pp.17–8.

[355] Olive Wyon *The School of Prayer* (SCM 1943).

[356] Thomas Merton *The Sign of Jonas* (Sheldon Press 1953) pp.102–3.

[357] Isobel Kuhn *By Searching* (OMF 1957) p.79.

[358] Gerald Vann *To Heaven with Diana!* (Collins 1960) pp.51–2.

[359] Paul Tournier *The Adventure of Living* (SCM 1966) pp.38–9.

[360] John Climacus *The Ladder of Divine Ascent* tr. Colm Luibhead and Norman Russell (SPCK 1982; CWSp) p.139.

[361] Conflation & adaptation of Kallistos Ware, Introduction to John Climacus *The Ladder of Divine Ascent* (SPCK 1982; CWSp) pp.26–7 and *Mystic Treatises by Isaac of Nineveh* tr. A.J. Wensinck (Amsterdam 1923) pp.85–6.

[362] Ramon Lull *Blanquerna* tr. E. Allison Peers (Jarrolds 1926) ch.79.

[363] F. Ageno (ed) *Iacopone da Todi: Laudi* (Florence 1953) pp.341–2, quoted in John Saward *Perfect Fools* (OUP 1980) p.89.

[364] *The Spiritual Exercises of St Ignatius* tr. Louis J. Puhl SJ (Loyola University Press 1951) para.234.

[365] Philip Doddridge *The Rise and Progress of Religion in the Soul* (1745; Berwick 1818 edn.) pp.176–8.

[366] Carus p.523.

[367] *Journals and Letters of The Rev. Henry Martyn B.D.* ed. Samuel Wilberforce (1837) I, 446.

[368] Francis Ridley Havergal *Loyal Responses* (1878).

[369] Dr & Mrs Hudson Taylor *Biography of James Hudson Taylor* (OMF 1965) p.311.

[370] Charles de Foucauld, source not found.

[371] N.P. Grubb *C.T. Studd, Cricketer & Pioneer* (1933; Lutterworth 1970) p.163–5.

[372] Evelyn Underhill *Worship* (Fontana 1962 edn.) p.173.

[373] Watchman Nee *Release of the Spirit* (STL 1968) pp.12–13.

[374] John Wesley 'Directions for Renewing our Covenant with God' (1780) in *John & Charles Wesley* ed. Frank Whaling (SPCK 1981; CWSp

[375] Dugald Macfadyen *Alexander Mackennal, B.A., D.D.: life and letters* (1905) pp.122–3.

[376] Quoted in Paul Sangster *Dr Sangster* (Epworth Press 1962) p.294.

[377] J.E. Fison *Fire Upon the Earth* (Edinburgh House Press, 1958) p.72.

[378] Thomas Merton 'Sacred Art and the Spiritual Life' in *Disputed Questions* (Hollis & Carter 1961) pp.154–6.

[379] Anthony Bloom *God and Man* (Hodder & Stoughton 1971) pp.81–2.

[380] Thomas Brooks *Heaven on Earth* (1657).

[381] John Wesley *Works* (3rd ed. 1819–21) XIV, 360–1.

[382] John Newton to Mrs Wilberforce, September 1764, in Bull pp.74–5.

[383] Augustus Montague Toplady *Works* (1825) VI, 402–3.

[384] Charles Simeon in Carus pp.15–6.

[385] Origen 'Prologue to the Commentary on the Song of Songs' in *Origen* ed. Rowan A. Greer (SPCK: SWSp 1979) p.223.

[386] Augustine *Expositions on the Book of Psalms* (LF V, 149ff) on Ps.CV.3.

[387] Bernard of Clairvaux *On the Love of God* (Mowbrays 1982) pp.53–4.

[388] Ramon Lull *The Book of the Lover and the Beloved* ed. K. Leech (Sheldon 1978) p.29.

[389] Richard Rolle *Fire of Love* (Harmondsworth: Penguin 1972) pp.98ff.

[390] William Cowper *Poems translated from the French of Madame Guion* (Newport Pagnell, 1801).

[391] Henry Drummond *The Greatest Thing in the World* (Hodder & Stoughton 1980) pp.41–2.

[392] Abbé Henri de Tourville *Letters of Direction* intr. Evelyn Underhill (Mowbrays 1982) pp.72, 82–3.

[393] David Watson *Fear No Evil* (Hodder & Stoughton 1984) p.171.

[394] Bernard of Clairvaux *On the Song of Songs* Sermon 9:7. (Cistercian Fathers Series) I, 56.

[395] Julian of Norwich *Revelations of Divine Love* tr. Clifton Wolters (Harmondsworth: Penguin 1966) pp.120–1.

[396] Martin Luther, tr. Thomas Carlyle in *Fraser's Magazine*, 1831.

[397] Jean Calvin 'Commentary on Thessalonians' from *Calvin: Commentaries* ed. & tr. Joseph Haroutunian & Louise Pettibone Smith (SCM 1958: LCC XXIII) pp. 202–3.

[398] Menno Simons 'Reply to False Accusations' from *The Complete Writings of Menno Simons* ed. J.C. Wenger (Scottdale, Pennsylvania: Herald Press 1956) p.554.

[399] Bishop Hugh Latimer, letter from prison to Bishop Nicholas Ridley, source untraced.

[400] John of the Cross 'Dark Night of the Soul' 2.10.1,2 in *The Collected Works of St John of the Cross* ed. Kieran Kavanagh OCD and Otilio Rodriguez OCD (Washington DC: Institute of Carmelite Studies 1973).

[401] John Donne *Complete English Poems* ed. A.J. Smith (Penguin 1971) pp.314–5.

[402] John Donne 'The Second of my Prebend Sermons upon my five Psalms, Preached at St Pauls, January 29 1625/6' in P&S VII, 54.

[403] John Preston *The Breast Plate of Faith and Love* (1630).

[404] Richard Sibbes 'The Bruised Reed and Smoking Flax' in *Works* ed. Alexander Grosart (Edinburgh 1862–4; repr. BOT 1973) I, 64.

[405] Richard Sibbes 'The Bruised Reed and Smoking Flax' in *Works* I, 85–6.

[406] Thomas Goodwin *A Child of Light Walking in Darkness* (1636) in *Works* (Edinburgh: James Nichol 1861) III, 237, 330–1.

[407] Thomas Brooks *Precious Remedies against Satan's Devices* (1652).

[408] Thomas Brooks *Precious Remedies against Satan's Devices* (1652).

[409] *No more but my Love: Letters of George Fox, Quaker* ed. Cecil W. Sharman (Quaker Home Service 1980) p.4.

[410] Pascal *Pensées* tr. A.J. Krailsheimer (Penguin 1966) nos.192 & 212.

[411] Robert Leighton undated letter to an unnamed Lady in *Works* (James Duncan 1830) I, CXXXII–III.

[412] John Wesley to Charles, in cypher; source untraced.

[413] Charles Wesley *Hymns and Sacred Poems* (1742).

[414] Samuel Johnson *Rasselas, Poems and Selected Prose* ed. Bertrand H. Bronson 3rd edn. (New York: Holt, Rinehart & Winston 1971) pp.35–6.

[415] John Berridge to John Newton Oct. 18, 1771, in J.C. Ryle *The Christian Leaders of the Last Century* (Nelson 1873) p.242.

[416] Newton to Lord Dartmouth, March 1772, in *Letters of John Newton* (BOT 1960) pp.128–9.

[417] *Letters of John Newton* p.96.

[418] Søren Kierkegaard 'Works of Love' (1847) in *Parables of Kierkegaard* ed. T.C. Oden (Princeton UP 1978) p.71.

[419] Anti-Climacus in Søren Kierkegaard 'The Sickness unto Death' (1849) p.176 in *Parables of Kierkegaard* p.93.

[420] *The Journals of Kierkegaard* ed. Alexander Dru (Fontana 1958) p.245.

[421] Gerard Manley Hopkins *Poems and Prose* (Harmondsworth: Penguin 1953) p.61.

[422] Bishop Taylor Smith *The Keswick Week, 1926* p.65.

[423] Amy Carmichael *Toward Jerusalem* (SPCK 1936) p.85.

[424] Simone Weil 'The Love of God and Affliction' in *Waiting on God* (Fontana 1959 edn.) pp.93–4.

[425] Geoffrey T. Bull *When Iron Gates Yield* (Hodder 1976) p.188.

[426] Olive Wyon *Prayer* (Fontana 1962) p.80.

[427] Frank Lake *Clinical Theology* (Darton, Longman & Todd 1966) pp.733–4.

[428] Arthur Bennett *The Valley of Vision* (BOT 1975) p.72.

Notes on Sources

429 Alexander Solzhenitsyn *The Gulag Archipelago 1918–1956 [Vol.II] Parts III-IV* tr. Thomas P. Whitney (Collins & Harvill P. 1975) pp.615–7.

430 Basilea Schlink *Patmos* (Lakeland 1976) pp.104–5.

431 Dorothee Sölle *Revolutionary Patience* (Lutterworth 1979) p.34.

432 Jakob Hutter Letter III 'Brotherly Faithfulness' *Epistles from a Time of Persecution* (Plough Publishing House 1979) pp.56–7.

433 Lewis Bayly *The Practice of Piety* (3rd edn. 1613).

434 John Donne *Complete English Poems* ed. A.J. Smith (Penguin 1971) pp.347–8.

435 John Donne 'Preached at S. Dunstanes upon Trinity Sunday 1627' in *P&S* VIII, 53.

436 Samuel Rutherford to Robert Gordon of Knockbrex, Jan. 1, 1637; letter 76 in *Letters of Samuel Rutherford* ed. Andrew Bonar (Oliphant 1891) pp. 161–2.

437 *Lyra Germanica: Hymns for the Sundays and Chief Festivals of the Christian Year* (Longman 1855) pp.152–3.

438 Søren Kierkegaard *Christian Discourses* tr. Walter Lowrie (Oxford University Press 1940) p.116.

439 *George Macdonald, An Anthology* ed. C.S. Lewis (Fount 1983 edn.) p.91.

440 Marie-Louise Martin *Kimbangu: An African Prophet and his Church* (Blackwell 1975) p.83.

441 Dietrich Bonhoeffer *Letters & Papers from Prison*, enlarged edn. (SCM 1971) p.14.

442 Source untraced.

443 *The Life and Letters of Fr Andrew* ed. Kathleen E. Burne (Mowbrays 1948) p.118.

444 Paul Claudel d.1955, source untraced.

445 Agnes Sandford *Healing Gifts of the Spirit* (Evesham: Arthur James 1966) pp.50–1.

446 Frank Lake *Clinical Theology* (Darton, Longman & Todd 1966) p.799.

447 Helen Roseveare *Give me this Mountain* (IVF 1966) pp.159–60.

448 Richard Wurmbrand *Tortured for Christ* (Hodder 1967) p.52.

449 Michael Ramsey *The Christian Priest Today* (SPCK 1962) pp.92–3.

450 Francis MacNutt *Healing* (Notre Dame: Ave Maria 1974) pp.183, 187.

451 Ernesto Cardenal *Marilyn Monroe and other poems* tr. Robert Pring-Mill (Search Press 1975) pp.79–80.

452 Lesslie Newbigin *The Open Secret* (SPCK 1978) p.121.

453 Jim Wallis *The Call to Conversion* (Tring: Lion 1982) p.101.

454 *The Cloud of Unknowing* tr. Clifton Wolters (Harmondsworth: Penguin 1961) p.60.

[455] John Foxe *A Sermon of Christ Crucified, preached at Pauls Cross the Friday before Easter, commonly called Good Friday* (1570) pp.26–7.

[456] John Donne, sermon preached at Lincoln's Inn, in *P&S* III, 112.

[457] Samuel Rutherford to the Laird of Carleton, May 10, 1637; letter 169 in *Letters of Samuel Rutherford* ed. Andrew Bonar (Oliphants 1891; orig. pub. in 2 vols. 1863) pp.318–9.

[458] Charles Wesley *Hymns and Sacred Poems* (1749), I.

[459] John Newton to Miss Medhurst May 25, 1762; in Bull, 54.

[460] A.M. Allchin *Ann Griffiths* (Cardiff: University of Wales Press 1976) p.48.

[461] Narayam Vaman Tilak, source untraced.

[462] G.A. Studdert Kennedy *The Unutterable Beauty* (Mowbrays 1983 edn.) p.86.

[463] Written on the wall in the besieged Warsaw ghetto by an unknown Jew.

[464] Thomas Merton *The Seven Storey Mountain* (Sheldon Press 1948) pp.419–20.

[465] James E. Seddon *Hymns for Today's Church* (Hodder & Stoughton 1982) no.518.

[466] Aylward Shorter, Kimbu Village Prayer in *African Christian Spirituality* (Geoffrey Chapman 1978) pp.155–7.

[467] Hans Küng *Does God Exist?* (Collins 1980) pp.657–8.

[468] *Martyrdom of St Polycarp* tr. James A. Keist in ACW VI, 140–1.

[469] Athanasius *De Incarnatione*, 27 in *Contra Gentes and De Incarnatione* tr. R.W. Thornton (Oxford: Clarendon Press 1971; Oxford Early Christian Texts).

[470] *Early Christian Prayers* ed. A. Hamman (Chicago: H. Regnery, & London: Longmans 1961) pp.161–2.

[471] Sermon 252.9 in *Saint Augustine: Sermons on the Liturgical Seasons* tr. Sr. M.S. Muldowney RSM, FC vol.38.

[472] Augustine *Expositions on the Book of Psalms* (NPNF VIII, 402) on Ps. LXXXIV.8.

[473] John Climacus *The Ladder of Divine Ascent* tr. Colm Luibheid and Norman Russell (SPCK 1982; CWSp) p.145.

[474] *Inst.* 3.25.3.

[475] William Perkins *A salve for a sick man: or, a treatise containing the nature, differences and kinds of death* (Cambridge 1595).

[476] William Perkins *A salve for a sick man.*

[477] C. Winkworth (tr.) *Lyra Germanica: Second Series: the Christian Life* (1858) pp.225–6.

[478] John Donne 'The second of my Prebend sermons upon my five Psalms. Preached at St Pauls January 29 1625/6' in *P&S* VII, 68–71.

[479] John Donne 'Preached at Whitehall. February 29 1627/8' in *P&S* VIII, 191.

[480] Robert Bolton *Of the Four Last Things* (1635) pp.89–91.

[481] Richard Baxter *The Saints Everlasting Rest* (1649; 10th ed. 1669).

[482] Richard Baxter *The Saints Everlasting Rest* (1649; 10th ed. 1669) pp.41–4.

[483] John Wesley *A Collection of Hymns for the Use of the People called Methodists* (1780) no.65.

[484] Augustus M. Toplady *Works* (1825) IV, 273.

[485] Letter of July 6, 1780 on the death of his daughter in John Scott *Life of the Rev. Thomas Scott . . . including a Narrative Drawn Up by Himself* (4th ed. 1822).

[486] John Newton, appendix to 'Letters to a Wife' in *Works* (1824) V, 624–5.

[487] 'The Second Coming of Christ' in *Sermons of Robert Murray M'Cheyne* (BOT 1961; from *Additional Remains*, 1846) pp.71–2.

[488] *Letters of Catherine, Lady Buxton* collected by Lady Victoria Buxton, typescript.

[489] C.S. Lewis *The Great Divorce* (Geoffrey Bles 1946) p.66.

[490] Karl Barth *Dogmatics in Outline* tr. G.T. Thompson (SCM 1949) pp.134–5.

[491] E. Elliot *Through Gates of Splendour* (Hodder & Stoughton 1957) p.189.

[492] C.S. Lewis *A Grief Observed* (Faber & Faber 1961) p.16.

[493] Michael Hare Duke *The Break of Glory* (SPCK 1970) pp.19–20.

[494] H. Berkhof *Christian Faith* tr. S. Woudstra (Grand Rapids, Michigan: Eerdmans 1979) p.529.

[495] H. Berkhof *Christian Faith*, p.532.

[496] Ernesto Cardenal *Marilyn Monroe and Other Poems* (Search Press 1975) pp.75–7.

[497] Jacques Ellul *Apocalypse: The Book of Revelation* (Seabury 1977) p.172.

[498] Margaret Ford *Janani – the Making of a Martyr* (Lakeland 1978) pp.92–3.

[499] Jürgen Moltmann *Experiences of God* (SCM 1980) pp.31–3.

[500] Hassan B. Dehqani-Tafti *The Hard Awakening* (Triangle, SPCK 1981) pp.113–4.

[501] Misuno Genzo tr. Marjorie Tunbridge *Japan Christian Quarterly* Summer 1984.

[502] *The Odes of Solomon: the Syriac Texts* ed. & tr. J.H. Charlesworth (Missoula, Montana: Scholars Press 1977) pp.67–8.

[503] Clement of Alexandria, quoted by Y.M.J. Congar *I believe in the Holy Spirit* (Geoffrey Chapman 1983) II, 222.

[504] Augustine *Expositions on the Book of Psalms* (LF VI, 178) on Ps. CXXXVIII.2.

[505] Symeon the New Theologian *Hymns of Divine Love* tr. George A. Maloney SJ (Denville, NJ: Dimension Books 1978) p.14, relined and slightly altered.

[506] Joseph Addison in *The Spectator* no.453, August 9 1712.

[507] Prose tr. by A.M. Allchin in *Ann Griffiths* (Cardiff: University of Wales Press 1976) pp.34, 36, 39–40. Verse tr. by H.A. Hodges in *Homage to Ann Griffiths* (Church in Wales Publications 1976) p.59.

[508] John Henry Newman, in 'The Dream of Gerontius', *The Month* (June 1865), with first verse repeated at the end.

[509] Fyodor Dostoevsky notebook entry, in Konstantin Modulsky *Dostoevsky* tr. Michael A. Minihan (Princeton UP 1967) p.650.

[510] Misuno Genzo tr. Marjorie Tunbridge *Japan Christian Quarterly* Summer 1984.

Index of Authors

Index of Authors

Augustine Bishop of Hippo, N. Africa 354–430 *31, 52, 65, 71, 73, 121, 166, 200, 216, 306, 373, 396*

Balthasar, Hans Urs von German Roman Catholic theologian 1905– *158, 197*

Barrington-Ward, Simon General Secretary of CMS & Bishop of Coventry 1930– *51, 162*

Barth, Karl Swiss Protestant theologian in Basle 1886–1968 *45, 46, 383*

Basil the Great Cappadocian Father, Brother of Gregory of Nyssa 330–379 *30*

Baxter, Richard Puritan divine 1615–1691 *79, 220, 240, 256, 378*

Bayly, Lewis Bishop of Bangor d.1631 *202, 342*

Bediako, Kwame Ghanaian Presbyterian *252*

Bennett, Arthur Independent Church minister *337*

Berkhof, Hendrikus Dutch Reformed theologian at the University of Leyden *385, 386*

Berkouwer, G.C. (Gerrit Cornelius) Professor of Theology at the Free (Reformed) University of Amsterdam *210*

Bernard of Clairvaux Cistercian Abbot of Clairvaux 1090–1153 *307, 314*

Berridge, John Vicar of Everton; early Evangelical 1716–1793 *329*

Berryman, John Poet 1914–1972 *90*

Bogue, David Dissenter; a founder of the London Missionary Society 1750–1825 *260*

Bolton, Robert Puritan divine and scholar 1572–1631 *377*

Bonaventure Italian Franciscan theologian, the 'Prince of mystics' c. 1217–1274 *122*

Bonhoeffer, Dietrich German Lutheran theologian opposed to Hitler 1906–1944 *61, 134, 173, 193, 266, 349*

Booth, William Founder and first General of the Salvation Army 1829–1912 *193, 243, 264*

Boyle, Robert Founder of the Royal Society 1627–1691 *189*

Brainerd, David Missionary to the Red Indians 1718–1747 *80, 168*

Bridge, William Congregational pastor in Great Yarmouth 1600–1670 *255*

Brooks, Thomas Puritan congregational pastor d.1680 *41, 148, 222, 302, 323*

Brunner, Emil Swiss Protestant theologian in Zürich 1889–1966 *133*

Bucer, Martin Ecumenical reformer 1491–1551 *201*

Bull, Geoffrey T. English missionary in China 1921– *88, 334*

Bunyan, John Puritan preacher and allegorist 1628–1688 *77, 104, 125*

Buxton, Lady Catherine Former Quaker; wife of the philanthropist Sir Thomas Fowell Buxton 1814–1911 *382*

Caird, John Principal of Glasgow University 1820–1898 *261*

Calvin, Jean French reformer, largely based in Geneva 1509–1564 *104, 111, 146, 187, 201, 277, 316, 374*

Camara, Helder Pessoa Archbishop of Olinda and Recife, Brazil 1909– *117*

Carden, John CMS missionary and writer 1924– *138*

Cardenal, Ernesto Nicaraguan poet 1925– *354, 386*

Carey, William Baptist missionary; Professor of Sanskrit and Bengali, Government College, Calcutta 1761–1834 *241, 259, 281*

Carmichael, Amy Beatrice First Keswick missionary; founder of the Dohnavur Fellowship 1867–1951 *134, 333*

Carpmael, Patrick Poet *91*

Carretto, Carlo Italian Little Brother of Jesus; hermit in the Sahara *234*

Chadwick, Samuel Methodist minister; Principal of Cliff College 1860–1932 *154*

Charles, Br. of Jesus (Charles de Foucauld) Ex-soldier and hermit 1858–1916 *292*

Index of Authors

Charleton, Walter President of the College of Physicians 1619–1707 *55*

Cherry, Edith Gilling English poet 1872–1897 *116*

Claudel, Paul French Roman Catholic author and diplomat 1868–1955 *157, 351*

Clement of Alexandria; Greek theologian *c.* 155–*c.* 220 *395*

Clemo, Jack Cornish Calvinist poet and writer 1916– *61*

Confessions

  Barmen, Declaration of 1934 *264*

  Japan, United Church of Christ in 1967 *270*

  Korea, Christian Ministers in South 1973 *271*

  Westminster Assembly 1644 *41, 68, 188*

Costas, Orlando Costa Rican at the Eastern Baptist Theological Seminary, Philadelphia 1942– *272*

Cowper, William Poet and hymn-writer 1731–1800 *113, 308*

Cragg, A. Kenneth Assistant Bishop in Oxford; apostle to Islam 1913– *246, 247*

Cranmer, Thomas Archbishop of Canterbury; English reformer; compiler of the Book of Common Prayer 1489–1556 *185*

Cyprian Bishop of Carthage *c.* 200–258 *71*

Cyril Bishop of Jerusalem *c.* 315–386 *65, 143*

Dehqani-Tafti, Hassan Bishop in Iran, in exile in England 1920– *391*

Denney, James Free Church theologian 1856–1917 *131*

Devanesen, Chandran Indian writer 1917– *141*

Doddridge, Philip Nonconformist divine and hymn-writer 1702–1751 *209, 287*

Donne, John Metaphysical poet; Dean of St Paul's 1571–1631 *54, 67, 75, 112, 218, 318, 343, 344, 361, 376, 377*

Donovan, Vincent Holy Ghost Father, formerly in Tanzania 1926– *118, 178, 214*

Dostoevsky, Fyodor Russian novelist 1821–1881 *401*

Drummond, Henry Professor of Natural Science in the Free Church College, Glasgow 1851–1897 *309*

Edwards, Jonathan New England Calvinist minister and philosopher 1703–1758 *68*

Elliot, Elisabeth Former missionary to the Aucas in Ecuador 1926– *116, 383*

Elliot, Jim Missionary martyr to the Aucas 1927–1956 *383*

Ellul, Jacques French Reformed theologian; Professor of Social History at Bourdeaux 1912– *388*

Ephraem Syrus Syrian Deacon, teacher and exegete *c.* 306–373 *120*

Erasmus, Desiderius Reformer and Christian humanist *c.* 1469–1536 *103, 239*

Evagrius of Pontus Monk in Egypt from Pontus in Asia 345–399 *216*

Faricy, Robert L. American Jesuit, teaching Spiritual Theology in Rome 1926– *236*

Farrer, Austin Theologian; Warden of Keble College, Oxford 1904–1968 *195*

Fison, J.E. (Joe) Bishop of Salisbury 1906–1972 *300*

Ford, Margaret Secretary to Janani Luwum 1937– *389*

Forsyth, P.T. (Peter Taylor) British Congregationalist 1848–1921 *44, 132, 209*

Fox, George Founder of the Quakers (Society of Friends) 1624–1691 *255, 324*

Foxe, John Martyrologist 1516–1587 *360*

Francis of Assisi Extraordinary monk, founder of the Franciscans 1181–1226 *36, 52*

Franck, Johann German Burgomaster, poet and hymn-writer 1618–1677 *204*

Fraser, J.O. (James Outram) 'of Lisuland', South West China 1886–1938 *227, 245*

Index of Authors

Fynn 20th century *49*

Gairdner, W.H. Temple CMS missionary in Cairo 1873–1928 *245*

Genzo, Misuno Paraplegic poet from Tokyo, communicating with a code based on movement of his eyelids 1937–1984 *392, 401*

Gill, Eric Roman Catholic sculptor, letterer and engraver 1882–1940 *60*

Giuliani, Maurice French Jesuit theologian 1916– *229*

Goodwin, Thomas Independent divine; President of Magdalen College, Oxford 1600–1679 *75, 149, 322*

Gregory of Nazianzus Cappadocian Father 329–389 *372*

Gregory of Nyssa Bishop of Nyssa, younger brother of Basil c. 330–c. 395 *276*

Gregory Palamas Archbishop of Thessalonica, exponent of *hesychasm* (interior quiet) 1296–1359 *216*

Gregory Thaumaturgus Bishop of Neo-Caesarea c. 213–c. 270 *166*

Griffiths, Ann Welsh Calvinist–Methodist poet 1776–1805 *364, 399*

Guigo II Prior General of the Carthusians d.1193 *97*

Hailsham, Lord Lord High Chancellor of Great Britain 1907– *234*

Hammarskjöld, Dag Danish Secretary-General of the United Nations 1905–1961 *89*

Hare Duke, Michael Bishop of St Andrews 1925– *384*

Haslam, William Perpetual Curate of Baldiu, Cornwall d.1905? *83*

Haughey, John C. American Jesuit writer 1930– *160*

Havergal, Frances Ridley Hymn-writer, poet and linguist 1836–1879 *58, 290*

Hebraeus, Bar Jacobite Syrian bishop and philosopher 1226–1286 *146*

Herbert, George Anglican priest and poet 1593–1633 *97*

Hopkins, Evan Henry A founder of the Keswick Convention 1837–1918 *130*

Hopkins, Gerard Manley Jesuit poet in N. Wales 1844–1889 *59, 60, 108, 332*

Hutter, Jakob Moravian Anabaptist d.1536 *341*

Ignatius of Loyola Basque Spaniard; founder of the Society of Jesus (the Jesuits) 1491–1556 *287*

Innocent III Pope 1160–1216 *145*

Irenaeus Bishop of Lyons c. 130–c. 200 *97, 276*

Isaac of Stella Cistercian Abbot of Stella, nr. Poitiers c. 1100–c.1169 *36, 277*

Isaac of Nineveh (Isaac the Syrian), Bishop of Nineveh d.c. 700 *34, 216, 285*

Jay, William Dissenting minister in Bath 1769–1853 *115*

Jewel, John Bishop of Salisbury; early Anglican apologist 1522–1571 *202*

John Climacus Abbot of Sinai c. 579–c. 649 *66, 285, 374*

John of the Cross Spanish mystic; exponent of the Negative Way 1542–1591 *278, 317*

Johnson, Samuel Poet, lexicographer, conversationalist 1709–1784 *328*

Julian of Norwich (Lady or Mother Julian) English mystic c. 1342–1420 *37, 54, 314*

Kempis, Thomas à Augustinian Canon and ascetic writer c. 1380–1417 *123*

Kidner, F. Derek Anglican Evangelical Biblical scholar 1913– *269*

Kierkegaard, Søren Danish philosopher; 'existentialist' 1813–1855 *83, 114, 331, 332, 347*

Kimbangu, Simon Congolese Christian imprisoned for 20 years 1889–1951 *213, 348*

King, Edward Bishop of Lincoln 1829–1910 *115*

King, Martin Luther American Baptist minister and Civil Rights campaigner 1929–1968 *267*

Kitamori, Kazoh Japanese theologian, at the Tokyo United Theological

Index of Authors

Nee, Watchman (Ni To-Sheng) Independent Chinese church leader 1903–1972 *295*

Neill, Stephen Missionary statesman and writer 1900–1984 *247*

Neumarck, Georg German lyric poet and hymn-writer; secretary to the Ducal archives at Weimar 1621–1681 *346*

Newbigin, J.E. Lesslie Bishop of the Church of South India; ecumenical statesman 1909– *251, 355*

Newman, John Henry Tractarian leader, later Cardinal 1801–1890 *400*

Newton, John Evangelical minister, hymn writer and abolitionist 1725–1807 *106, 169, 190, 257, 280, 303, 330, 363, 381*

Nicolai, Philipp German Lutheran pastor in Hamburg 1556–1608 *375*

Nouwen, Henri J.M. Dutch priest and theologian, now at Harvard Divinity School 1932– *176*

Origen Alexandrian theologian *c.* 185–*c.* 254 *239, 306*

Ostorodt, Christopher *166*

Owen, John Dean of Christ Church, Oxford; Puritan theologian and statesman 1616–1683 *150*

Pascal, Blaise French Jansenist writer 1623–1662 *41, 76, 112, 324*

Patrick Second Bishop of Ireland, and patron saint *c.* 390–*c.* 460 *31*

Payne Smith, Robert Evangelical Dean of Canterbury and orientalist 1819–1895 *192*

Perkins, William Puritan founding father 1558–1602 *255, 374, 375*

Pilgrim, The Anonymous nineteenth-century Russian Orthodox writer *225*

Polycarp Witness of St John the Apostle; martyr at Smyrna *c.* 69–*c.* 155 *372*

Preston, John Master of Emmanuel College, Cambridge; Puritan preacher and statesman 1587–1628 *67, 203, 220, 279, 319*

Ramsey, A. Michael Archbishop of Canterbury 1904– *270, 353*

Riedemann, Peter Member of the Hutterian Brethren *253*

Robinson, John Separatist minister in England and Leyden 1575–1625 *188*

Rolle, Richard English mystic and hermit *c.* 1295–1349 *308*

Roseveare, Helen English missionary in the Congo 1925– *352*

Rothe, Johann Andreas Pietist minister, friend of Zinzendorf in Herrnhut, breaking away later 1688–1758 *105*

Rutherford, Samuel Scottish Presbyterian divine *c.* 1600–1661 *345, 361*

Sanford, Agnes White Episcopalian lay lecturer on prayer and healing 1897–1982 *351*

Sangster, William Edwin Robert Methodist minister and leader 1900–1960 *300*

Sayers, Dorothy L. Writer and novelist 1893–1957 *47*

Schaeffer, Francis A. Founder of the L'Abri Fellowship 1912–1984 *159, 176*

Schillebeeckx, Edward Dutch Dominican theologian 1914– *212*

Schlink, Basilea Founder of the Darmstadt Mary Sisters 1904– *87, 339*

Scott, Thomas Biblical commentator 1747–1821 *190, 380*

Seddon, James Edward BCMS missionary in Morocco and hymn-writer 1915–1983 *366*

Seraphim of Sarov Russian monk, Staretz of Sarov 1759–1833 *151*

Seyler, Athene English actress 1899– *108*

Sheikh, Bilquis Moslem Pakistani convert to Christianity now resident in America 1916– *90*

Shepard, Thomas English and New England Puritan, co-founder of Harvard University 1604–1649 *113*

Sheppard, David S. Evangelical, Bishop of Liverpool 1929– *272*

Index of Authors

Shorter, Aylward 'White Father' missionary in E. Africa 1932– *367*

Sibbes, Richard Master of St Catharine's College, Cambridge, Puritan preacher 1577–1635 *167, 219, 279, 320*

Simeon, Charles Leader of the Evangelical Revival in Cambridge 1759–1836 *57, 82, 83, 113, 129, 170, 191, 258, 281, 289, 305*

Simons, Menno Dutch Anabaptist, founding father of the Mennonites 1496–1561 *316*

Sölle, Dorothee German theologian, founder of 'Political Evening Prayer' 1929– *339*

Solzhenitsyn, Alexander Russian novelist, in exile in America 1918– *338*

Song, Choan Seng Taiwanese theologian, at the Pacific School of Theology, Berkeley 1929– *161*

Southwell, Robert Poet and Roman Catholic martyr 1561–1595 *40*

Spurgeon, C.H. (Charles Haddon) Baptist minister of the Metropolitan Tabernacle 1834–1892 *115, 171, 192, 225*

Stott, John R.W. Rector of All Souls, Langham Place, Biblical expositor, Evangelical statesman 1921– *271*

Studd, C.T. (Charles Thomas) One of the Cambridge Seven (1885); founder of World Evangelisation Crusade 1861–1931 *293*

Studdert Kennedy, Geoffrey A. ('Woodbine Willie') First World War Chaplain and poet 1883–1929 *132, 364*

Suenens, Leon Joseph Belgian Cardinal and spokesman for 'Charismatic Renewal' 1904– *161*

Sundar Singh, Sadhu Charismatic Indian Christian convert 1880–1929 *85*

Symeon the New Theologian Abbot of St Mamas, nr. Constantinople 949–1022 *101, 102, 396*

Taylor, Edward American Puritan pastor and poet *c.* 1645–1729 *205, 207*

Taylor, James Hudson Founder of the China Inland Mission 1832–1905 *58, 242, 291*

Taylor, J.V. (John Vernon) General Secretary of CMS and Bishop of Winchester 1914– *160, 174, 211, 229*

Taylor Smith, Bishop Keswick preacher; Chaplain General to the forces 1860–1938 *333*

Temple, William Archbishop of Canterbury 1881–1944 *155, 246*

Tertullian African Church Father *c.*160–*c.*225 *120, 164*

Theophan the Recluse Russian Bishop and Staretz 1815–1894 *225*

Thielicke, Helmut German Protestant theologian in Hamburg 1908– *63, 117*

Thomas, R.S. (Ronald Stuart) Welsh poet and minister 1913– *63*

Tilak, Narayan Vaman Master Indian hymn-writer 1862–1919 *364*

Todi, Iacoponi da Italian Franciscan poet and lay brother *c.* 1230–1306 *286*

Toplady, Augustus Montague Calvinist author and hymn-writer 1740–1778 *189, 304, 380*

Torrance, T.F. (Thomas Forsyth) Professor of Christian Dogmatics in Edinburgh 1913– *134, 196, 213*

Tournier, Paul Swiss psychologist and writer 1898– *283*

Tourville, Abbé Henri de French parish priest and Director 1842–1903 *309*

Tozer, A.W. (Aiden Wilson) American pastor of the Alliance Church, Chicago 1897–1963 *157, 174, 195, 228, 249*

Traherne, Thomas English metaphysical poet 1637–1674 *55, 56*

Tugwell, Simon Dominican, Regent of Studies at Blackfriars, Oxford 1943– *232*

Turner, Steve Poet and rock journalist 1949– *163*

Tyndale, William Bible translator, reformer, martyr 1494–1536 *184*

Index of Authors